D1927841

African American Males and Education

Researching the Convergence of Race and Identity

A Volume in
Contemporary Perspectives on Race and Ethnic Relations

M. Christopher Brown, *United Negro College Fund*
T. Elon Dancy II, *University of Oklahoma*

Contemporary Perspectives on Race and Ethnic Relations

M. Christopher Brown and T. Elon Dancy II, Series Editors

Filling in The Blanks: Standardized Testing and the Black-White Achievement Gap Standardized Testing and the Black-White Achievement Gap (2011)
by Keena Arbuthnot

The Brother Code: Manhood and Masculinity Among African American Men in College (2012)
by T. Elon Dancy II

African American Males: Researching the Convergence (2012)
edited by T. Elon Dancy II and M. Christopher Brown II

African American Males and Education

Researching the Convergence of Race and Identity

Edited by

T. Elon Dancy II
University of Oklahoma

and

M. Christopher Brown II
Alcorn State University

IAP

Information Age Publishing, Inc.
Charlotte, North Carolina • www.infoagepub.com

Library of Congress Cataloging-in-Publication Data

African American males and education : researching the convergence of race and identity / edited by T. Elon Dancy II and M. Christopher Brown II.
p. cm.
Includes bibliographical references.
ISBN 978-1-61735-941-5 (paperback) — ISBN 978-1-61735-942-2 (hardcover) — ISBN 978-1-61735-943-9 (ebook) 1. African American young men—Education. 2. African American men—Education. 3. African American men—Education (Higher) 4. African American young men—Social conditions. 5. African American men—Social conditions. I. Dancy, T. Elon. II. Brown, M. Christopher.
LC2731.A33 2012
371.829'96073—dc23

2012024581

Printed in the United States of America

Dedication

For the "educators" of my youth for whom no book of this scope existed; for Zawadi who enlivens and embraces my scholarly passion and human mission; and for my colleagues, students, and friends, may this volume inform your thinking and inspire new actions that improve the educational spaces of African American males. Learn consistently, live authentically, and love unapologetically.

— ted2

For my cousins and their questions about race and identity; for the new cadre of faculty researching African American males who must yet unlearn methodology, uncover "truths", and unmask themselves; and for my progeny birthed through academic midwifery, nurtured through role molding, and matured through frientoring.

— mcb2

CONTENTS

12.07.21

PART III: THE NEXUS OF IDENTITY

PREFACE

The issues defining the relationship between African American males and education remain complex. Associated with each issue are multiple questions and problems facing African American males, their families, their communities, and educational context. For instance, research points to a number of K-16 pipeline issues affecting African American male students, including underachievement and cognitive paralysis, discipline challenges, low socioeconomic status background, and disparate college access and retention, among other issues. Although there has been substantial discussion about the plight of African American male participants and personnel in education, only modest attempts have been made to center analysis of identity and identity intersections in the discourse. Additionally, more attention to African American male teachers and faculty is needed in light of their unique cultural experiences in educational settings and expectations to mentor and/or socialize other African Americans, particularly males.

African American Males in Education: Researching the Convergence of Race and Identity addresses these gaps. This book emerges at a time when new social dynamics of race and other identities are shaping, but also shaped by, education. Over time, this cyclical relationship between identity and education is further complicated by power systems and multiple identities of participants in education. Educational settings consistently perpetuate racial and other forms of privilege among students, personnel, and other participants in education. For instance, differential access to social networks still visibly cluster by race, continuing the work of systemic privilege by promoting outcome inequalities in education and society.

African American Males and Education: Researching the Convergence of Race and Identity, pp. ix–xii

Race is often situated at the core for African American identity as race has historically marginalized this group for hundreds of years. While race is a primary identity in society and education, we recognize that race also interconnects with gender, class, and other identities. Accordingly, educational policy and practice must engage both primary and intersecting identities of students in order to fully serve them. Unfortunately, current national "attempts" to attend to the troubles African American males face in education have been surface efforts at best.

Educational settings must center understanding about African American males' historical identities as well as the evolving complexities of this group's racial constructions and intersecting identities. In this effort, defining race is important. Rather than a biological makeup, race is better understood as a power system in which skin color derives its significance from social, historical, and political contexts. Accordingly, an analysis of race in education must involve meanings that educators ascribe to students who are members of racially diverse groups. However, if racial identity (or any identity for that matter) is socially constructed then it may also be reconstructed. In this book, we push our understanding of identity and intersections and ponder two broad issues: (1) how education may participate in the process of reconstructing racial and other identities for African American males and (2) how this process is directly tied to addressing disparate outcomes among this group in education.

Since individuals have raced, classed, gendered, sexually oriented, spiritual, and other identities and selves (i.e., students, daughters, sons, employees), there are also many social worlds. Educational settings represent just one of the worlds in which multiple identities emerge and intersect. The word "convergence" is intended to capture the ways in which the intersecting identities of African American boys and men's lives interact, interface, and interrupt society and education. Central to our thinking is that African American boys and men are privileged in society by their gender and underprivileged by their race (African American or Black). In this book, educational settings are reenvisioned as systems of privilege and African American males viewed as both privileged and oppressed in these settings.

Because African American males' educational woes are deeply rooted in societal ills, editors embraced manuscript submissions from multiple disciplines, fields, and perspectives including history, psychology, sociology, anthropology, African and African American studies, women and gender studies, K-12 education, higher education, and college student affairs. Chapter authors employ various identity analyses in describing how African American males engage unique challenges in educational settings. Across chapters, attention is paid to the ways that socioeconomic status intersects with race in reproducing educational privilege, disparate trends among schools, colleges, and communities, and educational experiences among African American males. In addition, book chapters highlight research and scholarship that attempt to address core questions in educational policy and practice.

In Part I, the chapters look historically, culturally, and contextually at African American male identity issues in society and education. More specifically, narratives about race and intersectionality largely drive this discourse. In Part II, the chapters focus on the ways in which African American males uniquely teach, learn, and transform in educational settings. Part III gazes empirically into the experiences of various African American male groups at the intersection of culture and identity. Throughout the volume, each chapter meditates on the possibilities for the critical engagement and success of African American male participants in education.

No book on any topic is exhaustive; likewise, there are many topics, subjects, research questions, and contexts that are unaddressed in this book. This book offers both scholarly and practical sustenance to educational settings where various stakeholders must engage one of education's important student groups—African American males. In this effort, the book includes a strong balance of quantitative and qualitative inquiries as well as theoretical and scholarly papers. In recognizing the book's limitations, we simultaneously hope to inspire an empirical corpus of literature on the evolving African American male experience in America's schools, colleges, and society.

PART I

RACIAL AND CULTURAL CONTEXTS

CHAPTER 1

SO MANY QUESTIONS, SO LITTLE ANSWERS

Toward an Empirical Corpus of Literature on African American Men in College

T. Elon Dancy II

INTRODUCTION

Accountability in higher education is the topic of a number of scholarly papers, essays, and reports. These reports inquire about the effectiveness of higher education in teaching and preparing students for twenty-first century professional, social, and civic futures. Institutional shareholders (i.e., general public, students, businesses, governments, and other organizations) are increasingly holding colleges accountable for shaping better outcomes in college students (Burke, 2005). Current economic downturn in America places more emphasis on accountability in higher education given increasingly scarce resources and individuals' increased college enrollment to improve their economic positions. Notwithstanding, many perceive 4-year colleges as places which privilege some students while

African American Males and Education:
Researching the Convergence of Race and Identity, pp. 3–27

marginalizing others. Student groups hardly bear out these effects like African American men who have quickly become one of colleges and universities most elusive groups.

In its issue published Winter 2006/2007, The *Journal of Blacks in Higher Education* reignited conversations about how graduation rates among African American college women continue to outpace those among African American college men. In the journal's report, newer trends describing the enrollment and graduation rates among African American students were presented. The document, based on an analysis of National Collegiate Athletic Association (NCAA) data, reported that the graduation rates for African American women have continued to rise while graduation rates among African American college men are both unstable and significantly lower when compared to African American women. More specifically, African American women have improved their college completion rate from 34% in 1990 to 47% in 2006 (*The Journal of Blacks in Higher Education,* 2006/2007). Between 2001 and 2006, the graduation rate for African American college men has precariously hovered around 36%. In the report's conclusion, the journal revisits challenges to African American men's trajectory to the college degree as generally found in higher education research.

The issues defining and setting the context for understanding the relationship between African American men and colleges are complex ones for researchers. For nearly 20 years, research has sought to explain falling and/or dismal retention rates among African American college men. With attention to a new era of higher education accountability, this article is disciplined by the following questions: How has higher education research and scholarship shaped the field's understanding about African American men in college? Among this work, what pieces inform the field's core questions about this group's enrollment, retention, and completion? On what topics are research and scholarship clustering? What gaps remain or persist, and what questions go unanswered? Closer attention is paid to studies of gender and gender differences among college students that center or discuss the experiences of African American men in college.

THE ISSUE REVISITED: GENDERED TRENDS PAST TO PRESENT

African American men's educational attainment, enrollment, and persistence trends fall significantly below those of the general college student population and below that of African American women (Brown & Hurst, 2004). These trends persist despite race-based admissions, affirmative action hires for faculty and staff, and scholarships to increase collegiate access. Despite these trends, recent evidence suggests college-bound and college-enrolled African American men increasingly grow more confident in their intellectual and cognitive abilities (Allen, Griffin, Jayakumar, Kimura-Walsh, & Wolf, 2007). These trends baffle higher education institutions and challenge researchers to expose the causes and propose recommendations.

According to a report issued by the Frederick D. Patterson Institute of the United Negro College Fund, the rates at which African American men complete college are alarming. Enrollment of African American students in historically Black colleges/universities (HBCUs) and historically White institutions (HWIs) increased but was disproportionately gendered in the years following *Brown v. Board of Education* (1954).[1] In 1955, African American men comprised 55% of African American undergraduate enrollment while African American women comprised 45% (M. C. Brown & Hurst, 2004). In 1976, 35% of African American high school graduates who enrolled in college were African American men compared to 32% of African American women (Brown & Hurst, 2004). Between 1976 and 2000, the percentage of African American men who were enrolling in college began to decline sharply. By 2000, African American men who had graduated high school were enrolling in colleges at the same rate as they were in 1976 while African American women who had graduated high school were enrolling in college at an increased rate of 11% (Brown & Hurst, 2004). Over the last 30 years, African American women's enrollment in college has increasingly outpaced African American men's enrollment. Meanwhile, the college enrollment among African American men who were high school graduates continued to decrease. Today, African American men account for only 37% of African American undergraduate participation in higher education while African American women account for 63% (Brown & Hurst, 2004).

To be sure, the rate at which African American men attained the bachelor's degree has increased by 52% from 1977 to 2000. However, the rate at which African American women attained bachelor's degrees has increased by 112% in the same period (Brown & Hurst, 2004). Another report also observes that African American men are not persisting to and through the latter stages of the postsecondary pipeline (Harper, 2006). Harper (2006) reports that between 1977 and 2003, the most significant gains in African American men's degree attainment occurred at the associate's degree, not the bachelor's level. Analysis in this report also reveals that White men earned at least ten times more postsecondary degrees than did African American men in 2003. However, new trends offer optimism in conversations about African American men in college but also perplex an overall picture about this group.

African American men's self-ratings of their abilities may have increased over the past 30 years. In a study of self-perception trends among African American men who were college freshmen, African American men reported high educational aspirations as well as high self-confidence in their academic abilities and leadership skills during the high school-to-college transition (Allen et al., 2007). Specifically, Allen and colleagues found that African American men who were college freshmen were likely to rate themselves in the top 10% of all students their age regarding academic ability, math ability, writing ability, drive to achieve, and leadership ability. Three significant self-rating trends (academic ability, leadership ability, and intellectual self-confidence) are identified over a 30-year period for African American male college freshmen. In 1971, 34.5% of college-enrolled African American men believed they ranked in the top 10% of college students regarding academic ability. This percentage rate increased to 64.2% in 2004. In 1971, 43.5% of college-enrolled African American men believed they ranked in the top 10% of college-enrolled students regarding leadership ability. In 2004, 68.5% of African American men believed they ranked in the top 10% of college-enrolled students regarding leadership ability. In 1971, 44.2% of college-enrolled African American men believed they ranked in the top 10% of college students regarding their confidence in their intellect. By 2004, 75.5% of college-enrolled African American men believed they ranked in the top 10% of college students regarding confidence in their intellectual abilities (Allen et al., 2007).

Research also argues that African American men who choose to attend HWIs express slightly greater confidence in their academic abilities than their counterparts entering HBCUs (Allen et al., 2007). Allen and colleagues report that, in 2004, 66.4% of HWI-enrolled, African American male freshmen rated themselves above average regarding academic ability in comparison to 60.5% of HBCU-enrolled, African American male freshmen. Over the past 3 decades, African American men enrolled in HWIs also rated themselves more highly than African American men enrolled in HBCUs regarding leadership ability and intellectual self-confidence (Allen et al, 2007).

At the turn of the century, however, virtually no differences existed in the ways in which African American men perceived their abilities. In 2004, 68.9% of African American men who chose HBCUs and 68.2% of African American men who chose HWIs rated themselves in the top 10% regarding their leadership ability (Allen et al., 2007). Seventy-eight percent of African American men attending HBCUs rated themselves in the top 10% of their peers regarding intellectual self-confidence. In comparison, 73.9% of African American men enrolled in HWIs rated themselves similarly. This study also found African American women to feel less confident about their academic abilities than men albeit African American women's academic performance was superior. In 2004, African American men rated themselves more highly than African American women in terms of their academic ability (64% versus 61%), leadership ability (69% vs. 65%), and intellectual self-confidence (76% versus 65%) (Allen et. al, 2007).

In short, Allen and colleagues (2007) report that many African American men who come to college perceive their self-confidence and aspirations highly. Notwithstanding, African American men are disadvantaged in the collegiate pipeline in ways that impact persistence, retention, and degree attainment disparately. For decades, African American men who attended HWIs ranked their self-perceptions more highly than their counterparts enrolled in HBCUs. However, the retention rates among African American men enrolled in HWIs lag behind those rates among African American men enrolled in HBCUs (Davis, 1994).

Institutional context aside, African American men's retention rates are dismal across institutions of higher education. Mortenson (2001) reports that, in 2000, the college retention rate for African American men was 33.8%. In other words, 66.2% of African American men disenrolled before completing the requirements for the bachelor's degree. In fact, the rate at which African American men continued college is reported as the lowest among all raced and gendered groups (Mortenson, 2001). The following sections add context and color to report data.

Historical Context

The African American male college experience began with the turbulence of discrimination and exclusion of African Americans in educational contexts throughout the Reconstruction and Civil Rights eras (Dancy & Brown, 2007). This intolerance against African Americans ran rampant across America as society sent clear messages that integration was opposed (Anderson, 1988; Anderson, 2002; Brown & Freeman, 2004). Slave states maintained separate educational structures that provided African American students with a subordinate education until the Civil Rights era. Southern institutions of public higher education barred African Americans as a matter of law (Anderson, 2002). Free states used institutionalized racism to send similar messages (Anderson, 2002; Brown & Freeman, 2004). Even progressive southern Whites who advocated formal education for African American children proposed a specialized trade education for African Americans (Anderson, 2002). Northern institutions barred African Americans as a matter of educationally and socially rationalized practices (Anderson, 2002).

Desegregation initiatives focused on changing the racial demographics of the student and staff composition post-*Brown v. Board of Education* (1954). Desegregation processes often reveal the vestiges of legalized segregation. The *United States v. Fordice* (1992) case sent a clear signal to the nineteen southern and border states that more than racial neutrality and good faith efforts would be necessary under the law to demonstrate that the effects of the prior system of segregation had been eradicated. After years of what postsecondary education had assumed to be race neutral mission statements and admission requirements, the *Fordice* case declared that the mere existence of predominantly African American and White institutional enrollments represented a remnant of legal segregation (Brown, 1999). The Supreme Court held that the state of Mississippi's race-neutral policies and good faith efforts had not fulfilled its obligation to dismantle the state's dual higher education system. The *Fordice* ruling shifted the collegiate desegregation compliance framework from one of fiscal and academic equity to one of mission redesignation and racial recomposition of student populations (Brown, 1999).

Colleges, among other societal institutions, inherited the challenge of righting the effects of past wrongs. The perennial discourses on collegiate desegregation highlight this challenge. Notwithstanding, state coordinating boards and institutional boards of trustees are moving forward with implementing collegiate desegregation compliance initiatives (Brown & Freeman, 2004). The result is a collection of ad hoc policies and practices which promote changing the statistical composition of the student population within the corresponding institutions based solely on race—transdemography (Brown & Freeman, 2004).

Transdemography offers colleges dominated by both Black and/or White enrollments an opportunity to enrich the student campus context and to encourage intercultural communication within the academic environment (Brown, 1999). However, transdemography simultaneously portends to eradicate the rich campus culture for which HBCUs have been lauded, with scant implications for campuses populated primarily by White constituents (Brown & Freeman, 2004; Fleming, 1984; Roebuck & Murty, 1993). Current collegiate desegregation initiatives have as their primary aim attracting White students to historically Black colleges and universities (HBCUs) (Brown, 1999a; Brown & Freeman, 2004). As an interesting turn, existing compliance plans proffer limited resources or support for targeting significant increases in African American student attendance at the historically White institutions (HWIs) within the respective states. Collegiate desegregation has morphed into a transdemographic enrollment initiative. It is important for researchers and administrators to attend to the unintended consequences that have and continue to emerge from these shifting enrollments, terrains, and possibly paradigms. Extant empirical data bear out the disparate effects of the above described contexts on African American males.

African American Men go to Integrated Colleges: Sexed Work of the 1970s

After *Brown v. Board of Education* (1954) and the turbulent Civil Rights Movement, scholars increasingly studied African American students across colleges and universities, particularly those that were historically White (Astin, 1977, 1982; Cope & Hannah, 1975; Fleming, 1984; Nettles, 1985; Willie & McCord, 1972). Early post-*Brown* era research largely contextualized understanding about African American men in college within broader scholarship about African American students' experiences in college. Prior to this period, research on African American students considered their experiences in Black colleges (in which most were enrolled) (Willie & McCord, 1972). In the 1970s, less attention was paid to gender differences among African American students given less disparate enrollment and retention rates between African American men and women in college (Brown & Hurst, 2004).

Gail E. Thomas was one of few researchers in higher education who called attention to college choices in addition to academic, social, and otherwise affective experiences among sexed groups of African Americans. Based on Office of Civil Rights data (which involved approximately 3,068 higher education institutions), she responded to the field's questions about student enrollment. More specifically, her early work shed light on African American men's entry into college. Thus, her work shed light for how the field thinks about African American men's entry into higher education. In contextualizing her work, Thomas (1980b) noted that only 1% difference existed between African American women and men's college enrollment distributions. Specifically, African American women were 55% of the African American undergraduate population while African American men were 54% of that same population. She issued a clarion call for college access to be redefined due, in large part, to African American men and women who do not just "enroll somewhere" but instead access higher education at varied and more competitive levels than were assumed (Thomas, 1980b, p. 179). Thomas additionally called attention to the extent to which African American men and women were distributed in college, noting that enrollment was highly concentrated in Southern Black institutions. She additionally found that African American students largely majored in education and the social sciences, and that this group was underrepresented in science, technology, engineering, and mathematics (STEM) fields. College major choice, she argued, has import for expanding the field's thinking about access to higher education. This work, subsequently, was foundational in helping higher education to reenvision the goal of integration as engagement by encouraging colleges to develop programs that do more than racially mix student bodies.

In another study on college access, Thomas (1980a) noted that sex differences among African American students in college were not as distinct as sex differences among Whites in the 1970s. Prior to this longitudinal study of 13,925 high school seniors, sex differences among African Americans college access and entry were not previously investigated (Thomas, 1980a). Particularly, two findings are even more salient given a contemporary context of widely disparate college enrollment among African American women and men. First, Thomas found that one's sex did not produce a significant effect on choice to attend a historically or predominantly Black college in the 1970s. Second, she noted that African American men in college had a higher perception of college ability in comparison to African American women in college. Third, socioeconomic status background more greatly impacted African American men's decisions to pursue college enrollment than African American women. Thomas' work also evokes gendered (i.e., social) differences between the sexes (i.e., biological). In this study, high school class rank tended to impact African American boys' decisions to pursue higher education in comparison to African American girls for whom participation in particular high school curricula was more significant. Further, African American high school boys were also more likely than African American high school girls to attend college if a relative attended previously.

On the heels of Thomas' (1980a, 1980b) findings, scholars from psychological, anthropological, sociological and educational disciplines investigated why African Americans at all levels of education have difficulty learning, adjusting, and staying in historically White institutions post-*Brown* (Fleming, 1984; Fordham & Ogbu, 1986; Irvine, 1991). Comparative in nature, a body of literature emerged that compared African American men's experiences across institutional type (e.g., HBCU versus HWI). Findings clearly highlight African American students as marginalized in historically White contexts and satisfied in historically Black contexts (Brown & Freeman, 2004; Lamont, 1979; Roebuck & Murty, 1993; Willie & McCord, 1972). One book published in the 1980s *Blacks in College* (Fleming, 1984) would become a mainstay among empirical work on African American students generally and African American men in particular.

1980s and 1990s: African American Men in an Era of Comparative Work

Contexual Comparisons. African American men in college were implicated in much scholarship on African American college students generally in the

1980s and 1990s. At the center of much of this work is the institutional type (e.g., HBCU, HWI) interaction. A sizable portion of this work investigated early retention strategies at HWIs focused on the disparate academic performance of African American in comparison to White students (Allen, 1988; Cabrera, Nora, Terenzini, Pascarella, & Hagedorn, 1999; Donovan, 1984; Loo & Rolison, 1986; Nettles, Thoeny, & Gosman, 1986; Smedley, Myers, & Harrell, 1993). More recently, many researchers have compared HBCUs to HWIs to identify differences between contexts regarding the academic and social attainment and cognitive development of African American students (Allen, Epps, & Haniff, 1991; Berger & Milem, 2000; Bohr, Pascarella, Nora, & Terenzini, 1995; Cheatham, Slaney, & Coleman, 1990; Fleming, 1984; Nettles, 1987; Watson & Kuh, 1996). The overarching finding of most of these studies, with the exception of the Cheatham and colleagues' study, was that HBCUs are more successful at facilitating positive educational and social outcomes of African American students than are HWIs. Sociocultural, contextual, and student development literature reports that embracing and considering the culture of students is essential to their retention at HWIs (DeSousa & Kuh, 1996; Mallinckrodt & Sedlacek, 1987; Nettles et al., 1986; Tracey & Sedlacek, 1985). Faculty sensitive to African American cultures are also important. More specifically, close relationships with faculty are associated with better grades, higher levels of retention, and feelings of satisfaction with the university (Allen, 1988; Kuh, Douglas, Lund, & Ramin-Gyumek, 1994; Nettles & Johnson, 1987; Nettles et al., 1986; Sedlacek, 1987). Historically Black colleges and universities are often cited contexts where these trends are shaped.

HBCUs remain particularly effective at promoting African American postsecondary attainment (Brown & Freeman, 2004). Specifically, while HBCUs only enroll 16% of African American undergraduate students nationwide, they produce 28.5% of the baccalaureate degrees awarded to African American students (Brown & Hurst, 2004). Lamont (1979) posits that for many African American students, the HBCU is "culturally more congenial" than the historically White university (p. 32). Roebuck and Murty (1993) further suggest that "there is also a general level of satisfaction and camaraderie among [African American] students at Black schools that is not found among [African American] students on White campuses" (p. 15). In sum, the research agrees that African American students engage a more difficult trajectory to degree attainment in HWIs. African American students perceive HBCUs as more supportive and are therefore more likely to report satisfaction with collegiate experiences and persist to degree attainment.

Population Comparisons. A number of studies has compared African American students to students of other ethnicities, implicating African American men in findings and recommendations. Some of this work suggested that the ability to cope, the influence of sociocultural factors, and perceptions of White peers and faculty differentially affected African American and White college students (Allen et al., 1991; Nettles, 1991; Nettles et al., 1986; Smedley et al., 1993; Thotis, 1982). Research supported assertions that African American students who do not engage within supportive communities at HWIs often experience feelings of discomfort, social isolation, and stress (Feagin, Vera, & Imani, 1996; Fleming, 1984; Gossett, Cuyjet, & Cockriel, 1998; Lang & Ford, 1992; Ponterotto, 1990; Sailes, 1993). Researchers also investigated early retention strategies at HWIs focused on the disparate academic performance of African American in comparison to White students (Allen, 1988; Cabrera et al., 1999; Donovan, 1984; Loo & Rolison, 1986; Nettles et al., 1986; Smedley et al., 1993). Additionally, a number of studies suggest that the ability to cope, the influence of sociocultural factors, and perceptions of White peers and faculty differentially affect African American and White college students (Allen et al., 1991; Nettles, 1991; Nettles et al., 1986; Smedley et al., 1993; Thotis, 1982). Research supports assertions that African American students who do not engage within supportive communities at HWIs often experience feelings of discomfort, social isolation, and stress (Feagin et al., 1996; Fleming, 1984; Gossett et al., 1998; Lang & Ford, 1992; Ponterotto, 1990; Sailes, 1993).

Remembering "Blacks in College" 25 Years Later. One study is particularly salient in its comparative investigation of African American students in different collegiate environments as well as its attention to African American men. In 1984, psychologist Jacqueline Fleming completed a cross-sectional, multi-institutional study that compared freshmen and seniors in 15 institutions to obtain data about the social and intellectual gains of African American students in historically Black and historically White colleges. Fleming (1984) reported differences by race and gender in those collegiate contexts. Specifically, the data confirm that the dominance of men in general and the dominance of White men in particular are mainstays on college campuses. Furthermore, the data suggest that African American students are able to identify which student populations are most supported in the college.

In her study, Fleming (1984) writes that African American men are the "hardest hit" on historically White campuses (p. 141). Her research finds evidence of the eight following conditions to support her overarching hypothesis about African American men.

In HWIs:

1. African American men are predisposed to interacting with others in competitive ways which subsequently brings them emotional harm (p. 142).

2. African American men are unable to control feelings of detachment, depression, and low self-image relative to small numbers on campus (p. 142).
3. African American men are excluded inside and outside the classroom which constricts their intellectual gains and outcomes (p. 141).
4. African American men risk truancy and attrition if they socially or academically perform in less successful ways than others (competitive rejection) (p. 143).
5. African American men who feel unfairly treated may participate in in-class and out-of-class activities but only in emotional defense or out of aggression (p. 143).
6. African American men may display different aggressions (i.e., attempt to dominate women) as they internalize engagement problems (p. 143).

In HBCUs:

1. African American men act in very similar ways to White men at historically White colleges by showing less concern for others and constructing formal and informal attachments with faculty (p. 142).
2. African American men strive to remain content and complacent in historically Black collegiate environments because they feel a sense of control in an environment perceived as supportive (p. 142-143).

Fleming's (1984) *Blacks in College* was seminal in answering the field's core questions about both retention and completion of African American men in college. The large sample in this study (approximately 3,000 students) increased Fleming's ability to infer about African American students who attend both historically Black and White colleges in America. More broadly, this large-scale study was also a lynchpin in responding to persistent questions about whether African American students should receive or benefit from higher education (Gurin & Epps, 1975). In addition, Fleming was one of the first researchers of African American students in collegiate contexts to attempt to meaningfully describe the troublesome nature of gender in the lives of African American men in college.

As the 1990s approached, researchers noted trend increases among African American undergraduate enrollment in HWIs in comparison to HBCUs (Allen et al., 1991; Davis, 1994). At the same time, though, enrollment and retention rates among African American men were declining. In response, sociocultural, contextual, and student development literature encouraged historically White institutions to embrace and consider the culture of African American students if HWIs were generally interested in retaining these students (DeSousa & Kuh, 1996; Mallinckrodt & Sedlacek, 1987; Nettles et al., 1986; Tracey & Sedlacek, 1985). Research additionally emphasized the importance of positive faculty and student relationships. In fact, close relationships with faculty are associated with better grades, higher levels of retention, and feelings of satisfaction with the university (Allen, 1988; Kuh et al., 1994; Nettles & Johnson, 1987; Nettles et al., 1986; Sedlacek, 1987). In addition, several researchers provided data concerning the extent to which African American and minority students have been successful in negotiating the college pipeline (Astin, 1990, 1993; Pascarella & Terenzini, 1991; Tinto, 1994). Findings suggested that African American educational attainment in college largely relies on feelings of support and congruence with institutional norms.

Above trends are reflected in one of the most salient studies in the 1990s for understanding African American men's experiences in college specifically. Davis (1994) analyzed a data set on college students' academic and social experiences. More specifically, Davis examined how student background, college-level, and academic performance factors differentially affected 742 African American men who were enrolled in historically Black (55%) and White colleges and universities (45%). The study involved a sample of 4,094 students who attended 30 colleges and universities in the southern and mid-Atlantic states. Students in the study completed the Student Opinion Survey (SOS), a 109-item questionnaire addressing issues of college performance, behaviors, and attitudes.

Davis' study brings to mind similar intents as Fleming's (1984) work but maintains focus on African American men's experiences. Davis' work addressed the field's retention and completion questions by illustrating the influence of differences in college environment type (predominantly White and historically Black) on African American men's achievement and by showing the relative overall effects of student's precollegiate background characteristics, racial congruency variables, and college environmental factors upon the academic achievement. Significant differences were found in all of the variables in the study for African American men enrolled in predominantly White versus those enrolled in historically Black schools. African American men attending predominantly White institutions indicated less racial congruency between their high school/community and their colleges than did their peers attending historically Black colleges. Davis additionally found African American men attending Black colleges were more integrated into the academic life of the campus, got better grades, and perceived their colleges as providing more institutional support. African American men who had higher levels of academic integration apparently performed better academically. Academic integration, in particular, was the only college environment variable found to be a significant predictor of these student's grades at predominantly White colleges. During this decade, Davis' work is complemented with other qualitative work which described the role that barriers to social integration play in the college lives of African American men.

Racism as barrier to social integration for African American men in college was also described in the 1990s. For instance, sociologist Joe Feagin (1992) described campus discrimination against African American students in White colleges in his work. To answer the higher education field's questions of enrollment and retention, his study drew on in-depth interviews with two dozen college students, administrators, and faculty members from a larger study of 180 middle class African Americans. Apropos to African American men in college, Feagin found that African American men who attended colleges in cities with significant African American populations were victimized by campus police. Feagin contextualized this notion by asserting that police officers are trained to recognize demographic characteristics of potential criminals. According to Feagin's data, these characteristics indistinguishably point to "Black" and "male" identities and trouble African American college men's experiences.

Nuancing the Conversation: Recent Work on African American Men in College

The 1990s and 2000s were replete with pathological descriptions of African American men as "missing in action", "in crisis", or "endangered species" (Davis, 1994; Neal, 2005). In a similar vein, declines among African American male enrollment in college reached low points currently recognized in the field. These trends were largely the subject of writing about African American men in college that emerged afterwards (Cuyjet, 1997a, 2006). In *Helping African American Men Succeed in College*, for example, Cuyjet (1997b) describes campus and service programs that address engagement, retention and educational attainment issues for African American men in both collegiate contexts. This text also highlights practices that serve to enhance the in-class and out-of-class experiences for African American men. However, no qualitative data buttressed this work by providing the lived experiences of African American men in college. More recently, *African American Men in College* (Cuyjet, 2006) added to ideas about the engagement, retention and educational attainment of African American men. This writing highlighted many areas in which empirical work focused on African American men in college may be scaffolded.

Answering calls issued by recent commentary, Strayhorn (2008) added empirical evidence to inform higher education's more critical questions about academic achievement among African American men in college. In a similar vein as Davis (1994), Strayhorn employed quantitative methods to investigate the relationship between academic achievement, satisfaction with college, and students' supportive relationships. Strayhorn studied 219 African American men (most of whom were their first year of college) and found that socialization experiences (e.g., precollege and transition programs) increase African American males' satisfaction levels in colleges and universities. Strayhorn also found relationships with faculty to be supportive to African American men's overall college experiences, adding to scholarship that identifies faculty relationships as generally supportive to African American student experiences and particularly for African American men (Dancy & Brown, 2007; Fleming, 1984; Roebuck & Murty, 1993).

High-Achieving African American Men. In the late 1990s and early 2000s, research and scholarship took an unexpected turn. Research clustered in attempting to disrupt stereotypes among African American men by writing about or implicating those in this group who were high achieving (Bonner, 2000; Fries-Britt, 1997, 1998; Harper, 2005, 2008). Fries-Britt (1997, 1998), who was largely the progenitor of empirical work on high-achieving African American students, analyzed data from intensive interviews with African American students who were participants in the Meyerhoff Program—a merit based program for students in math, science and engineering. This work was particularly salient in discovering academic and social experiences through which African American students (and African American men within this group) in science, math, and engineering were persisting. Study of high-achieving, African American men largely follows broader investigations of high-achieving African American students generally.

Harper's (2005, 2008) additional qualitative work investigated the experiences of high-achieving African American men in college. Specifically, Harper conducted interviews with 32 high achievers who attended six public colleges and universities with the goal of expanding the field's knowledge about African American men in college with the experiences of those who had "beat the odds." In his work, Harper found contributors to these men's decisions to actively engage out of class. Respondents were largely impacted by the following factors: (1) prior campus involvement during high school (2) examples older African American male college students set for respondents (3) desires to leave behind campus legacies (4) compulsions to advocate for issues affecting African American students, and (5) desires to learn more out of class. Further, he noted that out-of-class activities contributed to high-achieving African American men's overall experiences at predominantly White institutions.

Fundamentally, work on high-achieving African American men in college was refreshing in reenvisioning this group in ways other than academically and socially disadvantaged. However, given that nearly two-thirds of African American men who enroll in college do not complete, disadvantage was and remains the truer depiction of the majority of this group and more aptly holds higher education accountable in the ways articulated in the Spellings Report (Brown, 1999b; Dancy & Brown, 2007; Davis, 1994; Harper, 2006; Strayhorn, 2008). Study of nuanced populations of African American men in college must be extremely careful that desires to disrupt stereotypes do not suggest that the experiences of African American men in college are more rose-colored than the breadth of research presents.

Engaged African American Men in College. Membership in student organizations is generally found in the literature as facilitators of social and academic engagement in college (Guiffrida, 2003; Harper & Wolley, 2002; Kuh et al., 1994; Pascarella et al., 2006; Sutton & Kimbrough, 2001). In 2004, one study compared gender differences in student engagement among students who attended HBCUs (Harper, Carini, Bridges, & Hayek, 2004). The responses of 1,167 African American undergraduates (919 women and 248 men) attending 12 HBCUs (9 public and 3 private) who completed the National Survey of Student Engagement (NSSE) survey in 2000 or 2001 were analyzed. The data suggested that African American men devote insufficient time and effort to studying, reading, writing lengthy papers, preparing for class, and critically engaging assigned materials. However, these activities were inconclusively linked to the field's core question about retention. Therefore, further empirical investigation is required to preempt any premature indictment of HBCUs as lenient in shaping success outcomes in African American men enrolled in HBCU contexts.

More recently, a study described in Cuyjet's (2006) volume seeks to illustrate involvement experiences for African American men in college. In the study, 25 African American men at a predominantly White college in the South found that involvement in campus activities ameliorates the collegiate experiences of African American men (Brown, 2006). Addressing questions of retention, the study involved qualitative methods to identify the out-of-class activities that positively impact African American men at a historically White research university. African American men at this college identified engagement in student organizations, mentoring, and supportive relationships with each other as important for enhancing collegiate experiences.

Membership in collegiate fraternities is found to contribute to stronger racial identities (see Taylor & Howard-Hamilton, 1995). In fraternities, African American men have the opportunity to engage with other African American men and construct meaningful relationships built upon community and campus service. As Kimbrough (2003) describes, African American fraternities work to deconstruct the social, economic, and political issues that challenge African Americans in college and across communities. McClure's (2006) qualitative study of 20 African American men who joined an Black Greek-letter fraternity (BGLF) sought to add to what the field knows generally about the impact of this membership on African American men who attended a historically White university. McClure found that this Black Greek-letter fraternity served as a network of social support for African American men enrolled in a historically White university. The BGLF in this study also served as portal to a network of sympathetic alumni and to deeper understandings about African American history and culture. However, quantitative efforts considered the intersections among African American men, colleges, and fraternities.

Severtis and Christie-Mizell's (2007) work sought to understand the link between Greek-letter membership and graduation for African American and White students. Findings were drawn from study of 3,712 of individuals who had completed high school and had been enrolled in college. Respondents completed the General Social Survey (GSS), a survey which the National Opinion Research Center administered from 1972 to 2002. Nine percent (approximately 335) of the sample was African American. Particularly, the interaction between race and Greek membership on the probability of graduation was tested. In short, Greek membership was more significant to African Americans' college completion vis-à-vis Whites. Though this study did not produce a raced and sexed analysis of data, the study produced a raced analysis. Subsequently, this finding suggests that Greek membership aids colleges in retaining African American men. Severtis and Christie-Mizell's work, when paired with McClure's (2007) work, counter researcher suggestions that fraternities have run their courses in colleges (Kuh, Pascarella, & Wechsler, 1996).

Sealing Interstices: Future Directions for Research

The studies discussed above are salient for the field's understanding of activities that positively influence retention for African American men in college and lay groundwork for larger empirical study of African American men's involvement in college. This review and synthesis evokes a general way in which the field thinks about African American male collegians. However, higher education must know more about this population to effectively enroll, retain, and complete them. Concurrently, additional knowledge about this group will also aid the field in meeting demands for increased accountability to college-enrolled and college-bound students generally and African American men specifically. Below, areas are highlighted where higher education's critical questions about African American men may be developed, extended, and/or supported.

African American Men in Community Colleges. Albeit more African American men are enrolled in community colleges in comparison to 4-year colleges, men's enrollment in any college is decreasing. Research is needed to engage this trend for African American men who are enrolled or bound for community colleges. To be sure, this body of work is emerging and has not been completely ignored. For instance, Perrakis (2008) investigated, through quasi-experimental design, factors associated with academic success for approximately 175 African American men enrolled in community colleges in the Los Angeles Community College District. In this quantitative study, she found that academic preparation was a more significant factor impacting academic achievement (i.e., GPA) than students' races or sexes. Such findings additionally implicate K-12 education.

Pipeline Issues. K-12 schools, too, share the responsibility in conversations about African American male access to postsecondary education. More research that investigates African American males' transitions to postsecondary education is needed given suggestions that secondary education fails to adequately prepare them for college (Jackson & Moore, 2006; Ladson-Billings, 2007; Polite & Davis, 1999). Along these lines, Ladson-Billings (2007) recently critiqued Division I athletic colleges and universities are for providing athletic scholarships while failing to provide a "real" education and increasing likelihood of graduation among African American men and women. This failure is linked to an additionally problematic trend. She writes "at far too many Division IA colleges and universities, the graduation rate of African American student athletes exceeds that of African American students in the general student population (p. x)."

Pipeline research should also investigate socioeconomic contributors to African American male choices to attend community or technical colleges. The field knows that more African American males enroll in community colleges in comparison to 4-year colleges. However, research will benefit in uncovering if the strategies African American male high school students employ in choosing one over the other are purely economic. Additionally, postassociate degree outcomes should be explored to determine African American male next steps beyond community colleges. Ladson-Billings (2007) argues that most African American students who earn associate degrees do not persist to bachelor's degrees (which multiplies career options). Additional empirical evidence may compel higher education to increase recruitment efforts among African American men who hold associate degrees. This effort may increase African American male enrollment in 4-year colleges and increase flexibility in a downturned job market.

Cultural Work. Higher education institutions have to engage the cultural work of knowing African American male collegians and the diversity work of weeding hidebound ideologies that oppress this group. Colleges cannot wholly serve students they do not know. Raced and sexed trends of collegiate enrollment, persistence, and degree attainment may point to an innate or cultural struggle in the African American male psyche that draws this group's disparate outcomes. Recent work engages the complexities of manhood and masculinity among African American men as these concepts influence college choice, sensemaking of the college experience, college major selection, persistence, engagement, and how these variables are differently impacted by enrollment in an historically Black colleges and universities and historically White institutions (Dancy, 2012). Such cultural work potentially enlarges the field's understanding about the enrollment, engagement, and retention of this group.

Also, study is needed to investigate the meanings African American men construct through their friendship and informal relationships with each other and other diverse students. These may inform institutions more clearly about attitudes toward diversity and, thus, give institutions insight into the ways in which they can shape similar experiences institution-wide. Such an empirical investigation would build upon research which identifies men's friendship groups as sites to study openness to diversity (antonio, 2004). These relationships not only inform African American men's worldviews but, structured properly, potentially represent retention initiatives.

Gay and Bisexual African American Men in College. Little research is offered on the unique experiences of African American gay, bisexual, and transgender (GBT) men in college. Instead, research has largely focused on the plight of White gay men and women. Recently, Washington and Wall (2006) reviewed the literature around sexual identity development to offer suggestions for how institutions of higher education can provide support to GBT African American men. Researchers argue that African American GBT men experience difficulty engaging in college because they perceive their presence as despised across many collegiate organizations specifically and the college campus broadly (Washington & Wall, 2006). Recommended initiatives include acknowledging and collaborating with gender-sensitive organizations on campus. Washington and Wall (2006) write that merging racial and sexual diversity events are more inclusive ways of engaging GBT African American men. More empirical evidence is needed to inform the experiences about this obscure group of college students and compel colleges to expand thinking and services around this group.

CONCLUSION

In this article, attention is paid to empirical work that centered or implicated African American men's experiences in college. Unfortunately, most writing on African American men in college is relegated to book chapters (i.e., Cuyjet's *African American Men in College,* 2006), monographs, and nonrefereed academic periodicals. After review, it is clear that much more empirical work is needed to address the field's core questions of enrollment, retention and graduation of African American men. Scholarship on African American men in college appears to cluster at poles—critical research and advocacy research. On one hand, critical research on African American men in college clusters along themes that paint validated, albeit disparaging, portraits of African American men's college experiences. These themes include maladjustment, racism, complacency, and disengagement. On the other hand, advocacy research on African American college men has primarily focused on defending the identities of many African American college men (e.g., high-achieving or student leaders). In doing so, advocacy research pushes against stereotypes about the kinds of African American men that enroll in American colleges and universities. At the same time, though, these studies incur multiple questions about the relevance of the research to understanding African American men in college experiences writ large.

Many of the implications of studies in this review do not suggest the investment of institutional financial resources as much as administrators, staff, and faculty are begged to critically interrogate individual and system-wide value systems as these affect, via space, service and pedagogy, African American men in college. Institutional shareholders who serve African American men should remain cognizant that colleges are reflections of the broader society, often mimicking society's thinking and actions. When African American men arrive on campus, they should find institutional climates both open and attuned to embracing difference.

Researchers must provide additional empirical evidence to bridge gaps in the field's knowledge about African American men. Methodologically, more large-scale quantitative and qualitative work on African American men is needed to engage the breadth and depth of this group's experiences. Researchers must dedicate themselves to asking questions intended to shape the field's understanding about how to connect African American men to college and facilitate their progress through it. New directions for research will potentially inform widely regarded interventions for working with African American men (e.g., mentoring programs, lecture series, and "rap sessions"). Additional empirical work on college-enrolled or college-bound African American males also potentially informs institution-wide policy around campus diversity and hiring practices, student services, as well as faculty and curriculum development. With these outcomes in mind, scholars must conduct empirical work on African American men to shape in the field more responsible interventions and initiatives in a new era of accountability as articulated in the Spellings Report.

NOTE

1. The phrase *historically White institution* is not a misnomer. Rather, it is used intentionally to describe and refer to the legitimate and legal practices of racial segregation in postsecondary institutions prior to the *Brown* litigation and its precedent cases.

REFERENCES

Allen, W. (1988). The education of Black students on White college campuses: What quality the experiences? In M. Nettles (Ed.), *Toward black undergraduate student equality in American higher education* (pp. 57-86). Albany, NY: State University of New York Press.

Allen, W., Epps, E. G., & Haniff, N. Z. (Eds.). (1991). *Colleges in Black and White: African American students in predominantly white and in historically Black public universities*. Albany, NY: State University of New York Press.

Allen, W., Griffin, K. A., Jayakumar, U. M., Kimura-Walsh, E. F., & Wolf, D. S. (2007, April). *Ebony and the ivory tower: Trends in the socioeconomic status, achievement, and self-concept of black male freshmen between 1971 and 2004*. Paper presented at the American Education Research Association, Chicago, IL.

Anderson, J. (2002). Race in American higher education: Historical perspectives on current conditions. In W. A. Smith, P. G. Altbach, & K. Lomotey (Eds.), *The racial crisis in American higher education: Continuing challenges for the twenty-first century* (pp. 3-22). Albany: NY: State University of New York.

antonio, a. (2004). When does race matter in college friendships? Exploring men's diverse and homogeneous friendship groups. *The Review of Higher Education, 27*(4), 553-575.

Astin, A. W. (1977). *Four critical years: Effects of college of beliefs, attitudes, and knowledge*. San Francisco, CA: Jossey-Bass.

Astin, A. W. (1982). *Minorities in higher education: Recent trends, current prospects, and recommendations*. San Francisco, CA: Jossey-Bass.

Astin, A. W. (1990). *The Black undergraduate: Current status and trends in the characteristics of freshmen*. Los Angeles, CA: University of California, Graduate School of Education.

Astin, A. W. (1993). *What matters in college?: Four critical years revisited*. San Francisco, CA: Jossey-Bass.

Berger, J. B., & Milem, J. F. (2000). Exploring the impact of historically black colleges in promoting the development of undergraduates' self-concept. *Journal of College Student Development, 41*(4), 381-394.

Bohr, L., Pascarella, E. T., Nora, A., & Terenzini, P. T. (1995). Do black students learn more at historically black or predominantly white colleges? *Journal of College Student Development, 36*(1), 75-85.

Bonner, F. A. (2000). African American giftedness: Our nation's deferred dream. *Journal of Black Studies, 30*(5), 643-663.

Brown, C. (2006). The impact of campus activities on African American college men. In M. Cuyjet (Ed.), *African American men in college* (pp. 47-67). San Francisco, CA: Jossey-Bass.

Brown, M. C. (1999). Ebony men in the ivory tower: A policy perspective. In V. Polite & J. E. Davis (Eds.), *African American males in school and society: Practices and policies for effective education* (pp. 122-133). New York, NY: Teachers College Press.

Brown, M. C., & Freeman, K. (2004). *Black colleges: New policies and perspectives for practice*. Westport, CT: Praeger.

Brown, M. C., & Hurst, T. (2004). *Educational attainment of African American males post-Brown v. Board of Education*: The Frederick D. Patterson Institute of the United Negro College Fund, Fairfax, VA.

Burke, J. (2005). *Achieving accountability in higher education: Balancing public, academic, and market demands*. San Francisco, CA: Jossey-Bass.

Cabrera, A. F., Nora, A., Terenzini, P. T., Pascarella, E., & Hagedorn, L. S. (1999). Campus racial climate and the adjustment of students to college. *Journal of Higher Education, 70*(2), 134-160.

Cheatham, H. E., Slaney, R. B., & Coleman, N. C. (1990). Institutional effects on the psychosocial development of African American college students. *Journal of Counseling Psychology, 37*, 453-458.

Cope, R., & Hannah, W. (1975). *Revolving college doors: The causes and consequences of dropping out, stepping out, and transferring*. New York, NY: Wiley.

Cuyjet, M. (Ed.). (1997a). Helping African American men succeed in college. *Helping African American men succeed in college: New directions for student services* (Vol. 80, pp. 1-4). San Francisco, CA: Jossey-Bass.

Cuyjet, M. (1997b). *Helping African American men succeed in college* (Vol. 80, pp. 1-4). San Francisco, CA: Jossey-Bass.

Cuyjet, M. (2006). *African American men in college*. San Francisco, CA: Jossey-Bass.

Dancy, T. E. (in press). *The brother code: Manhood and masculinity among African American men in college*. Charlotte, NC: Information Age.

Dancy, T. E., & Brown, M. C. (2007). Unintended consequences: African American male educational attainment and collegiate perceptions after *Brown v. Board of Education*. *American Behavioral Scientist, (51)*7, 984-1003.

Dancy, T. E., & Brown, M. C. (2008). Unintended consequences: African American male educational attainment and collegiate perceptions after Brown v. Board of Education. *American Behavioral Scientist, 51*(7), 984-1003.

Davis, J. E. (1994). College in black and white: The academic experiences of African American males. *Journal of Negro Education, 63*(4), 620-633.
DeSousa, D. J., & Kuh, G. D. (1996). Does institutional racial composition make a difference in what black students gain from college? *Journal of College Student Development, 37*, 259-267.
Donovan, R. (1984). Path analysis of a theoretical model of persistence in higher education among low-income black youth. *Research in Higher Education, 21*, 243-252.
Feagin, J. (1992). The continuing significance of racism: Discrimination against Black students in White colleges. *The Journal of Black Studies, 22*(4), 546-578.
Feagin, J., Vera, H., & Imani, N. (1996). *The agony of education: Black students at White colleges and universities*. New York, NY: Routledge.
Fleming, J. (1984). *Blacks in college*. San Francisco, CA: Jossey-Bass.
Fordham, S., & Ogbu, J. U. (1986). Black students' school success: Coping with the "burden of acting White." *The Urban Review, 18*(3), 179-205.
Fries-Britt, S. (1997). Identifying and supporting gifted African American men. *New Directions for Student Services*(80), 65.
Fries-Britt, S. (1998). Moving beyond Black achiever isolation. *Journal of Higher Education, 69*(5), 556-576.
Gossett, B. J., Cuyjet, M. J., & Cockriel, I. (1998). African Americans' perception of marginality in the campus culture. *College Student Journal, 32*, 22-32.
Guiffrida, D. A. (2003). African American student organizations as agents of social integration. *Journal of College Student Development, 44*(3), 304-319.
Gurin, P., & Epps, E. (1975). *Black consciousness, identity, and achievement: A study of students in historically Black colleges*. New York, NY: Wiley.
Harper, S. (2005). Leading the way: Inside the experiences of high-achieving African American male students. *About Campus, 10*, 8-15.
Harper, S. (2006). *Black male students at public flagship universities in the U.S.: Status, trends, and implications for policy and practice*: The Joint Center Health Policy Institute, Washington, DC.
Harper, S. (2008). Realizing the intended outcomes of Brown: High-Achieving African American male undergraduates and social capital. *American Behavioral Scientist, 51*, 1030-1053.
Harper, S., Carini, R. M., Bridges, B. K., & Hayek, J. (2004). Gender differences in student engagement among African American undergraduates at historically Black colleges and universities. *Journal of College Student Development, 45*(3), 271-284.
Harper, S., & Wolley, M. A. (2002). Becoming an "involving college" for African American men: Strategies for increasing African American male participation in campus activities. *Association of College Unions International Bulletin, 70*(3), 16-24.
Irvine, J. J. (1991). *Black students and school failure: Policies, practices, and prescriptions*. New York, NY: Praeger.
Jackson, J. F. L., & Moore, J. (2006). African American males in education: Endangered or ignored? *Teachers College Record, 108*(2), 201.

Journal of Blacks in Higher Education. (2007). Black women outpace Black men in college. Retrieved from http://www.jbhe.com/preview/winter07preview.html.

Kimbrough, W. (2003). *Black Greek 101: The culture, customs, and challenges of Black fraternities and sororities*. Madison, NJ: Fairleigh Dickinson University Press.

Kuh, G. D., Douglas, K. B., Lund, J. P., & Ramin-Gyumek, J. (1994). *Student learning outside the classroom: Transcending artificial boundaries*. Washington DC: George Washington University Press.

Kuh, G. D., Pascarella, E., & Wechsler, H. S. (1996). The questionable value of fraternities. *The Chronicle of Higher Education, 42*(32), A68.

Ladson-Billings, G. (2007). Entering the pipeline: The pre-k-12 challenge to equally prepare students for higher education. In J. F. L. Jackson (Ed.), *Strengthening the African American educational pipeline: Informing research, policy, and practice* (pp. ix-xi). Albany, NY: State University of New York Press.

Lamont, L. (1979). *Campus shock: A firsthand report on college life today.* New York, NY: Dutton.

Lang, M., & Ford, C. A. (1992). *Strategies for retaining minority students in higher education*. Springfield, IL: Thomas.

Loo, C. M., & Rolison, G. (1986). Alienation of ethnic minority students at predominately White institutions. *Journal of Higher Education, 57*(1), 58-77.

Mallinckrodt, B., & Sedlacek, W. E. (1987). Student retention and the use of campus facilities by race. *National Association of Student Personnel Administrators, 24*(3), 28-32.

McClure, S. M. (2006). Voluntary association membership: Black Greek men on a predominantly White campus. *Journal of Higher Education, 77*(6), 1036-1057.

Mortenson, T. (2001). College participation by gender age 18 to 24, 1967 to 2000. *Mortenson Research Seminar on Public Policy Analysis of Opportunity for Postsecondary Education, 109*, 1-6.

Neal, M. A. (2005). *New Black man*. New York, NY: Routledge.

Nettles, M. (1985). *The causes and consequences of college students' performance: A focus on Black and White students' attrition rates, progression rates and grade point averages*. Nashville, TN: Tennessee Higher Education Commission.

Nettles, M. (1987). Black and White college student performance in majority White and majority Black academic settings. In J. Williams (Ed.), *Title IV regulation of higher education: Problem and progress* (pp. 49-63). New York, NY: Teachers College Press.

Nettles, M. (1991). Racial similarities and differences in the predictors of college student achievement. In W. Allen, E. Epps, & N. Z. Haniff (Eds.), *College in Black and White* (pp. 75-91). Albany, NY: State University of New York Press.

Nettles, M., & Johnson, J. R. (1987). Race, sex, and other factors as determinants of college students' socialization. *Journal of College Student Personnel, 28*(6), 512-524.

Nettles, M., Thoeny, A. R., & Gosman, E. J. (1986). Comparative and predictive analyses of Black and White students' college achievement and experiences. *Journal of Higher Education, 57*(3), 289-318.

Pascarella, E. T., Edison, M., Whitt, E. J., Nora, A., Hagedorn, L. S., & Terenzini, P. T. (2006). Cognitive effects of Greek membership during the first year of college. *NASPA Journal, 33,* 254-259.

Pascarella, E. T., & Terenzini, P. T. (1991). *How college affects students.* San Francisco, CA: Jossey-Bass.

Perrakis, A. I. (2008). Factors promoting academic success among African American and White male community college students. *New Directions for Community Colleges, 2008, 142,* 15-23.

Polite, V., & Davis, J. E. (1999). *African American males in school and society: Practices and policies for effective education.* New York, NY: Teachers College Press.

Ponterotto, J. G. (1990). Racial/ethnic minority and women students in higher education: A status report. In J. G. Ponterotto, D. E. Lewis, & R. Bullington (Eds.), *Affirmative action on campus* (pp. 45-59). San Francisco, CA: Jossey-Bass.

Roebuck, J. B., & Murty, K. S. (1993). *Historically Black colleges and universities: Their place in American higher education.* Westport, CT: Praeger.

Sailes, G. A. (1993). An investigation of Black student attrition at a large, predominantly White, midwestern university. *The Western Journal of Black Studies, 17,* 179-182.

Sedlacek, W. E. (1987). Black students on White campuses: Twenty years of research. *Journal of College Student Personnel, 28,* 485-495.

Severtis, R. E., & Christie-Mizell, C. A. (2007). Greek-letter membership and college graduation: Does race matter? *Journal of Sociology & Social Welfare, 34,* 95-117.

Smedley, B. D., Myers, H. F., & Harrell, S. P. (1993). Minority-status stresses and the college adjustment of ethnic minority freshmen. *Journal of Higher Education, 64*(4), 434-452.

Strayhorn, T. L. (2008). The role of supportive relationships in facilitating African American males' success in college. *NASPA Journal, 45*(1), 26-48.

Sutton, E. M., & Kimbrough, W. (2001). Trends in Black student involvement. *NASPA Journal, 39*(1), 30-40.

Taylor, C. M., & Howard-Hamilton, M. F. (1995). Student involvement and racial identity attitudes among African American males. *Journal of College Student Development, 36*(4), 330-335.

Thomas, G. E. (1980a). Race and sex differences and similarities in the process of college entry. *Higher Education, 9*(2), 179-202.

Thomas, G. E. (1980b). Race and sex group equity in higher education: Institutional and major field enrollment statuses. *American Educational Research Journal, 17*(2), 171-181.

Thotis, P. (1982). Conceptual, methodological, and theoretical problems in studying social support as a buffer against life stress. *Journal of Health and Social Behavior, 23,* 145-159.

Tinto, V. (1994). *Leaving College: Rethinking the causes and cures of student attrition* (2nd. ed). Chicago, IL: University of Chicago Press.

Tracey, T. J., & Sedlacek, W. E. (1985). The relationship of noncognitive variables to academic success: A longitudinal comparison by race. *Journal of College Student Personnel, 26,* 405-410.

United States v. Fordice, 112 S. Ct. 2727. (1992).

Washington, J., & Wall, V. A. (2006). African American gay men: Another challenge for the academy. In M. Cuyjet (Ed.), *African American men in college* (pp. 174-188). San Francisco, CA: Jossey-Bass.
Watson, L. W., & Kuh, G. D. (1996). The influence of dominant race environments on student involvement, perceptions, and educational gains: A look at historically Black and predominantly White liberal arts institutions. *Journal of College Student Development, 37*(4), 415-424.
Willie, C. V., & McCord, A. (Eds.). (1972). *Black students at White colleges*. New York, NY: Praeger.

CHAPTER 2

DREAMS FROM MY FATHER

President Barack Obama and the Reconstruction of African American Men's History and Studies—A Response to the Ford Foundation Report, *Why We Can't Wait*

Zachery T. Williams

For me, when examining African American men's history and studies, as a proposed area of inquiry, two things first come to mind: (1) the necessary critiques of Black feminist and womanist scholars in critiquing Black patriarchy and misogyny and (2) Historian W. E. B. Du Bois's famous, yet disturbing phrase and question: "How does it feel to be a problem?"

Most people in American society, including many African American Men themselves, view Black men and the history and study of such as a problematic in need of handling. I have encountered many Black women intellectuals who expression suspicion that such a project is designed to reify and resurrect the old demons of Black male oppression in a twenty-first century form. Of course, portrayals in popular culture and media

African American Males and Education:
Researching the Convergence of Race and Identity, pp. 29–55

characterizations of Black men fully support this notion of Black men as problem, to be feared, not trusted, and avoided at all costs.

However, while I find substantive grounding with my sisters' relevant critiques, many of whom are my mentors, colleagues; others my wife, mother, grandmother, aunt, and other relatives; friends; I depart on the view of Black men and Black men's historical experience as being solely chalked up to one act of oppression after another. As an historian and as an African American man, myself, I have been compelled into lifelong quest in search of Black men. Who are we really? What has made us do what we have done over all these centuries, decades, years, months, days, hours, and seconds?

To answer such a question, I needed an approach and a power symbol that at the same time represented a real flesh and blood, contemporary, challenging figure of an African American man, who walked the walk and talked the talk: Enter biography and autobiography; Enter President Barack Obama. I remember reading essays on Black history and culture by Joyce A. Joyce, entitled, *Black Studies as Human Studies*, where she, from a literary standpoint, alluded to the centrality of viewing the African American historical experience through the lens of a human-centered approach (Joyce, 2005).

After reflecting on the meaning of the snippets of Joyce's work that I read, I began meditating on Du Bois's challenging question and the reverse of that: How could we turn the problem, that is the African American male/man into a human? Enter history. In this work, the pioneering work of Dr. Darlene Clark Hine and countless other Black women scholars, including Rosalyn Terborg-Penn, Sharon Harley, Beverly Guy-Sheftall, Leslie Alexander, and countless other Black women scholars (feminists and womanists) alike has been highly instructive in providing a model of vision through the development of Black Women's history and studies.

As I have examined the lives of African American women, it has taken me to the point of turning inward, trying to answer the critiques levied against Black men, past and present. It has led me to wanting to search through the biographies, autobiographies, writings, correspondence, and life records of named and nameless Black men in America.

President Obama's coming of age story and personal journey is not unlike that of many African American males and men, such as myself, designed to search for our roots and discover ourselves in the process. The fact that makes Obama's journey so compelling is that his was inwardly initiated, whereas many Black men often find the space and motivation in a jail cell or toward the very end of our lives if we make it there.

In beginning to digest the meaning of President Obama's important autobiographical account, I have reflected on my own personal journey of manhood, noting the trials and triumphs as well as those who left an imprint on them. Growing up in Greenwood, South Carolina, I grew up, in the mid-1970s, around the decline of the Black power movement, under the tremendous influence of a community of loving caring folk. However, for much of my early years, like Barack, my own biological father was not directly involved in my life, leaving my mother, grandmother, aunt, and uncle (when he was not overseas stationed in the military) to raise me; and raise me they did with courage, sacrifice, wisdom, and a whole lot of tough love.

As I begin to grow older, reaching my teen years, I too had my own desire to find myself, first through the wonderful women who guided my life; secondly, through images of African American men figures, introduced by visits to the local public library, inspired by Haki Madhubuthi's work (Madhubuthi, 1990, 2002) and by sitting at my grandmother's feet on Sunday afternoon, after church, watching the South Carolina ETV program *Jobman Caravan*, a program that featured important aspects of contemporary Black life, including significant moments in Black history and culture.

For me, when I began reading Barack Obama's *Dreams From My Father*, I empathized with his story and I also saw myself in it, locating my own situation in the places where he indicated his own (Obama, 1995, 2006). After getting over the obvious pain of not having my father around regularly, I came to the point in my life that I just wanted to know him, and thus hopefully come to know myself. My father was never completely absent in the traditional sense of the term, for I experienced time with him throughout my childhood. It was just that much of my early formation occurred without his constant imprint, something that soon became necessary for me. In the interim, a stepfather stepped in and became that constant male figure for me into my adult years. Even as I was grateful for this influence of my stepfather, I wanted to know my biological father more closely. Fortunately for me, I did not have to lose my father as President Obama did to have the opportunity at reconciliation with him. Over the years, we have become very close and he is a trusted spiritual advisor for me. As I came to understand him and his story, I came to understand my story, all that I inherited from him, and was challenged to know what I owed to my own children, now 5-year-old daughter Zion and 1-year-old daughter Zipporah.

Along the time, I came of age as a teenager, I also discovered the wonderful world of African American history books in the public library, a mile away from my grandmother's house. There I came across books that would change my life, and in the process, provide living models of what being a man could mean. I began reading Malcolm X's autobiography, Ebony magazine founder John H. Johnson's *Succeeding Against the Odds* (Johnson, 1989), Richard Wright's *Native Son* (Wright, 1940), Ralph Ellison's *Invisible Man* (Ellison, 1952), and most notably Benjamin Elijah Mays' *Born To Rebel*. It was Mays's *Born to Rebel* (Mays, 1987), highlighting the life of the influential religious leader, theologian, Dean of the school of religion at Howard University, long-time president of Morehouse College, a native of my home county, that made the most indelible literary imprint on me (Mays, 1987). Soon, Dr. Mays' story and philosophy became a way of life for me, forming a motto that I live by to this day: "born to rebel" (but in a good way). I so emulated Dr. Mays that I wanted to go to Morehouse College (like most young Black men in South Carolina during the early 1990s) and one day become a college president. I did get accepted, although I never went because of monetary and other reasons (I can tell you my Morehouse College story if anyone is interested). Regardless, the impact of Dr. Mays' story and example continued to have an impact on my life even into my collegiate years at Clemson University, where under the tutelage of historian mentor Dr. Henry Lewis Suggs, I made the decision to become an historian of the African American experience. Years later, I would publish my very first scholarly article on Benjamin Mays and contemporary Howard Thurman in what was then known as *The Journal of African American Men* (*Journal of African American Studies*).

Although I had to stitch them together like a quilt, those biographies, novels, stories, histories, helped support the living stories I gleaned from elders in my community, at church, and in my own family. Soon, I came to understand the complicated experience of all these Black men, many, like my father, were without their fathers for important periods of time. As I reflected on their stories, I came to a question: Was the sum of Black men's lives, especially those I encountered in my teen years, only reduced to that which was troubled; or was there something more, something richer, deeper, more infinitely human?

Noted theologian Howard Thurman, mentor to countless Black men and women of the civil rights generation, mastered a spiritual meditative practice that he defined as the "inward journey." Much of Thurman's published writings incorporate themes of his life in works including *For the Inward Journey*, *Jesus and the Disinherited*, and others (Thurman, 1949; 1961).

During the early part of the twenty-first century, President Barack Obama has come to represent a renewed image and reality for Black males and men—Black father, husband, leader, orator, role model. The President along with First Lady Michelle Obama and the First daughters, Malia and Sasha, have come to signify shifting identities for Black women, the Black family, and Black children. His meteoric rise has opened new possibilities and new questions regarding the experience of African American men (African American or American African as Kenyan Historian Ali Mazrui would say). *Dreams From My Father*, for me, epitomizes how biography, autobiography, and human studies, in general, can provide the conceptual building blocks for a twenty-first century African American men's history and studies. In fact, the work of V. P. Franklin, Roland Williams Jr., and Kenneth Mostern, in the area of autobiographical studies, evidence increasing efficacy of using this medium to distill the contours of the lives of African Americans (Franklin, 1995; Williams, 2000; Mostern, 1999). Amiri Baraka, interviewed in a documentary on the life of Richard Wright, discussed the usefulness of autobiography as a medium whereby African Americans could accurately distill the contours of their lives. In keeping with this notion, Baraka paraphrased James Baldwin saying "My life is a witness. I'm not making this up. My life is a witness" (California Newsreel, 1994).

I take two major lessons, among others, away from *Dreams From My Father*. (1) a journey of discovery of President Obama's father's legacy and (2) a journey to find himself in the tradition of many of the Black men he read during his coming of age moments—Malcolm X, Richard Wright, James Baldwin, Ralph Ellison, etc. The second point raises for me a renewed understanding of another of W. E. B Du Bois's important phrases, that of double consciousness." In *The Souls of Black Folk*, Du Bois writes these timeless words:

> One ever feels his twoness—an American, a Negro; two souls, two thoughts, two unreconciled strivings; two warring ideals in one dark body, whose dogged strength alone keeps it from being torn asunder. The history of the American Negro is the history of this strife,—this longing to attain self-conscious manhood, to merge his double self into a better and truer self. In this merging he wishes neither of the older selves to be lost. He would not Africanize America, for America has too much to teach the world and Africa. He would not bleach his Negro soul in a flood of White Americanism, for he knows that Negro blood has a message for the world. He simply wishes to make it possible for a man to be both a Negro and an American, without being cursed and spit upon by his fellows, without having the doors of Opportunity closed roughly in his face. (Du Bois, 1999)

Could it have been that Du Bois, like many other Black men throughout history, while attempting to erroneously speak for the entire Black race, while silencing the voices of Black women—could he/they have been really, underneath all the race man talk, really have been giving a sort of disclosure or window into their own specific experiences as Black men? Unfortunately, this never fully comes out as such, and has continued to exist as definitive statements of the entire Black experience. What's to blame for this occurrence? Oppression? Pride? Guilt? What have Black men been deprived of in the process?

What is African American Men's History and Studies? Toward a Beginning Definition

This chapter argues for the reconceptualization of both our historical and contemporary understanding of African American manhood, one that goes beyond narrow discussions of sexuality and masculinity, or the mere representation of manhood. African American men's history and studies is an historical-based and interdisciplinary model that provides for the scholarly examination of Black men's lives and lived realities. African American men's history and studies offers a critical theory that encompasses all scholarship written by as well as about Black men. Moreover, it develops the basis for incorporating a sense of historical particularity into the gendered study of Black men, which examines the realities of Black men's lives, as they understood them, thus allowing them to speak for themselves. In positing the theoretical framework of African American men's history and studies, I attempt to reinterpret the gender of Black men, by acknowledging that Black men actually do have a gender. Such a theory is in dialogue with Black feminist thought as well as Africana Womanism, even as it carves out a particular space for the critical interrogation of Black men's lives. In fact, theories of Africana womanism and Black feminist thought provide the theoretical support needed to justify the scholarly and critical examination of Black men; a task which heretofore, has yet to be undertaken by Black men themselves.

In an attempt to develop a more comprehensive theory for understanding the multivaried contours, realities, and complexities of Black manhood in twentieth century America, this theory represents an interdisciplinary model, by combining literary, biographical, and autobiographical writings of Black men, historical accounts of their lives and times, correspondence with Black men, Black women, and other groups; as well as examinations offered by scholars of Black masculinity studies, sociology, psychology, Black feminist thought and Africana womanism, among other disciplines.

This work goes beyond contemporary studies of Black masculinity and American men, which in my estimation, marginalize the study of Black men by reducing such a study to a fixation on sexuality and representation, as the defining features of Black manhood. Just as it is erroneous to study the construction of race without critical considerations of the interplay of gender, and class, it is equally erroneous to study gender without examining the critical interplay between intellectual, spiritual, and physical dimensions.

This theory probes for deeper examinations of the souls and minds of Black men even as it seeks to more comprehensively understand the positive and negative physical ramifications attributable to men embodying Black skin and identity. The power of naming oneself, as Hull, Bell-Scott, and Smith (1982) assert in regards to Black women's studies, is in itself a political act.

Lastly, African American men's history and studies seeks to integrate a critical Black men's theology into its overall framework, one that uses as its standpoint the theological doctrine of humanity. It represents a critical Black men's theology that is in dialogue with womanist and Black feminist theology. It seeks to address the ways in which relevant religion and spirituality, historically, have molded the educational and character development of African American men, while at the same time addressing criticisms of the Black theology project raised by Jacquelyn Grant and other womanist theologians concerning the issue of gender in theological and Black church spheres—the public and private. Parallel to that understanding is the question of whether Black men have also possessed souls worthy of examination. Reading and critique of the writings of many Black men and women religious intellectuals will aid this endeavor.

As a Black man historian, theologian, and intellectual, my search for a critical theory that emanates from within Black men's experience has led me to the point of proposing Black men's studies. In the path-breaking book on Black men's studies to date, *The American Black Male: His Present Status and His Future*, edited by Richard Majors and Jacob Gordon, the late Clyde W. Franklin, in referencing the popular James Brown hit, "It's a Man's World," queried ... But is it a Black Man's world?" (Majors & Gordon, 1994). Understanding the socially constructed nature of manhood and womanhood in American culture, Franklin proceeded to ask whether Black males could ever be considered "men." In the same piece, Taylor argues that not until the late 1960s did Black men ever really get to initially exercise truly self-styled masculinity, often overcompensating such a masculinity to debilitating and destructive extremes—evidencing something many women's studies and masculinity studies scholars accurately label as "hypermasculine" representation.

Whether one speaks of the Southern Christian Leadership Conference, the Nation of Islam, Black Panthers, Black Christian churches, or any organization in Black life, the reality has been that as Richard Majors articulated, Black men, out of developing survival mechanisms, have developed the "cool pose," or macho sensibility in order to cope with the realities of violence and terror visited upon them and Black people generally. With this understanding in mind, it is difficult to believe, from a historical standpoint, individually and collectively, that the motivations of Black men have been solely mere reactions to or imitations of White manhood.

In the same volume edited by Majors and Gordon (1994), Manning Marable, probes this critical and confrontational men's identity in all of its necessary parts. Marable delineates the need for Black men to confront White history, the Black woman, and himself, in order to move beyond a limited fixation on stereotypical and narrow notions of manhood. Marable seems to call for the kind of comprehensive theory that African American men's history and studies seeks to provide.

Manning Marable in an essay entitled, "The Black Male: Searching Beyond Stereotypes," in Richard Majors and Jacob U. Gordon's *The American Black Male: His Present Status and His Future* (1994), poses a question and postulates an answer of what a Black man is in American society. Marable asks:

> What is a Black Man? Husband and father. Son and brother. Lover and boyfriend. Uncle and grandfather. Construction worker and sharecropper. Minister and ghetto hustler. Doctor and mineworker. Auto mechanic and presidential candidate. What is Black man in an institutionally racist society, in the social system of modern capitalist America? The essential tragedy of being Black and male is our inability, as men and as people of African descent, to define ourselves without the stereotypes the larger society imposes upon us through various institutional means perpetuates and permeates within our entire culture. Our relations with our sisters, our parents and children, and indeed across the entire spectrum of human relations are imprisoned by images of the past, false distortions that seldom if ever capture the essence of our being. We cannot come to terms with Black women until we understand the half-hidden stereotypes that have crippled our development and social consciousness. We cannot challenge racial and sexual inequality, both within the Black community and across the larger America society, unless we comprehend the critical difference between the myths about ourselves and the harsh reality of being Black men. (Majors & Gordon, 1994, p. 70)

In this provocative chapter, Marable lends credence to the need for a critical, progressive, African American men's history and studies. The only point of departure for me would be in the ordering of confrontations. Marable proposes an interpretive framework that confronts White history, Black women, and lastly has the Black man confronting himself. Conversely, the acts of self-critical confrontations should follow as such: Black men, Black women, White history, White men and White women. African American men's history and studies posits the notion that what has been left out of the gender studies equation is a methodical and self-conscious effort on the part of Black men, themselves, to deal with their own realities, history, and challenges. The texts and source material, needed in this vital undertaking are available, yet unmined.

Gloria T. Hull and Barbara Smith, elaborating on the politics and meaning of the Black women's studies, offers instructive tools for scholars of a critical African American men's history and studies. Hull and Smith stated the case for the field clearly, articulating:

> Merely to use the term "Black women's studies" is an act charged with political significance. At the very least, the combining of these words to name a discipline means taking the stance that Black women exist—and exist positively—a stance that is in direct opposition to most of what passes for culture and thought on the North American continent. To use the term and to act on it in a White male world is an act of political courage. (Hull et al., 1982, p. xvii).

In contextualizing the need for Black women's studies, the authors elaborate on the condition of Black women, which gives rise to the need for an area of study to examine that condition. They continue:

> Like any politically disfranchised group, Black women could not exist consciously until we began to name ourselves. The growth of Black women's studies is an essential aspect of that process of naming. The very fact that Black women's studies describes something that is really happening, a burgeoning field of study, indicates that there are political changes afoot which have made possible that growth. To examine the politics of Black women's studies means to consider not only what it is, but why it is and what it can be. Politics is used here in the widest sense to mean any situation/relationship of differential power between groups or individuals. (Hull, Bell-Scott, and Smith, p. xvii)

Similarly, Black men intellectuals, via the avenue of African American men's history and studies, must participate in the same sort of multilayered engagement.

Echoing the continuity in the Black women's studies project, subsequent Black women intellectuals have provided further foundational theory for that innovative discipline, informing a method that African American men's history and studies must learn from. In a 1997 interview on the subject of "Whither Black Women's Studies" noted feminist scholar Beverly Guy-Sheftall (1997), in support of the position of Hull, Bell-Scott, and Smith (1982), argued that feminism represented the most appropriate and effective vehicle for the furtherance of Black women's studies. Guy-Sheftall (1997) explains the history and reasoning behind this position. She argues:

> Black women's studies, almost from its inception, wanted to theorize about the oppression of women of African descent but also wanted very much to talk about the ways that Black women resisted. Black women's studies consciously and very explicitly wanted not to construct a discourse that primarily emphasized Black women's victimhood. At the same time though, Black women's studies advocates were up against the notion that Black women were in fact not oppressed and had not been victimized. So we had to find a balance between the two premises because within African American communities there's the notion that Black women have not been victimized at all, particularly vis-à-vis Black men. This was the difficult balance that Black women's studies had to negotiate. (Guy-Sheftall, 1997, p. 36)

By contrast, Black women intellectuals advancing the notion of African womanism, rose to challenge the idea that Black women's studies should find sole representation in a feminist voice. An oppositional voice to Black feminism, Clenora Hudson-Weems (1993) in the early 1990s introduced the concept of Africana womanism. In defining Africana womanism, in contrast to Black feminism, Hudson-Weems asserted in her 1993 work by the same name, the following:

> Neither an outgrowth nor an addendum to feminism, *Africana Womanism* is not Black feminism, African feminism, or Walker's womanism that some Africana women have come to embrace. *Africana Womanism* is an ideology created and designed for all women of African descent. It is grounded in African culture, and therefore, it necessarily focuses on the unique experiences, struggles, needs, and desires of Africana women. It critically addresses the dynamics of the conflict between the mainstream feminist, the Black feminist, the African feminist, and the Africana womanist. The conclusion is that *Africana Womanism* and its agenda are unique and separate from both White feminism and Black feminism, and moreover, to the extent of naming in particular, *Africana Womanism* differs from African Feminism. (Hudson-Weems, 1993, p. 24)

Hudson-Weems (1993), while providing justification for Africana womanism as a philosophy and theoretical construct from which to redefine Black women's studies, also provides in her work, a parallel justification legitimizing Black men's studies. In the tradition of Hudson-Weems (1993), other Afrocentric scholars such as Nah Dove have provided continuity for this particular ideological perspective within Black Women's Studies. Dove echoes Hudson-Weems in critiquing Black feminist thought for being narrowly focused and for its overreliance on European paradigms. Hudson-Weems writes:

> the Africana woman, in realizing and properly assessing herself and her movement, must properly name herself and her movement—Africana wom-

> anist and Africana womanism. This is a key step which many women of African descent have failed to address. While they have taken the initiative to differentiate their struggle from the White woman's struggle to some degree, they have yet to give their struggle its own name. (Dove, 1998, p. 515)

These conversations and heated debates, occurring within Black women's studies over the past 2 or 3 decades, have not commenced within African American men's history and studies. In fact, African American men's history and studies has yet to be intentionally defined.

While similar questions can and should be raised within scholarly circles of Black men's intellectuals, few have publicly arisen in such a way as to define an area as broad as what is proposed herein. Guy-Sheftall (1997) and Hudson-Weems (1993) seem to challenge Black men intellectuals to properly and effectively define a progressive, honest, and complex gendered reality for African American men in order to understand the ramifications of that history, rooted in various interlocking social contexts. Much of what has come to represent characteristic notions of the socialized nature of Black men, has, as a result, rendered many of these men as replicas of their former self, preferring instead to adopt a reclusive, hidden, and mysteriously cold posture. Currently, a blanket identification of African American men's history and studies with Black masculinity has positioned Black men as nonhumans, or at best iconic representations, to be examined and not necessarily understood. In the academy, Black masculinity studies has come to represent, in its totality, Black men's studies by default and without discussion, evidencing a lack of serious dialogue and constructive engagement within the community of men. In terms of nommo or naming, most Black men intellectuals cannot even bring themselves to the point of calling themselves men, which begs the question David Walker asked in his *Appeal in Four Articles: Together with a Preamble, to the Colored Citizens of the World, but in Particular and Very Expressly, to Those of the United States of* America: "Are we Men!! I ask you, O my brethren! Are We Men?" (Walker, 1830, 1993).

Perceptively, communications studies scholar Ronald Jackson raises a critical question against Black masculinist scholarship for its uncritical acceptance, approval and adoption of "the same cultural, social, and political agendas as traditional White masculinist scholarship." Jackson concedes that there exists shared theoretical commonalities between the study of White men and Black men, but forcefully argues that "there is a distinction that emerges where gender meets culture" (Jackson, 1997, pp. 731-732; Booker, 2000). While Black feminist thought is a critical aspect of Black women's history and studies, it, alone cannot embody such an area in its totality; it also needs to operate in dialogue with Africana womanism, and vice versa.

Comparatively, Black masculinity studies and Black sexuality studies represent legitimate and critical areas of investigation within the broader framework of African American men's studies. However, alone, these areas cannot completely "represent" African American men's history and studies, especially a holistic study of Black men and all of their/our complexities.

Similarly, as was the case with Black women's studies, to argue for the efficacy and legitimacy for Black men's studies as a field of study is "an act charged with political significance" (Hull, Bell-Scott, & Smith, 1982). However, it is uniquely politically charged considering the persistent labeling, association, and participation of Black men with White patriarchy. It is true that, in response to the continuing assault on Black manhood in America, either knowingly or unknowingly, Black men in varying manners have sought, in varying instances, to imitate repressive models of White masculinity and manhood. However, at no point in time in American history or cultural life, especially on a transnational level, have Black men and White men ever been considered on the same footing of social, economic, or political equality; much less having shared the same racialized, gendered, sociocultural experience.

Amidst Black men's reactionary rhetoric and imitation of White men's lives, seemingly lies a deeper and distinctive reality and history of Black men in America—one which has been projected beyond the national borders—yet one which has remained buried in the minds and souls of Black men. In "The World the Diaspora Made: C.L.R. James and the Politics of History" and *But a Local Phase of a World Problem: Black History's Global Vision,* Kelley (1999) provides scholarly justification for extending Black men's studies beyond the borders of America's nation-state. Kelley (1999) grounds the study of African American, in general, and Black men, in particular, in a transnational arena. Using examples of numerous Black women and men intellectuals, artists, and activists, including Carter Woodson, and Benjamin Brawley, a transnational understanding of the impact of Black men's lives, activism, and work is felt beyond the borders of nation where they, in the words of James Baldwin, are made invisible (Kelley, 1999).

In fact, Baldwin (1955), in *Notes of a Native Son,* offers a compelling account of his brief imprisonment in Paris in 1949. Baldwin, in a chapter entitled, "Equal in Paris," writes of a resolved understanding of his inability to escape the constrictions of race and manhood in Black:

> For, since I no longer felt that I would stay in this cell forever, I was beginning to be able to make peace with it for a time. On the 27th I went again to

> trial and, as had been predicted, the case against us was dismissed. The story ... finally told, caused great merriment in the courtroom, whereupon my friend decided that the French were 'great.' I was chilled by their merriment, even though it was meant to warm me. It could only remind me of the laughter I had often heard at home, laughter which I had sometimes deliberately elicited. This laughter is the laughter of those who consider themselves to be at a safe remove from all the wretched, for whom the pain of the living is not real.... (Baldwin, 1955, p. 158)

The voice of Baldwin speaks of a complex social reality experienced by Black men of reputation and those without, whom traveled abroad. Baldwin, a Black homosexual man, experiences encroachments upon his manhood on multiple levels and offers a stark example of a transnational Black man who knows the paradoxes of dehumanization at home and abroad, alongside moments of joy and peace. In addition to Baldwin, countless other examples exist and require extensive illumination. In a related sense, writer Ellis Cose characterizes this predicament experienced by Baldwin and countless other Black men as "envy," a mixture of jealously and desire projected upon Black men, then summarily internalized and reproduced through the cool pose attempt to reconcile, mask, and deal with this intrusion upon and denial of one's humanity (Cose, 2002; Majors & Billson, 1992).

Hence, there is a definite need to avoid essentializing any one identity of Black men as being representative of all Black men. Black Masculinity Studies, Black sexuality studies, Black male feminist theory, or an amorphous African American men's history and studies alone cannot define the complicated and multidimensional reality of varieties of Black men.

Despite the apparent difficulties of making this case, especially in the academy as it relates to the educational development of African American men, it is a necessary argument that must commence in light of the social significance of President Barack Obama on the reconstructed meaning of Black manhood in America and around the world. Even amidst controversy, within the African American community, Black men still possess a complex gendered identity, as theologian Dwight Hopkins (2003) reminds us in his classic work *Head and Heart: Black Theology: Past, Present, and Future.*

Hopkins asserts:

> Too many people within the African American community, church, and Black theology believe that gender concerns only women. When the gender issue becomes the center of discussion, most Black men, for example, become like corpses. Their tongues grow silent; their bodies drop to a limp posture; and their presence fades into a ghostlike absence. Gender, from their vantage point, relates only to Black women. If this logic is true, they

> reason, then it would be another example of Black male sexism to enter the conversation and dominate what is said and not said. The flip side of this belief is that African American men do have a gender, which is obviously false. Black men have a male gender, so gender refers to both men and women. (Hopkins, 2003, p. 91)

While I agree with Hopkins' (2003) basic argument, I do depart on one aspect, the aspect of linking the term "male" to a mature gender identity. Such a categorization fits a physiological definition, not an ontological and comprehensive identity orientation. However, as one considers the sociocultural and historical condition of Black men in America, past, present, nationally, and transnationally, Black men must reclaim the definition of their own gender identity and must define that as that of a "man." Even as it is agreed that the designation of "manhood" is a problematic social construction, so also it must be affirmed that the designation, "male" holds even more of a problematic, socially constructed connotation. The difference between the two has been interpreted by Black men psychologists such as Na'im Akbar, who argue that the term "male" translates more closely to "boy" and "mannish," both failed attempts at achieving manhood (Akbar, 1993). Fellow African American psychologist Joseph White has written extensively that Black men are in search of an identity and cultural space where they can freely be men, without what Du Bois calls "contempt and pity" (White and Cones III, 1999).

Even when one adopts an ambivalent gendered identity perspective illustrated by Claude Brown's character in his important novel, *Manchild in the Promised Land* (Brown, 1965), one has to go beyond maleness and masculinity in order to fully understand the enormous complexities constitutive of historical Black manhood. Recent research has demonstrated that economically marginalized sanitation workers in Memphis, Tennessee affirmed in thought and deed that they understood themselves to be, "men." Placards read, "I Am a Man," with no reference to male, manchild, or the equivalent (Estes, 2005; Honey, 2007).

To date, the area of Men's Studies has yet to develop consistent and comprehensive paradigm regarding Black men's specific histories and life experiences. The criticism Jackson leveled against Black masculinist scholarship holds sway here, evidencing a tremendous void in the literature of men's studies. Similarly, Whiteness studies has become increasingly ghettoized as many of its scholars have chosen to distance themselves from a careful critique of the historical and contemporary complexities and realities of White manhood in America compared with Black manhood. While some studies exist to refute such a claim, the majority of works, developed in recent years, clearly demonstrate an inability to confront head on that particular reality. While important, these studies fail to, comparatively, provide insightful analysis of the historical relationship between Black men and White men.

Few United States historians with the exception of David Roediger and Darlene Clark Hine, respectively, have entered the conversation to correct incomplete and inaccurate historical analysis offered by some social theorists and literary scholars. Consequently, the result of more Black men intellectuals choosing to bypass the issue of theorizing their own histories and critiquing themselves has intensified the criticism levied against them for historic and current irresponsibility and powerlessness. Much of the continued criticism could be attributed to the fact that more Black men remain outside of the realm of discourse occurring among gendered publics. Even amidst criticisms that Black men who assert an identity of agency are being patriarchal, it is imperative for Black men to enter the conversation (Roediger, 2002; 1998; Triaster, 2000).

In entering the engendering conversation, Black men must also confront the ghosts and demons of having to live up to the standard of White manhood in America and the contentious and multidimensional fallout that stems from this historic and often difficult relationship among men, involving issues of power, oppression, and domination. As a critical part of Black men's studies, this dialogue and study of the complex relationships among Black and White men, on social, psychological, physical, emotional, and religious/spiritual levels, intertwined in various subsets of study, what could be roughly called Black/White manhood studies, could offer much substantive matter that will unlock other aspects of the issue of manhood for both groups. Not only has White womanhood represented the standard bearer for womanhood in America since the founding of the republic, "White manhood, has always functioned as the standard bearer for what being a man in America means (Nelson, 1998; Morrison, 1992; Cole & Guy-Sheftall, 2003).

Further, the shadow of White manhood has continued to haunt Black men and women, in terms of hindering the development of other progressive models of manhood and womanhood, models that could repair broken social relationships within African American families and communities. As a result of this obvious void, from this Du Boisian internal and extraneous struggle within the souls, minds, hearts and bodies of Black men, have come the cool pose influenced masculinity tactics that have utilized representation, overrepresentation, sexuality, and other criteria to inadequately compensate for a meaningful, healthy gendered identity; the prevailing cool pose identity serves to reify popular culture images of Black men as the bad man, the brute, the thug, and the pimp, functioning as defense mechanisms, in an attempt to deal with the weight, burden, and seemingly impossible challenge of negotiating Black manhood in America (Bogle, 1989).

This shadowing of Black men, often by Black men ourselves, has contributed, in varying ways, to the "invisibility" and phantom-like existence that Ralph Ellison, Richard Wright, and James Baldwin (1952) and articulated so well in *The Invisible Man, Native Son*, and *Black Boy*. Such an existence has propelled Black intellectuals such as Ellison (1952), Albert Murray (1996, and Stanley Crouch (2004) to propose interpretive methods, that amount to neutral positional identities, identities that hopes to maintain a unity between the two selves Du Bois hoped would never be torn asunder.

In the process, the battle over manhood became a battle over representation and sexuality, with notions of religion/spirituality and intellect lost in a strange psycho-social-historical brew. In this sense, not only race has perplexed and plagued Black men of varying sexualities, religions, and intellects, it has also served to cast a veil over its connected and conjoined twin: gender.

For example, during the period historian Rayford Logan (1954) characterizes as "the nadir," Black men were not only targeted because they were "Black" but because they were men. The challenges of numerous historical moments forced Black men to assert either some self-defined negotiation of the Du Boisian dual identity or submerge any feeling at all. The realization of this uncomfortable and impossible positionality, has been decidedly stark for many Black men, rendering many muted copies of their former selves, unable to offer an effective response and resolution to the threat of White manhood. The inverse fear of Black manhood, or the uncritical adoption by Black men of patriarchal behaviors, could end in injury or death. As in the case of Emmet Till (Nelson, 2003), any assumed assertion of agency or authentic Black manhood posed too much for the wages of White manhood. Subsequently, Black men, in varying ways, chose to descend down into the underground, in a manner likened to Ellison's (1952) "invisible man." Today, the overpreoccupation and concentration on "masculinity" is reflective of such a reoccurring and sad trend in American life and culture. Instead of carving out new terrain, gender and cultures studies have chosen, thus far, to focus on illustrating, as opposed to fully understanding or interpreting the multidimensional historical reasoning for the escapism, rage, patriarchy, and silences of Black men (Black, 1997; Hale, 1998).

Much as Cornel West and Eddie Glaude set forth in *African American Religious Thought*, concerning the need for Black religious studies to reconceptualize its discipline, Black men's history and studies assumes a similar theoretical justification. West and Glaude's reconceptualization of Black religious studies, carves out a new integration of the important themes influencing Black religious thought. Among these areas include Black religious history, the sociology of Black religion, gender configurations, and the influence of cultural criticism on the study of Black religion. In a related vein, African American men's history and studies centrally situates the study of African American men's history, as the fulcrum fuelling the call for a new gendered discipline (West & Glaude, 2003).

To study Black men properly, one must do so from a transnational and interdisciplinary standpoint—one that examines critically, humanely, and holistically the music, writings, memoirs, achievements, shortcomings, etc of all Black men. In support of the conjoined Black men's history and studies project, Hine and Jenkins argue in the introduction to volume two of *A Question of Manhood: A Reader in U.S. Black Men's History and Masculinity*:

> It is hoped that the two volumes of *A Question of Manhood: A Reader in Black Men's History and Masculinity* will contribute to the growing interest in African American masculinities. Much erroneous information about Black men exists, and is widely circulated in the popular media, Most of it depicts Black men as negligent, criminal, and genetically prone to violence. But we have chosen historical essays that tell a more complex reality. They convey some sense of the depth and complexity of Black men's multifaceted experiences in the United States. Historically, the great struggle that has engaged Black men and women since the first days of their sojourn in the western world has been the survival of all peoples of African descent in the diaspora. As Aldon D. Morris wrote in the foreword to the first volume, we embrace and place before you 'the noble side of the notion of what it means to be a man." (Hine & Jenkins, 2000, p. 11)

While I agree with virtually everything that Hine and Jenkins offer concerning Black men and manhood in this statement, I still find the ideal of masculinity or masculinities as being inadequate, especially from a historical standpoint, which undergirds much of Black men's studies theory I pose here, of articulating and realizing the complete reality of Black men in America. Instead of contributing to the growing body of literature of a narrow African American masculinities, Perkins and Hine's groundbreaking study, serves as a foundational work in the area of African American men's history and studies, more broadly defined.

Further, African American men's history and studies must examine Black manhood as it appears in all walks of life. Not only should the field interpret "Great Black Men" of history and view Black men as objects of desire, envy, and property, but Black men's studies must examine all Black men as subjects and actors in their own unfolding historical drama, in all of our complexities, nuances, creative moments, and so on. For example, the songs of Black men soul singers, the lyrics of Black men hip-hop artists; the films of Black men movie directors, the pictures of Black men photographers, and the artwork of Black men artists are as relevant as the prose and scholarship of many of the works reviewed earlier; which are as relevant as my uncle's revelation about the joys and frustrations of his life. Henry Louis Gates has offered thirteen personal portraits of Black men although thirteen is not nearly enough to capture the diversity of experience embedded within that gender. African American men's history and studies stands to provide intellectual space for the continued interrogation of these diverse experiences of men.

MALCOLM X AND THE HERMENEUTIC OF HISTORY

Perhaps, one piece of the conceptual brick of critically and progressively examining Black men's lives is provided by philosopher/theologian, public intellectual par excellence Dr. Cornel West, with his "hermeneutic of history." Here, I parallel Dr. West's conceptual insights with the person and life of Malcolm X, in the hope that such a discussion may prove useful in reconstructing the concept and reality of African American men's history and studies.

Religious philosopher Cornel West, in *Prophecy Deliverance: An Afro-American Revolutionary Christianity*, coined and characterized the "hermeneutic of Afro-American history," a hermeneutic that Malcolm used successfully in his critique of Christianity and his recruitment for the Nation. West defines this hermeneutic:

> that focuses on the diverse conceptions of self-image and self- determination during the prolonged Afro-American entrance into the corridors of modernity: the long overdue reaping of the harvest that Afro-Americans helped cultivate, the seizing of opportunities previously closed, and the bruising encounter with the emptiness, sterility, and hypocrisy of postmodernity. (West, 1982, p. 69)

West further describes in the words of religious scholar Anthony Pinn, the terror and triumph of this experience through exodus, in the wilderness, and presently in exile. The terror of the African American experience involves the objectification of that experience and its people. West writes:

> When Afro-Americans are viewed as passive objects of history, Afro- American history is a record of the exclusion of a distinct racial group from the economic benefits and cultural dilemmas of modernity. Politically, this exclusion has meant White ownership of Afro-American persons, possessions, and progeny; severe discrimination reinforced by naked violence within a nascent industrial capitalist order; an urban enclaves of unskilled unemployables and semiskilled workers within a liberal corporate capitalist

> regime. Culturally, this has meant continual Afro-American degradation and ceaseless attempts to undermine Afro-American self-esteem. (West, 1993, p. 69)

Lastly, West underscores the nightside of this hermeneutic, one that examines African American people as subjects of history. West muses that when this is done:

> Afro-American history becomes the story of a gallantly persistent struggle, of a disparate racial group fighting to enter modernity on its own terms. Politically, this struggle consists of prudential acquiescence plus courageous revolt against White paternalism, institution-building and violent rebellion within the segregated social relations of industrial capitalism; and cautious reformist strategies within the integrated social relations of 'postindustrial' capitalism. Culturally, this has meant the maintenance of self-respect in the face of pervasive denigration. (West, 1982, pp. 69-70)

The discussion of the hermeneutic of history, as characteristic of Malcolm's transformative leadership model, takes on even greater relevance as it is applied to the development of a critical African American men's history and studies. Apart of this hermeneutic involved the concept of conversion. The experience of conversion is also central to articulating Malcolm's transformation into a more effective leader, evidenced by his continued maturation through experience and an insatiable appetite for African American history and other forms of knowledge. Religion scholar Anthony Pinn in his work, *Terror and Triumph: The Nature of Black Religion*, examines Malcolm's conversion experience into the Nation alongside his articulation of the related hermeneutic of what he calls the "ontological dimension," one similar to West's hermeneutic of history. In his examination of conversion, Pinn compares and contrasts the Black Muslim experience with the Black Christian. To Pinn, the motivation undergirding conversion in the Black Church can be found in "existential situations of pain, suffering, or injustice," which function as "a central impetus for recognizing the inner need for change, the core impulse for more meaning" (Pinn, 2003, pp. 166-167).

By contrast, in examining conversion accounts of members of the Nation of Islam, Pinn noted the milieu in which it evolved and flourished. The nation, beginning in the 1930s grew during the peak of the second Great Migration of the 1940s, and 1950s in deplorable socioeconomic conditions that left migrants disillusioned, wallowing in poverty and plagued by discrimination. In contrasting the two during this time period, Pinn determined that Christian conversions held more of a mystical nature to them whereas the nation's focus on concrete realities and manifested reason appealed to growing numbers of migrants disaffected and cynical about life in the ghettos of the urban north. Of course, the nation grew its largest in the urban north and Midwest as the south was still the bastion of Christianity and other areas of the country had not yet evolved an overriding religious sensibility as compared to its counterparts east. The discussion of conversion and the historical hermeneutic has direct application when applied to the theoretical reconstruction and merger of African American men's historical and contemporary experiences.

Malcolm utilized what Cornel West (1982) in, *Prophecy Deliverance*, characterizes as a "hermeneutic of history" that informed his encounter and critique of Christianity. Beyond the critique, which is a critical aspect, one must examine the need to apply the fundamental characteristics of this hermeneutic to the reconstruction of African American Men's historic and contemporary identities. Philosopher Alain Locke argued that self-criticism was the third dimension of African American culture. It must be noted that the self-critique, in question, is continuous and not simply applicable for a temporary period of time (Locke, 1950). Further, this critique is also not designed to be self-abnegating but self-affirming. In other words, the tool of self-critique must go toward lifting African American Men, and all of its varieties of community members, out of their inertia, apathetic stance, and constant state of oppression, toward a renewed, reconstituted humanity.

AFRICAN AMERICAN MEN'S HISTORY AND STUDIES: DOES IT REIFY BLACK MALE HEGEMONY?

There is no conflict between the assertion of a critical African American men's history and studies, Black feminist thought, and Africana womanism. Rather than displacing these much needed areas of Black women's studies. Black men's studies, in many ways evolves from the challenge and vision led by Black feminists and womanists. The discipline, instead of reintroducing hegemony, seeks to challenge it and examines Black men as a gender, instead of assuming what many consider to be the obvious. Much of the scholarly critique that has been brought to bear against Black men, has focused on the fact that Black men, overtly and subtly, sought to speak for Black women or similarly ignore their voices. In this sense, the generalized assertion that the Black experience was commiserate with a monolithic and archetypical Black man created more harm by not incorporating the sense of historical particularity which Black Men's Studies now calls for. Such an escapist policy within Black communities, adopted by Black men, served to create the groundswell of criticism precipitated by the feminist movement. In addition to calling for accountability with respect to patriarchy, Black men's studies attempts to demystify the amorphous "Black man" and "White man" and highlight specifics and name names.

For Black men to effectively come to grips with the challenges offered by Black feminism, Africana womanism, and womanist theology, they must first come to terms with their search for identity and with themselves. For the academy and seminary, this begins with the assertion of a decisive and multifarious theory which allows for inclusiveness while censoring none. Without such a theory, constructed in community and amidst various publics, all that will continue to exist will be monologues on one hand, and vehement denials and dismissals from Black men, on the other hand, who feel simultaneously defensive and yet, invisible, because they have never fully defined a comprehensive and progressive manhood.

Even the successes, achieved by Black men, have been attained at a price. Such minor successes have not failed to afford Black men a full acquisition of manhood as William H. Grier and Price M. Cobbs (1968) note in their classic 1968 work, *Black Rage*. In the probing chapter, "Acquiring Manhood, these psychologists insightfully characterize the dilemma inherent in the perpetual attempt of Black men to acquire manhood—one that is culturally specific and relevant. The authors argue:

> For the Black man in this country, it is not so much a matter of acquiring manhood as it is a struggle to feel it his own. Whereas the White man regards his manhood as an ordained right, the Black man is engaged in a never-ending battle for its possession. For the Black man, attaining any portion of manhood is an active process. He must penetrate barriers and overcome opposition in order to assume a masculine posture. For the inner psychological obstacles to manhood are never as formidable as the impediments woven into American society. By contrast, for a White man in this country, the rudiments of manhood are settled at birth by the possession of a penis and a White skin. This biological affirmation of masculinity and identity as master is enough to insure that, whatever his individual limitations, this society will not systematically erect obstructions to his achievements. (Grier & Cobbs, 1968, p. 59)

Fueled by the language of interchangeable and confusing confluences of sex and gender, the contemporary study of Black men has become lost in the postmodern moment, giving way to imaginary conceptualizations of manhood, devoid of sociohistorical reality; grotesque metaphorical studies, and empty studies of the symbolic meanings of Black masculinity, which prove elusive to the markers of Black reality. While doing so, the study of Black men has been poorly and insufficiently portrayed, allowing both the naming and the acquisition of manhood to remain amorphous, elusive, and escapable. Consequently, continued acceptance of this anonymity and lack of recognition of specific manhood(s), grounded in understandings of historical particularity, has served to place Black and White manhood in the realm of a fictional and figurative status, detaching and separating the general and romantic notions of manhood from the real voicing, articulation and recognition of real men with real pains, real problems, real loves, real dreams, real lives.

White and Black women led the way, specifically White and Black feminists, against the backdrop of the feminist and Black women's movement, in defining the gendered self. Now, Black men must give flesh to their bones of anonymity and tell which Black and White men they are speaking of and toward. White ethnic men have begun that discussion, albeit an incomplete one, as their voice continue to predominate the area of "Men's Studies." However, men's studies has failed to give visibility to the invisibility of Black men, with most studies concentrating on narrow discussions of the Black body and issues of sexuality, devoid of discussions and interrogations of Black men's minds and the souls of Black men. The closest works to date to more centrally address the gender dilemmas of Black men have been Marlon Ross' essay, "In Search of Black Masculinities" (Ross, 1998), Christopher Booker's *I Will Wear No Chain* (Booker, 2000), Ronald Jackson's, "Black 'Manhood' as Xenophobe," (Jackson, 1997) and Richard Majors and Jacob U. Gordon's landmark work *The American Black Male* (Majors & Gordon, 1994), among other works. With the current intellectual terrain mapped, Black men's studies is needed now more than ever.

While signaling important markers in the area of gender studies, a few of the works, which emphasize "male" to signify "man" and that concentrate solely on issues of "Black masculinity," demonstrate the inability of American men's Studies, especially Black men scholars, to move beyond masculinity. Despite these criticisms of masculinity studies, much of the current scholarship represent important parts of the evolving Black men's studies project, as evidenced by the critical and comprehensive subject matter of the issues which they cover, issues also of importance to Black men.

WHERE DO WE GO FROM HERE: CHAOS OR COMMUNITY?

In 1967, Martin Luther King, Jr. penned perhaps the most prophetic, eloquent, and yet, virtually least studied protest commentaries and most outstanding classics of American literature to date, *Where Do We Go From Here: Chaos or Community?* (King, 1967). King's account is as instructive to us as that of other outstanding Black men intellectuals, including James Baldwin, who instructed us in *The Fire Next Time*, *Notes of a Native Son* (Baldwin,

1963), and many other powerful works of personal commentary and autobiography from Black men, who were as different as the colors of the rainbow; yet beautiful and great in diversity. In addition, the example and legacy of theologian Benjamin Mays (2003), embodied in the Morehouse Man, offers an enduring model of progressive Black manhood, infusing theory with practical application and practice. Edward Jones, in his 1957 *Phylon Quarterly* article, entitled, "Morehouse College in Business Ninety Years—Building Men," reveals the core theoretical and practical aspects of Mays's program of making Black men. Jones' avocation of, and in-depth reference to the five principal values articulated by Mays during the Ninetieth Anniversary of the college, exemplify qualities that offer useful criteria for the contemporary theoretical and practical reconstruction of Black men and Black men's studies. This holistic plan consisted of qualities and characteristics that included maximum mental development, the development of men with "sound character and integrity," the foundation of "high religion in the life of the man," community responsibility, and self- and collective confidence in personal and communal Black manhood (Jones, 1957).

Mays's (2003) own emphasis on "knowledge of self" for the proper development of Black manhood offers a Christian based model that harkens back to Marcus Garvey's UNIA and parallels the program of the Hon. Elijah Muhammad and the Hon. Louis Farrakhan, as contextualized within the framework of the Nation of Islam. Other conversations must continue to connect the theoretical definitions of Black men's studies with the actual outcomes and practices that should emanate from them. There also should commence more courses on the study of Black men in community centers, church institutes and schools, colleges and universities, as well as national studies, reflective of a broader and more in-depth interdisciplinary theory of practice.

AFRICAN AMERICAN MEN'S HISTORY AND STUDIES AND THE FORD FOUNDATION REPORT, *WHY WE CAN'T WAIT*

Lastly, the Ford Foundation's 2008 report *Why We Can't Wait: A Case For Philanthropic Action: Opportunities for Improving Life Outcomes for African American Males* provides a three-part integrative model of engaging the enduring Black male crisis. This model encourages philanthropic groups to fund efforts in the areas of interdisciplinary research, grassroots programs, and public policy—proposing that these three individual silos work more closely together. Among its concrete recommendations is the establishment of a scholarly forum to engage issues and solutions concerning Black males as well as the development of a research clearinghouse on the Black male (Ford Foundation Report, 2008).

In the state of Ohio, similar to other states across the nation such as Georgia, there are a number of efforts under way to effectively address these educational and life crises facing Black men. Many programs and services are available at the collegiate level (Cuyjet, 2006). This effort undergirded Governor Ted Strickland statewide initiative for increasing the Graduation rate of Black males. Accordingly, my own institution, the University of Akron, with our Black Male Summit (April 3 & 4, 2009), my Pan African Studies class on African American men's history and studies, an African American male learning community, and other initiatives serve to provide solution-oriented models that can be duplicated throughout the state and nation, effectively empowering African American males and men.

President Barack Obama broke this strange silence of Black men by openly and honestly writing a memoir that sought to intentionally find himself, while locating himself within the tradition of Black and other men who impacted his life. *Dreams From My Father* is a story about discovery, reconciliation, liberation, and redemption, all vital components for all Black men and those who love and critique them, to reconstruct our understanding our of individual and collective paths.

POLICY RECOMMENDATIONS

1. Revive and/or create an African American Men's History and Studies journal.
2. Create an African American Men's History and Studies Research and Policy Institute, that provides interdisciplinary research; technical assistance to existing and newly formed programs impacting Black men; and plays a central role in constructing, evaluating, and implementing public policy, producing public policy briefs and white papers. Perhaps the institute could be named after a prominent figure such as Benjamin E. Mays, Malcolm X, Paul Robeson, or Howard Thurman.
3. Create African American Men's History and Studies classes at colleges and universities across the nation, modeled after the inaugural one taught, during the summer of 2008, in the University of Akron's Pan African Studies program.

REFERENCES

Akbar, N. (1993). *Visions for Black men*. Tallahassee, TN: Mind Productions & Associates

Baldwin, J. (1955). *Notes from a native son.* Boston, MA: Beacon Press.

Baldwin, J. (1963). *The fire next time*. New York, NY: Dial Press.

Black, D. P. (1997). *Dismantling Black manhood: An historical and literary analysis of the legacy of slavery.* New York, NY: Garland.

Bogle, D. (1989). *Toms, coons, mulattoes, mammies, and bucks: An interpretive history of Blacks in American films*. New York, NY: Continuum.

Booker, C. (2000). *I will wear no chain! A social history of African American males*. Westport, CT: Prager.

Brown, C. (1965). *Manchild in the promised land*. New York, NY: Macmillan.

Cole, J. B., & Guy-Sheftall, B. (2003). *Gender talk: The struggle for women's equality in African American communities*. New York, NY: Ballantine Books.

Cose, E. (2002). *The envy of the world: On being a Black man in America.* New York, NY: Atria

Crouch, S. (2004). Goose-loose blues for the melting pot. In T. Jacoby (Ed.), *Reinventing the melting pot: The new immigrants and what it means to be American* (pp. 271-284). New York, NY: Basic Books.

Dove, Nah. (1998, May). African womanism: An afrocentric theory. *Journal of Black Studies 28*(5), 515-539.

Dubois, W. E. B. (1999). The souls of Black folk. Retrieved from http://www.bartleby.com/114/1.html

Ellison, R. (1952). *Invisible man*. New York, NY: Random House.

Ford Foundation. (2008). *Why we can't wait—A case for philanthropic action: Opportunities for improving life outcomes for African American males* (2nd Ed.). Brooklyn, NY: Marcus Littles, Ryan Browers, & Micah Gilmer.

Franklin, V. P. (1995). *Living our story, telling our truths.* New York, NY: Oxford University Press.

Grier, W., & Cobbs, P. (1968). *Black rage.* New York, NY: Basic Books.

Guy-Sheftall, B., & Hammonds, E. M. (1997). Whither Black women's studies. Interview, *Difference: a Journal of Feminist Cultural Criticism, 9*(3), 31-45.

Hale, G. (1998). *Making Whiteness: The culture of segregation in the South, 1989-1940*. New York, NY: Pantheon Books.

Hine, D., & Jenkins, E. (Eds). (2000). *A question of manhood: A reader in U.S. Black men's history and masculinity, The nineteenth century: From emancipation to Jim Crow.* (Vol. 2). Bloomington, IN: Indiana University Press.

Honey, M. K. (2007). *Going down Jericho Road: The Memphis strike, Martin Luther King's last campaign*. New York, NY: W. W. Norton & Company.

Hopkins, D. N. (2003). *Between head and heart: Black theology, past, present, and future*. New York, NY: Palgrave.

Hudson-Weems, C. (1993). *Africana womanism: Reclaiming ourselves*. Troy, MI: Bedford.

Hull, G. T., Bell-Scott, P., & Smith, B. (Eds.). (1982). *All the women are White, all the Blacks are men, but some of us are brave: Black women's studies*. New York, NY: The Feminist Press.

Jackson, R. L. II. (1997, July). Black manhood as xenophobe: An ontological exploration of the Hegelian Dialectic. *The Journal of Black Studies*, 27(6), 731-750.

Johnson, J. H., & Bennett, L. (1989). *Succeeding against the odds*. New York, NY: Warner Books.

Jones, E. A. (1957). Morehouse College in business ninety years-building men. *The Phylon Quarterly, 18*(3), 231-245.

Joyce A. (2005). *Black studies as human studies: Critical essays and interviews*. Albany, NY: State University of New York Press.

Kelley, R. D. G. (1999). "But a local phase of a world problem:" Black history's global vision, 1883-1950. *The journal of American history, 86*(3), 1045-1077.

King, M. L., Jr. (1967). *Where do we go from here: Chaos or community?* New York, NY: Harper & Row.

Locke, A. L. (1950). Self-criticism: The third dimension in culture, *Phylon, 11(*4), 391-394.

Logan, R. (1954). *The Negro in American life and thought: The nadir, 1877-1901*. New York, NY: Dial Press.

Madhubuthi, H. (1990). *Black men: Obsolete, single, dangerous?: Afrikan American families in transition: Essays in discovery, solution, and hope*. Chicago, IL: Third World Press.

Madhubuthi, H. (2002). *Tough notes: A healing call for creating exceptional Black men: Affirmations, meditations, readings, and strategies*. Chicago, IL: Third World Press.

Madison, L. (Producer/Writer/Director). (1994). *Richard Wright—Black boy* [Documentary]. USA California Newsreel.

Majors, R., & Billson, J. (1993). *Cool pose: The dilemmas of Black manhood in America*. New York, NY: Touchstone.

Majors, R., & Gordon, J. U. (Eds.). (1994). *The American Black male: His present status and his future*. Chicago, IL: Nelson-Hall.

Mays, B. (2003). *Born to rebel: An autobiography*. Athens, GA: University of Georgia Press.

Morrison, T. (1992). *Playing in the dark: Whiteness and the literary imagination*. Cambridge, MA: Harvard University Press.

Mays, B. (2003). Born to reMostern, K. (1999). *Autobiography and Black identity politics: Racialization in twentieth-century America*. Cambridge: Cambridge University Press.

Murray, A. (1996). *The hero and the blues*. Visalia, CA: Vintage Press.

Nelson, D. M. (1998). *National manhood: Capitalist citizenship and the imagined fraternity of White men*. Durham, NC: Duke University Press.

Nelson, S. (Producer & Director). (2003). *The murder of Emmett Till* [Documentary]. United States: PBS

Obama, B. (1995). *Dreams from my father: A story of race and inheritance*. New York, NY: Times Books.

Obama, B. (2006). *The audacity of hope: Thoughts on reclaiming the American dream*. New York, NY: Crown Publishing.

Pinn, A. B. (2003). *Terror and triumph: The nature of Black religion*. Minneapolis, MI: Fortress Press.

Roediger, D. (1998). *Black on White: Black writers on what it means to be White*. New York, NY: Shocken Books.

Roediger, D. (2002). *Colored White: Transcending the racial past.* Berkeley, CA: University of California Press.

Ross, M. B., (1998, Fall). In search of Black masculinities. *Feminist Studies, 24*(3), 599-626.

Thurman, H. (1949). *Jesus and the disinherited.* Nashville, TN: Abingdon Press.

Thurman, H. (1961). *The inward journey.* New York, NY: Harper.

Triaster, B. (2000, June). Academic Viagara: The rise of American masculinity studies. *American Studies Quarterly, 52*(2), 274-304.

Walker, D. (1993). *David Walker's appeal in four Articles: Together with a preamble, to the coloured citizens of the world, but in particular, and very expressly, to those of the United States of America* (3rd ed.). Baltimore, MD: Black Classic Press.

West, C. (1982). *Prophecy deliverance: An Afro-American revolutionary christianity.* Philadelphia, PA: The Westminster Press.

West, C. (1993). *Race matters.* Boston, MA: Beacon Press.

West, C., & Glaude, E., Jr. (Eds.). (2003). *African American religious thought: An anthology.* Louisville, KY: Westminster John Knox Press.

White, J., & Cones III, J. (1999). *Black man emerging: Facing the past and seizing a future in America.* New York, NY: Routledge.

Williams, R. L. (2000). *African American autobiography and the quest for freedom.* Westport, CT: Praeger.

Wright, R. (1940). *Native son.* New York, NY: Harper & Brothers.

CHAPTER 3

BLACK BOYS AND BLACKBOARDS

Examining African American Males and Masculinity in Collegiate Spaces

M. Christopher Brown II

LET'S START BY SETTING THE RECORD STRAIGHT

The new millennium was ushered in with terror attacks on domestic soil, fiscal tensions in global markets, and uncertain terrain for the social landscape as it relates to public discourse and civic behavior. Despite the cacophonous declarations without data, documentation, or details, it is not true that the majority of the nation's African American college-aged males are engaged in the nightlife, counterculture, and/or prisons. Even data-rich periodicals and media outlets fail to have clear, concise, and uncomplicated data on the issue of African American male imprisonment.

Consider a report in the News and Views section of *The Journal of Blacks in Higher Education* (2003). The article "More Black Men Are in Jail Than

African American Males and Education:
Researching the Convergence of Race and Identity, pp. 57–72

Are Enrolled in Higher Education" was inaccurate and disseminated misleading information. Let me declare, *There are more African American males in college than in prison.*

Let us utilize the same two sources that *The Journal of Blacks in Higher Education* cites—the United States Departments of Justice and Education. The Department of Justice reported the total African American male prison population at 586,700 not 757,000. Moreover, the United States Department of Education listed African American male college enrollment at 635,300 students and not 604,200. In raw numbers, there are more Black men in college. However, the standard research convention is to calculate persons 18 to 25 as "college age." The United States Census, the National Center for Education Statistics, along with social scientists uses 18-25 as traditional college age.

Why do *The Journal of Blacks in Higher Education* and countless others continue to ignore this standard? What is to be gained from constructing an errant social reality around the educational state, place, and achievement of African American males? Given the near universal access to knowledge and data, how do the national media continue to perpetuate a distorted view of the educational achievement of African American males?

When the standard is used appropriately, the data reveals only 122,700 college-age Black males in prison. There are over five times more college-age African American men attending institutions of higher education than there are in prison. Further, the college enrollment rate among African American males has increased by 36% over the last 25 years (Dancy & Brown, 2008). In fact, for the 1990-2000 decade covered in the article, African American male college enrollment grew by more than 31% rather than the 25% reported. All evidence suggests that Black male college attendance rates continue to be headed in the right direction.

The import, impact, and implications of the errant and misguided research reports have created a distorted context related to the academic expectations and education policy. The attainment of African American males across the educational spectrum has critical importance for educators, policymakers, and society at large. National data trends display inconsistent and erratic performance by this population across postsecondary indicators. University faculty and researchers continue to offer explanations and/or implications for these educational trends. This chapter details the experiences of African American males in educational settings, the unique public history that gives context to their collegiate realities, and the role of effective practice in improving student performance.

THE SOCIAL CONTEXT OF EDUCATION FOR AFRICAN AMERICAN MALES

Like the historical ground from which they grow, schools and classrooms are not raceless nor have they ever been. They are the sites where the rules of race are taught and reinforced. There is a struggle in the realm of education that centers on its function. Much of this struggle also involves a need to distinguish between education and schooling. Schooling has as one of its goals to teach students about the ways of society so that they might be able to understand and participate in that society. This often leads to the perpetuation of inequalities of race (much less class or gender). The disaggregated data on African American males highlight the challenges of race in schools and colleges.

Before addressing the politically based discrepancies within educational settings, there must be some consensus on the purpose of education (primary, secondary, or higher). Underwood (2000) argued that schools "must prepare you to be a rational, reflective, and critical thinker. It should provide truthful knowledge about who you are and how you become a productive member of society" (p. 44). Being a rational, reflective, and critical thinker can be complex and require a solid base of knowledge about a subject. However, if most schools concentrate on a curriculum that centers on non-African American students, how can they be expected to relate to the subject, let alone think critically about its content? Moreover, how and in what ways do they promote college readiness, if at all?

The curriculum remains primarily concentrated within White American ideologies and perspectives. Rarely do African American students, much less African American male students, attend a public school that has a curriculum focused on their cultures and histories. This lack of a "relevant" education could perpetuate low academic achievement by this cohort of learners. Consequently, many of these students may not see the relevance or importance of schooling. Far too many teachers then view these students as underachievers or learning disabled. This is not true (Brown & Davis, 2000).

Like society at large, education within the United States must respond to the swelling population of students from myriad backgrounds and experiences. Consequently, the educational structure must also engage the complex nuances of multiple cultures, languages, and contexts within and without the classroom. The attempts to create a broad system of education that includes all persons have created visions of a culture in which many marginalized and oppressed groups are visible. Given the multiple dialogues from underrepresented groups, the mandate requires curricular changes which can unite all of the voices, and that will move society closer to the reality of universal education (Kincheloe & Steinberg, 1997).

The question that persists is whether all groups or persons experience education equally or equitably in this universe. The physical presence of African American students in a school or classroom does not necessarily connote fair and equitable treatment. While both school and collegiate desegregation in theory promote educational policies centered in equity of educational opportunity, both concepts fail to provide meaningful guidance for efficient student outcomes. This is guided by the history of disparate experiences for African Americans pursuing collegiate education.

The United States has undergone different conceptions of education as different and significant peoples have joined the population (Brown, Dancy, & Norfles, 2006). Without question, educating everyone in the twenty-first century will require curricular change. Hence, cultural/racial difference, both as a hallmark of American society and as an aspect of the higher-education curriculum, will continue to spawn debate and conceptual confusion. This conscious acknowledgement of race in an idyllically named colorblind society fodders dialectic between power, race, and hegemony that contours the definition, purpose, content, and pedagogy of primary schools and secondary institutions, not to mention colleges and universities.

The issues defining and setting the context for understanding the relationship between African American males and education are complex. Associated with each issue are multiple questions and problems facing Black males and their families—blood and fictive kin. Although there has been substantial discussion about the plight of Black boys in school, only modest attempts have been made to connect male lives to any meaningful understanding of masculinity and manhood. While the lives of Black males create much public interest (and fear) as evidenced by extensive national debate, media fixation, scholarly inquiry and social interventions, little attention is paid to more private matters. Indeed, private concerns are being voiced by families, friends, spouses, and lovers of Black males who at times benefit and fall victim to relationships with Black males that are fraught with economic and emotional challenges.

These precarious relations are facilitated by a combination of structural economic changes that have moved many industrial jobs off shore, demographic shifts in household arrangements and compositions, and changes in male role expectations as fathers, sons, spouses, and significant others. Nowhere is the confluence of social and political mandates, ideologies, and alleged pathologies more profound than in schooling. Because the discourse on Black males and their role performance is steeped in the hegemonic rhetoric of traditional constructions of masculinity, it fails to sensibly represent and elaborate on the diversity and complexity of Black male's lives and relations, particularly in the academic enterprise.

THE HISTORY AFRICAN AMERICAN MALE COLLEGIATE ACCESS

Educational opportunities were limited for African Americans prior to the Civil War. The problem of access was further complicated by the system of slavery operating in the South and the unquestioned racism of the North (Anderson, 1998). While some free African Americans attended "White colleges" in northern states, systematic postsecondary educational opportunities for African Americans were virtually nonexistent (Brown, 1999). In an effort to fill the void, northern missionaries, abolitionists, and educators began to establish colleges whose missions were devoted to the education of African Americans. The first such college to be officially chartered was Cheyney State University in Pennsylvania (founded in 1837). The aftermath of the war brought a proliferation of institutions targeted toward the newly freed African American population. More than two hundred HBCUs were founded or chartered by the year 1890 (Brown & Davis, 2000).

The year 1890 brought the passage of the Second Morrill Act. The first Morrill Act of 1862 provided federal support for state-level public higher education. The Morrill Act of 1890 mandated that those funds be inclusive of colleges and universities which enrolled African American students. Because of the practice of segregation in the South, many states elected to establish separate public HBCUs for the sole purpose of having a legal beneficiary for the federal support. These public HBCUs eventually were referred to as the 1890 institutions. This pattern led to a dual system of higher education in nineteen southern and border states (Alabama, Arkansas, Delaware, Florida, Georgia, Kentucky, Louisiana, Maryland, Mississippi, Missouri, North Carolina, Ohio, Oklahoma, Pennsylvania, South Carolina, Tennessee, Texas, Virginia, and West Virginia) which cemented the state and place of public HBCUs within the nation's higher education landscape.

This pattern of postsecondary educational opportunity persisted until a series of cases were filed by African American students seeking admission to "historically White institutions" (Brown, 1999). *Berea College v. Kentucky* (1908), *Pearson v. Murray* (1936), *Missouri ex rel. Gaines v. Canada* (1938), *Sipuel v. Board of Regents of the University of Oklahoma* (1948), *Sweatt v. Painter* (1950), and *McLaurin v. Oklahoma State Regents for Higher Education* (1950) each involved African American plaintiffs seeking to integrate a "White college." The preceding higher education integration cases served as jurisprudential planks for *Brown v. Board of Education of Topeka* (1954). The Supreme Court ruled in the *Brown* (1954) decision that school settings restricted by race were unconstitutional. This case began the seemingly elusive quest to desegregate public education.

While desegregating public schools proved difficult, the disestablishment of the dual postsecondary education model remained even more complex. Title VI of the Civil Rights Act of 1964 was proffered in an attempt to provide federal support for the cumbersome efforts aimed at desegregating colleges and universities. Subsequent litigation was filed to bolster the federal government's authority under Title VI—*Adams v. Richardson* (1972) and *United States v. Fordice* (1992). Both of these cases sought to enlist the federal government in resolving the issues surrounding collegiate desegregation compliance within the nineteen southern and border states. Despite the continued significance of race in civic and social contexts, education researchers, school personnel, and policymakers have yet to construct meaningful lenses for the assessment, interpretation, and intervention of race in colleges, schools, or social institutions.

The story of African American males in educational spaces is good and bad. African American males are both admired and despised in schooling and collegiate contexts (Davis, 2000). Recently, the *New York Times* and other popular media have touted the "Crisis of the Black Male" with a bittersweet glee. However, the collegiate experiences of African American men are ignored as journalists, politicians, and public commentators focus on the experiences of African American men in ghettos or prisons. Without question the African American male has enticed the United States's societal and intellectual imagination (Akbar, 1991; Hare & Hare, 1985; Kunjufu, 1988; Madhubuti, 1990). Sadly, too much of the enticement has resulted in pathological discourses on dysfuctionality. Likewise, the unfortunate tendency of education research to focus on the educational "problems" rather than "successes" of African American males leads to deficit model research studies that muddy the water on Black males' experiences in collegiate settings.

The research literature is replete with findings that clearly highlight African American students as marginalized across collegiate contexts. Trends that describe African American male educational attainment, enrollment, engagement, and attrition disturb higher education institutions and challenge researchers to expose the causes and propose recommendations. These trends persist despite race-based admissions, affirmative action hires for faculty and staff, and scholarships to increase collegiate access.

WHAT THE RESEARCH SAYS ABOUT AFRICAN AMERICAN MALES IN COLLEGE

Research on African American males is widely implied in the larger discourse on African Americans in college. After *Brown v. Board of Education*

(1954) and the turbulent Civil Rights Movement, many scholars began to study the experiences of African American students on historically White college campuses (Astin, 1977, 1982; Cope & Hannah, 1975; Davis, 2004; Fleming, 1984; Nettles, 1985; Pascarella & Terenzini, 1991). Likewise, other scholars from psychological, anthropological, and educational disciplines began to investigate the reasons why African Americans at all levels of education, have difficulty learning, adjusting, and staying in historically White institutions post-*Brown* (Fleming, 1984; Fordham & Ogbu, 1986; Irvine, 1991; Willie & McCord, 1972). Several researchers provided data concerning the extent to which African American and minority students have been successful in negotiating the college pipeline (Astin, 1990, 1993; Nettles, 1991; Tinto, 1994). However, few researchers turned their attention to the questions related to how African American males perceive college and persist to educational attainment (Davis, 1994; Davis & Polite, 1999; Fleming, 1984). And, while a significant number of African American males attend historically White institutions as athletes, even research about this subgroup is slow to emerge (Adler & Adler, 1991).

Tinto's (1975, 1987, 1994) theory, though challenged, offers an explanation that may lend insight into why African American males choose to remain in college or leave. Tinto posits that students' perceptions of the college experience relate to the degree that they engage in the college's social and academic communities and that negative perceptions of the college experience become predictors of attrition. As such, African American males who perceive any inconsistency between themselves and the institution will experience more difficulty becoming integrated and therefore are less likely to stay in college. Tinto (1994) proposed that some form of both academic and social integration were necessary to positively impact collegiate perceptions because the two, though different, are interrelated. Any difficulty becoming integrated on either level has an adverse effect. In 1994, Tinto endorsed the creation of communities in college to enhance the classroom experience. Greatly interested in his scholarship, scholars who have tested Tinto's model also confirm strong relationships among attitudes and behaviors and negotiating college (Bean, 1983; Pascarella & Terenzini, 1983).

Similarly, Fleming's (1984) study explored how African American students intellectually and psychosocially experience different college environments introduces a conversation about African American male perceptions of college. Scholars of note continue to cite a 20-year analysis, though their research about African American male collegiate perceptions though Fleming's analysis is unfettered. Fleming posits that African American males are unable to maintain controlled feelings of detachment in historically White colleges due to their subdominance and small numbers. In other words, African American males exhibit aloof behavior to cope with a lack of representation and power on campus. Fleming introduces the term *competitive rejection* to describe the ways in which African American men upon entry of college perceive themselves as least congruent with other students regardless of race and gender. African American males perceive themselves as less significant in comparison to other ethnic groups in college. Fleming's study also suggests that African American men's negotiation of competition in social and academic college contexts detrimentally affects their engagement, collegiate perceptions, and educational attainment.

Therefore, an African American male who experiences academic or social failure at a historically White college is at greater risk for attrition than White males or females and/or African American females who experience similar failures. Fleming's findings suggest that African American men risk truancy and attrition due to a loss of intellectual motivation and low self-image. Fleming's work, for example, posits that African American men are unable to maintain controlled feelings of detachment in predominantly White colleges. These feelings are rooted in African American men's perceptions of themselves as less significant in relation to other ethnic groups in college. Fleming's work also suggests that African American men's negotiation of competition in social and academic college contexts detrimentally affects their engagement and persistence.

Fleming's research also suggests that African American males who attend historically Black colleges exhibit behavioral profiles indistinguishable from White males. African American male dominance tendencies gain prominence in the historically Black collegiate environment as they perceive the historically Black institution as a more familiar territory. This is due in part to informal attachments to faculty (Fleming, 1984). Davis' (1994) work also examines how African American men who attended historically Black colleges differ from those who attend historically White colleges and differences in academic success predictors for the two groups. The survey data in his study shows that African American males at Black colleges are successful in their pursuit of educational attainment and perceive their colleges as more institutionally supportive. Harper and colleagues (2004) used interview methods to investigate the experiences of African Americans in college. Findings show that African American men in HBCUs neglect to make use of out-of-class time and are more likely to disappoint their instructors than African American females.

Despite growing enrollments, the data on African American male attainment at historically White institutions remains disappointing at best and disturbing at worst. African American males may feel victimized by faculty, staff, and students, notwithstanding available institutional support services (Cuyjet, 1997; Davis, 1994; Harper et al., 2004). Research suggests that African American males are labeled as threatening, unfriendly, and less intelligent than any distinguishable segment in American society by the college experience (Cuyjet, 1997; Hopkins, 1997). Consequently, African American males must negotiate a historically White campus that perceives them as hostile, intellectually inferior, and fatherless, and that values them solely for their athletic skill (Dancy, 2005).

AFRICAN AMERICAN MALE COLLEGIANS, MASCULINITY, AND ACADEMIC PIPELINE

African American masculine identity literature is largely shaped by research on the experiences and behaviors of young African American boys. Research on African American males is widely implied in the larger discourse on African Americans in college. After *Brown v. Board of Education* (1954) and the turbulent Civil Rights Movement, scholars increasingly study African American students on historically White college campuses (Astin, 1977; 1982; Cope & Hannah, 1975; Davis, 2004; Fleming, 1984; Nettles, 1985; Pascarella & Terenzini, 1991). Scholars from psychological, anthropological, and educational disciplines investigate the reasons why African Americans at all levels of education, have difficulty learning, adjusting, and staying in historically White institutions post-*Brown* (Fleming, 1984; Fordham & Ogbu, 1986; Irvine, 1991; Willie & McCord, 1972). Several researchers provide data concerning the extent to which African American and minority students have been successful in negotiating the college pipeline (Astin, 1990; Astin, 1993; M. Nettles, 1991; Tinto, 1994).

The marginalization and sorting of the schooling process therefore forces teachers to recontextualize what is currently known or believed about African American males in school. Educational settings must be redefined and revamped in order to accommodate diverse student populations. The policies and practices implemented in P-16 education have substantial impact on the quality and quantity of African American male students who complete high school, college, and/or enter the global workforce (Hodgkinson, 1985). The "flow" within the academic pipeline of elementary and secondary education is critical to the lifelong outcomes and possibilities in higher education and beyond. For African American male students, the academic pipeline leading to higher education has the greatest importance (Brown & Davis, 2000).

According to the Michael Nettles (1987), African American students overall are not excelling at a satisfactory level within desegregated systems of elementary, secondary, and higher education across the nation. He further argues that this persistent level of underachievement impacts their opportunity for social mobility and economic stability. What has gone unexplored in the era of desegregated compulsory and collegiate schooling is the significant role of education as a source of empowerment. However, empowerment only occurs when educational settings provide students with a sense of ownership and belonging. African American students do not by-and-large feel a sense of ownership and/or belonging to the desegregated school (see Kunjufu, 1988). As African American male students proceed through the P-16 academic pipeline, public school settings must seek to accommodate their diverse educational needs. Educational differences must not be treated as educational deficits. Failure to acknowledge the importance of self-affirmation through security and serendipitous learning through liberty evinces disempowering, desegregated educational settings which ill-serves African American male students.

From another perspective, Lisa Delpit (Halsey, Lauder, Brown, & Wells, 1997) argues that African American students must be granted participation in the "culture of power." Delpit asserts five aspects of this culture of power that can be considered key points to the matriculation of African American students in P-16 public education. They include the following: (1) issues of power are enacted in classrooms; (2) there are codes or rules for participating in the structures of power; (3) the rules of the culture of power are a reflection of the rules of the culture of those who have the power; (4) if you are not already a participant in the culture of power, being told explicitly the rules of that culture makes acquiring power easier; (5) those with power are frequently least aware of—or at least willing to acknowledge its existence, while those with less power are often most aware of its existence (p. 583). By asserting the importance of knowing the rules of the culture of power, Delpit (Halsey et al., 1997) sets the stage for preparing African American students for the right kinds of access and opportunities. Teachers are charged with formally overseeing the transference of cultural knowledge, traditions, and values to their students. However, this is merely the beginning of their duties. They are also responsible for nurturing and protecting both the student and her/his intellectual curiosity (Brown, 2000; Brown, Davis, & McClendon, 1999).

Far too many African American males (as well as other marginalized groups) are educated in classrooms whose curricular content ignore if not nullify their existence. The relationship between these students and society is often an ahistorical, repressive, and often stereotypical fashion (Castenell & Pinar, 1993; Hall, 1997). As a result, these students come to be viewed as anomalies who detract from the focus on learning rather than participants who are seamlessly woven into the fabric of the educational setting. Because the experiences of African American males are often not perceived as necessary within the educational setting, the personhood of these students is often devalued, ignored, and displaced. Efforts by teachers, administrators, and concerned others to undo the academic and social experiences ripple effect for African American males requires a thorough analysis of the status of the pipeline and the nature of empowerment.

SUPPORTING AFRICAN AMERICAN MALES IN EDUCATIONAL SPACES

Myriad roles and functions exist for teachers who endeavor to support their students—instruction on content, inspiration toward resilience, and impartation of support and encouragement. Teaching has goal-oriented forms and manners of being which attempt to maximize student growth and development, academically, professionally, and otherwise. As such it must be viewed as a nurturing process in which the teacher serves as a role model, teacher, sponsor, encourager, counselor, and friend to the students with the end goal of promoting the latter's professional and/or personal development. Each of these functions must be carried out within a context of a continuing, caring relationship between the teacher and student. The mission of supporting requires the teacher to perform specific roles and exhibit given behaviors. Although the roles and behaviors are varied there are tripartite modes of teacher support that capture the sum of all the requisite activities (Brown, 2000; Brown, Davis, & McClendon, 1999). The three modes of supporting are academic midwifery, role molding, and frientoring.

Academic midwifery is the way in which teachers assist their students in producing new ideas and scholarly insights. It is related to the formal instructional and advising responsibilities of a professor, but advances to a role of supporting. Teachers must bring to life the sleeping potential within their students that without assistance would otherwise be wasted. This is particularly important for African American male students. Although absent from the literature on teacher duties, one of the greatest responsibilities is the care of the intellectual soul of our students. Teachers must assist students in giving birth to intellectual ideas, methods of inquiry, and professional practices that are transformative. As previously mentioned, teaching is not just about helping students regurgitate what you know, but also includes aiding students as they learn their way serendipitously.

The next modality requires all teachers, but especially teachers of African American males, to move beyond role modeling to role molding. Role molding differs from academic midwifery in that the focus shifts from theoretical, abstract, and cognitive to practical, pragmatic, and applied. "Role modeling" suggests that one serves as a symbolic figure of what is possible or aspired. Conversely, "role molding" is the active engagement of a teacher in shaping the lives of their students into the academic and social shapes or patterns which the students' desire. At this juncture it is necessary to offer a warning. Faculty must be leery of trying to mold students into what they wish for the students to be. (If you recall Malcolm X wanted to be a lawyer, but his teacher wanted him to be a carpenter.) Under role molding the support is to aid the student in carving out their own niche. This is extremely difficult for many White teachers who may have limited understanding of other groups' cultural interests. The role molder is to teach through confirming and questioning the usefulness and appropriateness of student activities, maintaining a focus on the student's desired educational goals or career ambitions.

The last mode in the supportive teaching is frientoring. Frientoring is the unique nexus between mentoring and friendship. As such, it is the frientoring function of supporting relationships that is the most complex. This complexity is exacerbated by the presence of African American males. This complexity is generated by the asymmetrical nature of the teacher-student relationship. Traditionally, friendly interactions between teachers and students have been discouraged because the position of teachers as superior partners and students as inferior partners raises ethical questions for many academics (Smith & Davidson, 1992). Hence out-of-class friendships between teachers and students are discouraged. Given the sexualized racial paranoia of American society (Brown, Dancy, & Davis, 2007; Dancy & Brown, 2008), friendly relations between White female teachers and Black male students are often met with heightened scrutiny and skepticism. However, discouraging out-of-class relationships between teachers and students runs contrary to the idea of supporting student academic growth and personal development. In frientoring, the teacher provides guidance and wisdom, while the student provides respect and reverence for the interactions. Frientoring allows each person to feel as though they are giving of themselves and simultaneously receiving intellectual and emotional reinforcement. Supporting African American male students requires friendly relations between teachers and students.

The supporting modes of academic midwifery, role molding, and frientoring are central to the effective supporting of African American male students in specific, and all students in general. By bringing to life the buried cognitive thoughts of the students, shaping them into studious inquirers, and providing them genuine access to our professional lives, we create an atmosphere where students will aspire to serve comparable roles in the lives of future students. Each of the tripartite modes requires care and support, experiential learning, collaboration, and commitment to both the students and the profession (Valadez, 1998). Consequently, teachers must rethink their roles as supporters and encouragers of students (Brown, 2000). John Bean (1998) writes, "Only if we reimagine our work, can we serve the soul of the world" (p. 511). The tripartite modes serve to promote and advance the educational experiences of African American students and others.

CONCLUDING THOUGHTS

African American male participation in college remains scant across both historically Black and White campuses. Higher education still needs to make significant improvements to make in admitting, enrolling, and completing more African American males from college at all levels. Consequently, all colleges, without respective to history or predominant population, must begin or continue to create and improve the campus environments in which African American males experience their college days. Given what we know, historically Black colleges remain one of the best models for this type of contextual intervention. Other models include campus student centers or spaces designed as safe-havens and/or that focus on student adjustment and engagement. Both entities provide resources and opportunities critical to African American male retention, completion, and civic success.

Without substantive intervention on the part of all institutions, African American males may be largely absent from the history of colleges and universities in America in the twenty-first century. To the extent that institutions of higher education can provide culturally responsive learning communities, perceptions of disinterest and disengagement by and among African American males on campus will diminish. The future requires the participation of all of our nation's citizens, including African American males. Colleges and universities play a critical role in preparing African American males to assume important roles in the academic, economic, and civic realities of the United States and global community.

REFERENCES

Adams v. Richardson, 351 F.2d 636 (DC Cir. 1972).

Adler, P. A., & Adler, P. (1991). *Backboards and blackboards*. New York, NY: Columbia University Press.

Akbar, N. (1991). *Visions for Black men*. Tallahassee, FL: Mind Productions & Associates.

Anderson, J. (1998). *The education of Blacks in the south, 1860-1935*. Chapel Hill, NC: University of North Carolina Press.

Astin, A. W. (1977). *Four critical years: Effects of college of beliefs, attitudes, and knowledge*. San Francisco, CA: Jossey-Bass.

Astin, A. W. (1982). *Minorities in higher education: Recent trends, current prospects, and recommendations*. San Francisco, CA: Jossey-Bass.

Astin, A. W. (1990). *The Black undergraduate: Current status and trends in the characteristics of freshmen*. Los Angeles, CA: University of California, Graduate School of Education.

Astin, A. W. (1993). *What matters in college?: Four critical years revisited*. San Francisco, CA: Jossey-Bass.

Bean, J. (1998). Alternative models of professorial roles: New languages to reimagine faculty work. *Journal of Higher Education, 69*(5), 496-512.

Bean, J. P. (1983). The application of a model of turnover in work organizations to the student attrition process. *Review of Higher Education, 6*(2), 129-148.

Berea College v. Commonwealth of Kentucky, 211 U.S. 45 (1908).

Brown, M. C. (1999). *The quest to define collegiate desegregation: Black Colleges, Title VI compliance, and post-Adams litigation*. Westport, CT: Bergin & Garvey.

Brown, M. C. (2000). Involvement with students: How much can I give? In M. Garcia (Ed.), *Succeeding in an academic career: A guide for faculty of color* (pp. 71-88). Westport, CT: Greenwood.

Brown, M. C., & Davis, J. E. (2000). *Black sons to mothers: Compliments, critiques, and challenges for cultural workers in education*. New York, NY: Peter Lang.

Brown, M. C., Dancy, T. E., & Davis, J. E. (2007). Drowning beneath a rising tide: How America leaves its disadvantaged students behind. In S. P. Robinson & M. C. Brown (Eds.), *The children hurricane Katrina left behind: Schooling contexts, professional preparation, and community politics*. New York, NY: Peter Lang.

Brown, M. C., Dancy, T. E., & Norfles, N. (2006). A nation still at risk: No child left behind and the salvation of disadvantaged students. In F. Brown (Ed.), *No child left behind and other special programs in urban school districts* (pp. 341-364). Oxford, England: Elsevier.

Brown, M. C., Davis, G. L., & McClendon, S. (1999). Mentoring graduate students of color: Myths, models, and modes. *Peabody Journal of Education, 74*, 105-118.

Brown v. Board of Education of Topeka [Brown I], 347 U.S. 483 (1954).

Castenell, L. A., & Pinar, W. F. (Eds.). (1993). *Understanding curriculum as racial text: Representations of identity and difference in education*. Albany, NY: State University of New York.

Civil Rights Act of 1964, Pub. L. No. 88-352, 78 Stat. 241.

Cope, R., & Hannah, W. (1975). *Revolving college doors: The causes and consequences of dropping out, stepping out, and transferring*. New York, NY: Wiley.

Cuyjet, M. (Ed.). (1997). *Helping African American men succeed in college: New directions for student services* (Vol. 80). San Francisco, CA: Jossey-Bass.

Dancy, T. E. (2005). Madness or elitism? African Americans who reject HBCUs. *Black Issues in Higher Education, 22*(5). 82.

Dancy, T. E., & Brown, M. C. (2008, March). Unintended consequences: African American male educational attainment and collegiate perceptions after *Brown v. Board of Education. American Behavioral Scientist*, 984-1003.

Davis, J. E. (1994). College in Black and White: The academic experiences of African American males. *Journal of Negro Education, 63*, 570-587.

Davis, J. E. (2000). Mothering for manhood: The (re)production of a Black son's gendered self. In M. C. Brown & J. E. Davis (Eds.), *Black sons to mothers: Com-*

pliments, critiques, and challenges for cultural workers in education. New York, NY: Peter Lang.

Davis, J. E., & Polite, V. (1999). *African American males in schools and society: Policies and procedures for effective education.* New York, NY: Teachers College Press

Davis, R. D. (2004). *Black students' perceptions: The complexity of persistence to graduation at an American university.* New York, NY: Peter Lang.

Fleming, J. (1984). *Blacks in college*. San Francisco, CA: Jossey-Bass.

Fordham, S., & Ogbu, J. U. (1986). Black students' school success: Coping with the "burden of acting White." *The Urban Review, 18*(3), 179-205.

Hall, P. M. (Ed.). (1997). *Race, ethnicity, and multiculturalism: Policy and practice*. New York, NY: Garland.

Halsey, A. H., Lauder, H., Brown, P., & Wells A. S. (Eds.). (1997). *Education: Culture, economy, and society.* Oxford, England: Oxford University Press.

Hare, N., & Hare, J. (1985). *Bringing the black boy to manhood: The passage.* San Francisco, CA: Black Think Tank.

Harper, S. R., Carini, R. M., Bridges, B. K., & Hayek, J. C. (2004). Gender differences in student engagement among African American undergraduates at historically Black colleges and universities. *Journal of College Student Development, 45*(3), 271-284.

Hodgkinson, H. (1985). *All one system: Demographics of education, kindergarten through graduate school.* Washington, DC: The Institute for Educational Leadership.

Hopkins, R. (1997). *Educating Black males: Critical lessons in schooling, community, and power.* Albany, NY: State University of New York Press.

Irvine, J. J. (1991). *Black students and school failure: Policies, practices, and prescriptions*. New York, NY: Praeger.

Kincheloe, J. L., & Steinberg, S. R. (1997). *Changing multiculturalism*. Bristol, PA: Open University

Kunjufu, J. (1988). *To be popular or smart: The black peer group*. Chicago, IL: African American Images.

Madhubuti, H. (1990). *Black men: Obsolete, single, dangerous?* Chicago, IL: Third World Press.

McLaurin v. Oklahoma State Regents for Higher Education, 339 U.S. 637 (1950).

Missouri ex rel. Gaines v. Canada, 305 U.S. 337 (1938).

More black men are in jail than enrolled in higher education [Editorial]. (2003, Autumn). *The Journal of Blacks in Higher Education, 41,* 62.

Morrill Act of 1890, Ch. 841, 26 Stat. 417.

Nettles, M. (1987). Black and white college student performance in majority white and majority black academic settings. In J. Williams (Ed.), *Title IV regulation of higher education: Problem and progress* (pp. 49-63). New York, NY: Teachers College Press.

Nettles, M. (1991). *Assessing progress in minority access and achievement in American higher education*. Denver, CO: Education Commission of the States.

Nettles, M. T. (1985). *The causes and consequences of college students' performance: A focus on Black and White students' attrition rates, progression rates and grade point averages*. Nashville, TN: Tennessee Higher Education Commission.

Pascarella, E. T., & Terenzini, P. T. (1983). Predicting voluntary year persistence/withdrawal behavior in a residential university: A path analytical validation of Tinto's model. *Journal of Educational Psychology, 75*, 215-226.
Pascarella, E. T., & Terenzini, P. T. (1991). *How college affects students*. San Francisco, CA: Jossey-Bass.
Pearson v. Murray, 182 A. 590 (1936).
Sipuel v. Board of Regents of the University of Oklahoma, 332 U.S. 631 (1948).
Smith, E. P., & Davidson, W. S. (1992). Mentoring and the development of African American graduate students. *Journal of College Student Development, 33*(6), 531-539.
Sweatt v. Painter, 339 U.S. 629 (1950).
Tinto, V. (1975). Dropouts from education: A theoretical synthesis of recent research. *Educational Research, 45*, 89-125.
Tinto, V. (1987). *Leaving college: Rethinking the causes and cures of student attrition*. Chicago, IL: University of Chicago Press.
Tinto, V. (1994). *Leaving College: Rethinking the causes and cures of student attrition* (2nd. ed.). Chicago, IL: University of Chicago Press.
Underwood, E. (2000). From son to mother? Intellectualizing the personal. In M. C. Brown & J. E. Davis (Eds.), *Black sons to mothers: Compliments, critiques, and challenges for cultural workers in education* (pp. 35-49). New York, NY: Peter Lang.
United States v. Fordice, 505 U.S. 717, 112 S.Ct. 2727 (1992).
Valadez, J. R. (1998). The social dynamics of mentoring in graduate education: A case study of African American students and their graduate advisors. In H. T. Frierson (Ed.), *Diversity in higher education* (pp. 129-140). Stamford, CT: JAI.
Willie, C. V., & McCord, A. (Eds.). (1972). *Black students at White colleges*. New York, NY: Praeger.

PART II

CLASSROOMS AND PEDAGOGY

CHAPTER 4

WHO AM I? I AM WHO YOU SAY I AM

Black Male Identity and Teacher Perceptions

Denise L. Collier and V. Lawson Bush

September 20, 2007 approximately 20,000 people marched in Jena, Louisiana in protest of six African American male students initially charged with second-degree murder and conspiracy for a schoolyard brawl. The protesters charged that this was excessive and discriminatory prosecution. In addition, the protesters reminded the media that White students who engaged in fights and hung nooses in a tree, which incited racial tension at the school, were never charged with a crime. The Jena Six calamity filled the airwaves for several months before becoming yesterday's news. Several months after the melee, the lead defendant became involvement with other legal issues and unfortunately eventually attempted suicide. The facts now show that the Jena Six news coverage was full of inaccuracies, sensation, and under reporting. However, the frenzy around this case highlighted the general, all too typical storyline of African American males and punishment.

African American Males and Education:
Researching the Convergence of Race and Identity, pp. 75–100

To date, successfully engaging and teaching African American male students in educationally constructive ways remains one of the most urgent and elusive issues facing the educational system in the United States. Unfortunately, to be an African American male student in the United States is to be placed at risk of suspensions, expulsions, special education placement, marginalization, and, ultimately, school failure (Davis, 2003; Ferguson, 2000; Polite & Davis, 1999). There is no shortage of literature describing the alienation, disengagement, high dropout rates, and underachievement of African American male students (Davis, 2003; Dunbar, 1999; Duncan, 2002; Ferguson, 2000; Irvine, 1990; Polite & Davis, 1999). Recently, Holzman (2006) reported that nationwide an alarming 55% of African American males do not graduate from high school with their cohort; and in some large, urban school districts, the numbers are higher (Greene, 2002). However, despite this and other ominous achievement data, arguably the most pressing issue with respect to African American male students is the increasingly devastating discipline statistics and the dearth of literature, policies, and actions aimed at improving the predicament.

The overarching purpose of this current qualitative case study is to illuminate one of the most pervasive problems in the field of education: the over punishment of African American male students in educational settings, and how teacher perceptions may contribute to this phenomenon. Additionally, we are interested in the capacity of teacher perceptions to impact student relationships. Therefore we were guided by the following research questions: (a) what perceptions and beliefs do teachers have about African American male students and how, if it at all, these beliefs intersected with the classroom management strategies and the discipline outcomes of their African American male students? and (b) what is impact of teacher perceptions on how African American male students are viewed and engaged by their peers and how these perceptions may also influence how African American boys view themselves?

BACKGROUND

In almost every major city in the United States, African American male students are overrepresented in suspensions and expulsions. Figure 4.1 displays the extent of the problem in many urban districts. For instance, in Dallas, African American male students make up 17% of the student population, and 31% of school suspensions and 43% of expulsions. In Charlotte, African American male students make up 22% of the student population, and 49% of school suspensions and 61% of expulsions. The pattern holds in Los Angeles, with African American males making up 6% of the student population and an astounding 18% of the suspensions and

19% of expulsions (Holzman, 2006). The United States Department of Education reports that 25% of all African American male students had been suspended at least once over a 4-year period, and they are 2.6 times more likely than White males to be suspended from school (Schiraldi & Ziedenberg, 2001). Racial disproportionality in suspensions and expulsions is also a consistent finding in the literature (McFadden, Marsh, Price, & Hwang, 1992; Raffaele Mendez, Knoff, & Ferron, 2002; Skiba, Peterson, & Williams, 1997; Wu, Pink, Crain, & Moles, 1982). Yet, Skiba, Michael, Nardo, and Peterson (2000) conclude, "studies have yet to find racial disparities in misbehavior [are] sufficient enough to account for the typically wide racial differences in school punishment" (p. 6). Their findings suggest that African American males do not necessarily misbehave more than other students, notwithstanding disproportionate punishment statistics. Unfortunately, despite the conclusions of Skiba et al. and the current suspension and expulsion data, there is a dearth of literature detailing successful classroom management practices and large-scale, sustainable institutional reform that even has the potential for creating more equitable and successful discipline outcomes for African American male students.

The Larger Issues

The extent of African American males discipline problems must be situated in the larger life and schooling outcomes and their social/political context in order to understand the critical need for the current study.

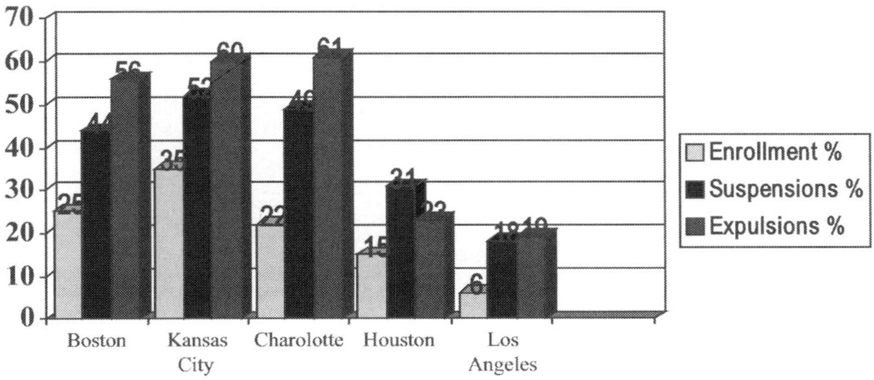

Source: (Holzman, 2006)

Figure 4.1. African American discipline statistics.

Research has shown that African American students are suspended more often than others for infractions that are subjective in nature (Skiba et al., 2002); and even when other students commit the same infraction, African American students are frequently given harsher punishments than White students (Gregory, 1996; McFadden et al., 1992; Shaw & Branden, 1990; Skiba & Knesting, 2001), suggesting the over punishment is indeed a problem. This trend is also seen in the juvenile justice system (Kennedy, 2001). In fact, the most salient aspect of the school discipline gap is its mirroring of the juvenile and adult justice system with respect to the disproportionate rates of African American males being punished.

In 2000, African American children comprised approximately 13% of the total number of children under 18 years old (National Center for Educational Statistics, 2003); but nationally they represented 26% of school age children arrested, 30% of the cases in juvenile court, 45% of youth in juvenile detention, and a devastating 46% of the cases waived to criminal court (Osher, Sims, & Woodruff, 2002). Ironically, despite the fact that violent crimes and homicides also decreased during this period (Levitt, 2004), according to the United States Department of Justice (1997), between 1990 and 1997 the imprisonment rate for African Americans skyrocketed by more than 50%, with African American males constituting the majority of the increase. If the current levels of incarceration persist, an African American male in the United States would have about a 1 in 3 chance of going to prison during his lifetime, while a Latino male would have a 1 in 6 chance and a White male would have a 1 in 17 chance of going to prison (Bureau of Justice Statistics, 2003).

Comparing school discipline outcomes with juvenile and prison statistics is not an excessive leap. The replacement of graduated discipline policies with zero tolerance policies has created dire consequences for African American males. First, suspensions and expulsions, similar to incarceration rates, have dramatically increased. For example, in Chicago, 6 years after zero tolerance policy enactment, there have been 150 times more proposed expulsions, going from 100 students in the year 1993 to 1,500 students in the year 2000, with an overwhelming amount of the students being African American males (Applied Research Center, 2000). Secondly, studies have also shown a relationship between "preventative discipline" and higher incarceration rates, especially among poor African American and Latino men (Tonry, 1999). A study by the Center for Disease Control (1994) found that "out of school" youth (suspended and expelled youth) of all races are more likely to become engaged in physical fights, use drugs, engage in sexual intercourse, carry weapons, and engage in other troublesome behavior.

The problems created by the disparate punishment of African American males have coalesced into what researchers have termed the *School-to-*

Prison Pipeline, a theory referring to institutional policies and practices that, according to a number of scholars (Christle, Jolivette, & Nelson, 2005), perpetuate a clear and unabated path to prison for large numbers of African American males. The movement possibly illuminates one of the darkest sides of the educational system, the fluid *pipeline-to-prison* created by the discipline procedures and policies meted out to mostly African American male students. It also suggests that addressing issues of behavior and discipline with African American boys is paramount in changing the schooling experience and life outcomes of African American males.

The ill effects of the consistent removal of African American males from the regular education program for behavior issues have been highlighted in recent literature (Skiba et al., 2003). The aforementioned discipline gap statistics (suspensions and expulsions) and subsequent consequences provide only a small moiety of how behavioral issues consistently remove African American males from academic opportunities. The disposal of African American males into special education classes, alternative schools, and a mélange of district-created character, behavior, and social skills classes and programs can be traced to behavioral issues and are often de facto disciplinary measures. Of particular concern are the disproportionate numbers of African American males identified as emotionally disturbed, a behavior disorder special education classification.

According to Holzman (2006), in Oakland, African American males make up 22% of the student population and 60% of the students labeled emotionally disturbed. The pattern holds in Boston, where African American males make up 25% of the student population and 57% of the students labeled emotionally disturbed. Oswald, Coutinho, and Best (2002) conclude that African American males are more likely than any group and 5.5 times more likely than White females to be identified as severely emotionally Disturbed (SED). Emotional disturbance is loosely defined as a persistent maladaptive behavior that interferes with learning, including the inability to maintain satisfactory relationships, having inappropriate feelings, a general mood of unhappiness, and physical symptoms and fears of personal or school problems. The subjective nature of this definition leaves the identification of emotionally disturbed students up to the beliefs, whims, and judgment of the referring teacher and his/her ability to sway the student study team. In fact, empirical and conceptual work points to questionable referral processes (Foster, 1990; Serwatka, Deering, & Grant, 1995); biases in assessments (Hilliard, 1991; Reid, 2001); and cultural discontinuity and nonsynchronization (Gay, 2000; Irvine, 1990) as factors causing the overrepresentation of African American males labeled emotionally disturbed and placed in other soft special education categories.

The overrepresentation of African American males in special education is significant because this label relegates large numbers of African American males to special day classes that isolate them from regular education curriculum and the general school population because of perceived behavior problems. In addition, the graduation rate of emotionally disturbed students is only 27.5% (Osher et al., 2002). Simultaneously, 45.9% of youth on probation, 67.5% of the youth incarcerated, and 88% of youth put in residential treatment centers are classified as having some sort of emotional disturbance (Snyder & Sickmund, 1999). It is difficult to discern which comes first: the emotional disturbance, delinquency, or low educational attainment; but it is evident that there is a link between these factors, underscoring the need to discontinue the labeling of large numbers of African American males.

CONCEPTUAL FRAMEWORK

The importance of teacher belief systems, racism, and perceptions has been part of closing the achievement gap literature for decades. A seminal, yet controversial study by Rosenthal and Jacobson (1968) was one of the first to examine the effect of teacher perceptions on student achievement. In that study, teachers were told that some students were "intellectual bloomers." At the end of the school year, these students scored significantly higher than other students on academic measures. Their findings, dubbed the *Pygmalion Effect*, indicated that student academic outcomes were indeed affected by teacher perceptions and expectations. Similarly, Good and Brophy (1980) concluded that early in school, teachers form different expectations for different students based on a litany of factors, including race, socioeconomic status, sex, speech patterns, appearance, and parents. Teachers then began to behave differently toward different students. If this differential treatment is consistent throughout the schooling of a student, according to Good and Brophy, the treatment begins to affect the student's self-concept, levels of aspirations, achievement, and, more germane to the present study, interactions and classroom conduct.

For the conceptual framework of the current study, the researchers considered the above research on expectations and perceptions central to understanding the phenomenon that causes African American males to be over punished, because these expectations and perspectives frame how teachers respond to and construct educational opportunities for African American male students. In addition, the conceptual framework of this study considers the issue of race and racism, discussed below, essential to understanding this phenomenon. It is the fusion of these two streams of research that frames this study's conceptual framework, which is a declaration that African American male students to most are *beyond love*.

Beyond Love

Weiner (2003) theorizes that there are two paradigms alive at many urban schools with respect to classroom management. Paradigm one is the *cultural deficit* paradigm. This paradigm blames the parenting skills, cultural norms and mores, morals, and communities for the behavioral issues and academic performance of low-income students of color. The pervasiveness of paradigm one is substantiated by empirical data. Diamond, Randolph, and Spillane (2004) concluded in their study that teachers refused to take any responsibility for the learning and achievement of African American students because of their deficit beliefs about African American students' families, motivation, and limited skills, which they believe undermine their ability to teach them. Weiner postulates that this paradigm actually perpetuates the status quo, which is the acceptance of White culture and ideologies as a normalized state of affairs, because this paradigm relinquishes control, blame, and responsibility of teachers and institutions for the underachievement and over punishment of African American students.

Conversely, Weiner's second paradigm, *contextual analysis*, shifts the blame away from student deficiencies and concentrates on the deficiencies of teachers and educational institutions inability to meet the needs of certain populations. Paradigm two, which guides the conceptual framework of the current study, challenges the status quo and suggests that it is not the "pernicious" culture and/or behavior of students, but racism and teachers devaluing students' cultural milieu and its subsequent manifestations and the teacher's negative perceptions and beliefs that are the root of the problem. From these lenses, the overrepresentation of African American males in suspensions, expulsions, and other punishments requires addressing issues of race, racism, perceptions, and culture that have added to their predicament. In addition, this paradigm acknowledges that negative beliefs and perceptions of African American males are so crystallized that they are unfortunately considered by many *beyond love* (Delgado, 1996; Duncan, 2002), agents in their own demise and destruction and therefore unworthy of sympathy, concern, or love.

In order to empirically approach the *beyond love* status, the context of race, racism, and oppression must be considered; therefore, the conceptual framework of this study draws upon critical race theory. Critical race theory has its roots in legal scholarship (Bell, 1992; Delgado, 1995; Crenshaw, Gotanda, Peller, & Thomas, 1995). This theory critiques the traditional discourse on race and racism related to (in this case) education by examining how educational theory and practice is used to marginalize people of color (Bell, 1992; Delgado, 1996; Delgado & Stefanic, 2001; Duncan, 2002; Solórzano & Yosso, 2001). Critical race theorists' empirical and conceptual work suggests that racism inculcates every aspect of American social structures and that racism is so endemic that often times its insidious nature and outcomes are hidden under seemingly objective information and race neutral politics.

LITERATURE REVIEW

Despite the fact that African American males are grossly overrepresented in instances of punished behavior, classroom management textbooks and models reveal that race and cultural issues regarding discipline are given little or no discussion. Most research regarding classroom management and discipline takes a decidedly functionalist viewpoint, which leaves the phenomena of culture, race, and racism set apart from classroom interactions. However, there is great deal of research that concludes that cultural discontinuity and race related issues between the mostly White teaching staff and African American males is a major factor in the underachievement and disproportional punishment (Irvine, 1990; Townsend, 2000). There is also an overwhelming amount of research noting that race and culture are indeed relevant to behavior (Gilbert & Gay, 1985; Hilliard, 1995; Tyler, Boykin, Boelter, & Dillihunt, 2005). In fact, differences in behavior between African American and White students have been noted upon school entry; this is also a highly consistent finding in the literature (Hosp & Hosp, 2001; Pigott & Cowen, 2000; Zimmerman, Khoury, Vega, Gil, & Warheit, 1995). Hilliard (1976) concludes that research related to behavior issues that does not account for the imposition of race and culture on behavioral patterns is likely beset with problems.

Cultural responsiveness has recently emerged as a new and compelling area of research (Irvine, 1990; Gay, 2000; Ladson-Billings, 1995). Scholarship in this area gleans much of its conceptual framework from the work of scholars who have linked cultural dissonance to poor academic achievement and disproportional punishment. Culturally responsive teaching is defined as adjusting how one teaches to match the needs and experiences of students, using students' cultural knowledge, prior experiences, frames of reference, and performance styles to make learning encounters more relevant and effective (Gay, 2000). Initial research in this area has shown promise for improving the academic and disciplinary outcomes for students of color. The theory of culturally responsive teaching addresses cultural dissonance in the classroom by insisting that teachers must be able to construct classrooms that have relevance and meaning to students' culture and social/political context (Howard, 2003). Literature refers to cultural responsiveness by a variety of descriptors, including culturally relevant, synchronized, congruent, centered, contextualized, and mediated (Gay, 2000). In recent years, the theory of culturally responsive and/or relevant teaching has yielded an impressive body of theoretical and empirical literature; and recently, work has been presented calling for culturally responsive institutions, not simply pedagogy (Johnson & Bush, 2004).

A new stream of research has identified culturally responsive classroom management (Gay, 2006; Monroe & Obidah, 2004; Weinstein, Curran, & Tomilson-Clark, 2003). This research has begun to outline more effective classroom management strategies for students of color. However, to date, this literature has not specified issues concerning African American male students and their particular context and characterization, which are discussed below, in America. This study sought to fill this void. In addition, given the overwhelming discipline and achievement data of this particular group, as compelling as culturally responsive literature is, and although its literature base discusses sociopolitical issues, it may not be sufficient to explain the phenomenon that causes overrepresentation of African American males in punishment because of their unique social, political, historical, and economic context in the United States.

Scholars conclude that negative media portrayals of African American males as violent, hypersexual, disrespectful, lazy, unintelligent, and threatening are ubiquitous (Carby, 1998; Davis, 2003). Therefore, as teachers and the general public construct spoken and unspoken rationalizations for the overrepresentation of African American male students in punishment, explanations like anger, too much television, hip hop culture, immorality, gang affiliation, poverty, and a general desire to be *cool* become acceptable. Moreover, even as scholars attempt to unpack the complexity of the overrepresentation of African American males in punishment using seemingly deterministic models, their research leads to issues such as parental neglect and abuse (Singer, 1996); academic difficulties (Hirschi, 1969); self-fulfilling prophecies brought about by labeling (Casella, 2001); maladaptive and unhealthy male identities (Poissant & Alexander, 2000); and African American students' resistance and cultural opposition to schooling (Fordham & Ogbu, 1986) as the causes of their behavioral issues. While all of these explanations on the surface appear to have merit in certain situations, they also serve to call into question the resiliency, intelligence, home life, and culture of African American males, consequently leaving the role of teachers and institutions and belief systems, racism, and perceptions with respect to the overrepresentation of African American males in punishment under theorized and empirically fragmented.

METHODS

The centrality of race in this study required a methodology grounded in critical race theory so that there could be "greater ontological and epistemological understanding of how race and racism affect the education and lives of the racially disenfranchised" (Parker & Lynn, 2002, p. 42). Critical race methodology, described in the conceptual framework, is also often aligned with the qualitative methodologies. Thus in this current study, case study methodology was adapted to a multicase study (Bogdan & Biklen, 2003); therefore, it is an in-depth examination of more than one teacher.

Study Site

Potential schools were selected that had a reputation of having difficulties with African American children or for the deleterious treatment of African American students. Selection was accomplished similarly to the nomination process put forth by Foster (1997). However, instead of asking for effective schools and/or educators, we sought out schools with negative reputations because we wanted schools that did not seem to be meeting the needs of African American male students. Nominations were requested from (a) parent coordinators, who field complaints from parents; (b) specialists and advisors, who observe in classrooms; and (c) directors, who supervise principals.

The school sites were then narrowed based on three other criteria. First, the school's African American population had to be between 30% and 70%. Second, the school had to suspend and/or expel proportionately more African American male students than any other group, which was established using district data. Third, the school had to have a variety of teachers with respect to age, background, and experiences.

Park Avenue Elementary School.[1] The school is situated in the middle of an area with thousands of low-income apartments in Southern California. This area is commonly referred to as the "Maze" and has a reputation for gang violence, crime, drugs, and poverty. The school is 50.4% African American and 48.7% Latino. Ninety-five percent of the students are on free or reduced lunch. In 2000, the school suspended 64 African American students and four Latino students for an average of 3 days. During the 2004-2005 school year, 10 African American students and one Latino student were suspended, also with an average of 3 days for each suspension. Over the past 2 decades, Park Avenue Elementary School has also developed a reputation for underachievement and their State test scores over the past few years have contributed to pejorative public perception.

Participants

The participants were four teachers from Park Avenue Elementary School. Literature suggests that the negative schooling experiences of African American male students begin around fourth grade (Kunjufu, 1985). In addition, there is a large amount of literature detailing the "fourth grade slump," particularly in urban schools (Chall & Jacobs, 2003; Sweet & Snow, 2003). Consequently, we wanted to study fourth grade teachers; but we were interested in seeing any differences that might occur in the third and fifth grades as well. Therefore we sought teachers, who taught third, fourth, or fifth grade who were female teachers in order avoid gender as a factor in the analysis, and who were not resource or special education teachers. The following four teachers participated in the study: *Kim Walt, a* 32-year-old White female teacher who has been teaching for 4 years and is currently teaching third grade; *Lucy Cab*, a 38-year-old White female teacher who has been teaching for 15 years and is currently teaching fifth grade; *Mary Union*, a 35-year-old African American teacher who currently teaches fourth grade and has been teaching for 6 years and; *Stacy Bean*, a 33-year-old White female teacher who teaches fifth grade and has been teaching for 10 years.

Sources of Data and Procedures

The data were gathered by the lead researcher using participant observations, interviews, and document analysis during the 2005-2006 school year over a 6-month period. The majority of the observations took place in the participants' classrooms. These observations were not limited to specific settings or times. Instead, they took place at various times during the instructional day in order to improve sampling as suggested by Bogdan and Biklen (2003). Observations also were conducted during lunch, recess, assemblies, graduation rehearsal, and on career day. Not all of the observations were preplanned. Following the procedure of Foster (1997), each interview question was not prewritten per se, but each interviewee was asked similar questions based on a set of questions and an outline, unless a question was related to something specifically from an observation, interview, or document related to a particular participant. Copious notes were made during each interview; and most interviews were tape recorded and then transcribed, except for two unscheduled impromptu interviews, where notes subsequently were doubled checked with the interviewee for accuracy. Observations and follow-up interviews, both open-ended and informal (Bogdan & Biklen, 2003), took place during the remainder of the school year in various locations, including at the school site, at coffee houses, and in the homes of participants. The primary and secondary documents collected and analyzed included posted student work; notes to parents; notes to teachers; assignments; school/district discipline policies; classroom rules and consequences; public records; student work discussed in class; and any artifact or information related to discipline, classroom management, and/or punishment.

Data Analysis

As suggested by Strauss and Corbin (1998), simultaneous data collecting, notetaking, coding, comparing and creating theories, and referring to relevant extant literature took place; hence, the data and the theory could be described as emergent, and this information was used to plan future data collecting modes and opportunities. As data collection and field notes creation continued a list of strategy codes (Bogdan & Biklen, 2003) were created. Informal interviews with teachers were used to make sure that the data from such strategy codes were not simply the researchers' judgment but also a reflection of the participants' intent. According to Merriam (2001), constructing categories (and codes) is "largely an intuitive process;" in this case, constructing categories was systematic and constant. Units of information were merged into categories and/or codes only to combine them again to make sense of the data and begin developing theories.

FINDINGS AND ANALYSIS

We found that many of the pejorative beliefs, attitudes, and stereotypes that are pervasive in the larger society concerning African American boys and men permeate the walls of elementary classrooms impacting how teachers perceived and engage them. In this section we first present our findings on the teachers' perceptions of African American male students. We place the participants on a continuum of beliefs and perceptions which loosely builds upon the work of Banks' (1991) *Dimensions of Multicultural Education* and Lindsey, Nuri-Stacys, and Terrell's (1999) *cultural proficiency continuum*. Next, we discuss the link between teacher perceptions and their treatment of students as we describe how African American males in the study were targets of differential treatment. Last, we explore the influence of how the teachers' perceptions and differential treatment of African American males influences how they are viewed by their peers and ultimately how they perceive themselves.

Teacher Beliefs and Perceptions

The combination of interviews, observations, and documents allowed for an opportunity to collect a wide range of data to capture the underlying beliefs of the participants and how these beliefs intersected with the practice.

It was the lack of authentic caring (see Noddings, 1984, 1995; Valenzuela, 1999) that informed the decision to place Ms. Cab and Ms. Bean at the extreme ends of the perception continuum (see Table 4.1). Their comments regarding African American males and actions in their classroom create hostile environments for their African American male students. For example, Ms. Cab said that her students were "lazy," loud, had an "attitude," and would not take responsibility for their actions. She described African American parents as too "blasé" and commented that their expectations were too low. She also considered the physically restrictive school environment as a problem for African American males. However, she also stated that her kids had "no long term gratification" or impulse control. She commented that they acted like "jackasses" and that some were "unteachable."

With relationship to Ms. Walt, however, the data paint a very disturbing and yet perplexing picture. In her interviews and in the many exchanges with Ms. Walt, she did not say openly disparaging remarks about her African American male students, nor their families or communities. We would even venture to say that, in many ways, she meant well. Yet, her lack of engagement and lack of care, as evidenced by *targeting* African American male students was indicative that, although she did not say negative remarks about her students, she was clearly not in paradigm one.

One of the most pervasive findings in this study was that teachers used African American males as a classroom management strategy. When it was time to quiet their students or go onto the next activity, three of the participants often used African American male students as a discipline strategy in order to control the rest of the students. By this, we mean they would find or *target* an African American male student talking, even though others were talking, call his name, and, by virtue of this admonishment, quiet the rest of the class. This constantly occurred in Ms. Walt's classroom. Throughout observations, Ms. Walt's students were often loud

Table 4.1. Continuum of Beliefs and Perceptions

Paradigm	*Participant Placement*	*Perceptions and Beliefs*	*Practices and Outcomes*
Paradigm one Cultural deficit paradigm	Cab	Negative perceptions and beliefs of African American males are accepted as true	Teachers target African American male students
	Bean	Negative perceptions and beliefs of African American males are accepted as partially true	African American male students are sometimes targeted and responded to ineffectively
Grey area	Walt	Negative Perceptions of African American male students are seen as possibly problematic and short sided	Teachers do not necessarily respond appropriately to African American male students and/or are too permissive
Paradigm two Institutional deficit paradigm	Union	Negative perceptions of African American male students are seen as problematic	Teachers respond positively to African American male students and are in some ways responsive to their culture and context
		Negative perceptions of African American males are seen as racist	Teachers respond positively to African American male students and are responsive to culture and context. Teachers are advocates for African American male students

and off task. She was the one participant whose classroom we would actually describe as painfully out of control. By this we mean the students in her class were often off task, too loud to hear directions, and generally disruptive. But, instead of dealing with *all* of the students that disrupted the class, Ms. Walt often looked around, chose one student, and then called that student's name and/or punished that one, instead of all of the students engaging in the unwanted behavior. The student most often *targeted* was an African American male.

On the other hand, Ms. Union, the African American teacher, seemed to be the only teacher that we could place in paradigm two, what we termed the *institutional deficit paradigm*. It is interesting that the only African American teacher turned out to be the participant who had the positive beliefs and perceptions regarding African American male students. This is not a surprising finding. Studies have found that increasing the numbers of African American teachers decreased corporal punishment, suspensions, expulsions, and assignments to special education courses (Jackson, 1999). Other research has noted the effectiveness of African American teachers with African American students (Foster, 1997; Ladson-Billings, 1994; Siddle Walker, 2001). Nevertheless, on one hand, it appears the shared experience of being an African American made Mrs. Union more sensitive and caring; but on the other hand, we realize that there are some African American teachers who are harmful and ineffective because they, like the other teachers in this current study, are also inundated with negative information and images of African American males.

A look at Table 4.1 reveals that although Ms. Union is in paradigm two, she is not at the positive edge of the continuum. The reason for this is that while she treated her students fairly and she had positive attitudes toward her students, she never advocated for them in an open forum. She was the most culturally relevant teacher and the one teacher that we would never describe as racist, oppressive, or complicit in the marginalization of her students, but she did not take the step to advocate for her students.

Differential Treatment

There is a variety of literature that declares that the ways in which teachers respond to students are based on a variety of factors. This line of research is nothing new in the arena of educational research. One of the most influential studies was by Good and Brophy (1978), who found that the reaction of teachers to students is based partly on their perception of students. Additionally, the findings of Darley and Gross (1983) suggest that teachers often act with "confirmatory bias," which is the tendency to make conclusions that are based on preliminary hypothesis despite contradictory evidence. To put it another way, teachers' beliefs about students from racial stereotyping actually drive their reactions or overreactions to students. Other research indicates that teachers react to students based on their previous history with a particular student, the immediate context, the tolerance level of the teacher, and the resources available for managing behavior disruptions (Skiba et al., 2003). Numerous scholars have indicated that White students are punished more for objective infractions and that African American children are suspended more for subjective infractions (Skiba, Michael, Nardo, & Peterson, 2000) and more severely punished for what most would consider less egregious acts, which numerous studies have substantiated (Gregory, 1996; McFadden et al., 1992; Shaw & Braden, 1990; Skiba & Knesting, 2001). Therefore, it is clear that students in general are responded to differently; but, in addition, it is fair to say that African American students in particular are perpetually victims of differential treatment.

The data from this current study affirm that differential treatment was a constant part of the classroom life for African American male students in three of the four participants' classrooms. Keeping in mind Ferguson's (2000) and Duncan's (2002) work and the depth of the criminalization, demonization, and adultification of men of African descent in America, data from the present study also reveal that this differential treatment may be linked to the participants' perceptions and ideologies.

The teachers, whose beliefs aligned with paradigm one, and therefore the two participants who seemed to have the most negative perceptions of African American males, applied differential treatment most regularly. What is important to note is that this *targeting* took place in only three of the four classrooms: Ms. Union did not target students. Although there were a couple of incidents where she called a student's name to stop a certain behavior, it was never in response to more than one student engaged in the same activity. In line with the work of Weinstein and colleagues (2003), who studied culturally relevant classroom managers, Ms. Union often used appropriate interventions to assist students with behavior difficulties. She was generally consistent and fair regardless of color or gender. Her interviews also confirm that this was purposeful. She stated, "People have less patience with African American men. They expect them to do wrong." Instead she believed teachers needed to "talk to them … give them a chance … let them learn from the experience." Therefore, their slate was wiped clean the next day. She did not target students, even those who seemed to need more intervention than others. At the same time, she was still firm and serious about students who were disturbing the class or, as she said, "not taking care of business." Her actions were reminiscent of those called *warm demanders*, as indicated by Irvine and Fraser (1998), Kleinfeld (1975), and others. This might also explain why there was less anger in her classroom. It also would put her in a very different paradigm with respect to beliefs and practice than Ms. Cab and Ms. Bean, in particular, which further substantiates the claim that perceptions appear to influence practice.

The following incident that took place under Ms. Bean's watch is a paragon example of differential treatment.

The one incident that struck us as the most egregious happened during a four-square game after lunch. All of the students were lined up at a square waiting for their turn. The students were excited. Many of them were jumping up and down and screaming. The teacher seemed to quickly become frustrated with the noise level and told the students that if they touched the line instead of standing behind the line, they would not be allowed to play. After about 3 minutes of student warnings, Devon, an African American male, stepped on the line. He was told that he could no longer participate in the four-square game. He sat on the ground after some back and forth with the teacher and watched the game from a distance. The students then temporarily calmed down and began standing behind the line.

About 5 minutes later, Juan, a Latino boy, stepped on the line. Two African American students immediately said, "Ohhhhhh, Ms. Bean, Juan stepped on the line." Ms. Bean said nothing. Juan then eventually stepped on the line again. This time instead of waiting for the children, the lead researcher told Ms. Bean that Juan stepped on the line. She looked at Juan and asked him to go to the end of line and then made a comment about how excited the students get during these types of activities.

The above example is significant for many reasons; however, what we find particularly important to this current inquiry is the response of the two other African American boys who are apparently acutely aware of the pervasiveness of differential treatment. In fact, *all* of the students noticed what was happening.

The Impact of Differential Treatment on Peers

One very rarely discussed phenomenon, which occurs at middle and high schools near Park Avenue, is the fights and other problems between Latina(o) and African American students. To date, there is little educational literature related to this phenomenon, which has become commonplace in many of the local high schools. During the school year in which this study took place, several incidents between Latina(o)s and African

Americans made local headlines. The District had created a new division dedicated to improving "human relations" between ethnic groups. Park Avenue had not reported many racial issues between students; however, classroom dynamics indicated that these students could be headed toward racial problems as teenagers because teachers did little in the classrooms to create community and tolerance in these elementary students, and also because teachers' negative perceptions of and responses to African American males, in particular, are being absorbed by the Latina(o) students. While Black and Latina(o) relations as they are associated with teacher perceptions was not the focus of this current project, the differential treatment of students along racial and gender lines is notable and must be explore in future research.

The differential treatment of Black students was mostly seen in Ms. Bean's and Ms. Sak's classrooms, but there were elements of this problem in all four classrooms. The extent of the tensions and problems varied from African American students not being able to secure partners to work on group projects, to the blatant shunning of African American male students, and the constant targeting of African American males while other students were free to talk and roam the classroom.

In Ms. Bean's classroom this dynamic was especially obvious. The first of note was a list of students of the month that was posted near the front of the classroom: Tasha Gordon, Gerardo Rodriguez, Maria Espinosa, "Big Juan" Campos, Carmen Diaz, and Martin Hernandez: no African American boys were given this distinction. This seemed like a small point, but it foreshadowed much of what would be seen in her classroom with respect to this issue. For example, during one observation in Ms. Bean's classroom, two Latinas were playing soccer with a balled up piece of paper. These girls were also talking and not seated in their assigned seats; they had actually been disengaged and talking for an hour. Interestingly enough, the teacher had spent the morning calling Dante's name (an African American boy) and making sure he was seated and working quietly. He was even warned that the principal would be given the names of students who would not be graduating because of their behavior, yet nothing was said to the two Latinas.

Meanwhile, an African American girl raised her hand. After being called on by Ms. Bean, asked, referring to the lead researcher, "What is her purpose for being here? After an explanation, she then asked a more succinct question directly to the lead researcher, "You are here to watch us right?" "Yes." She then looked at the two Latinas and said, "See, she is watching you guys." The African American girl was letting the two know that they were acting inappropriately and that others had probably noticed. The fact that she said nothing to Ms. Bean also meant that she might believe that Ms. Bean was not concerned with their behavior. Ms.

Bean did not say a word to the two Latinas who had been "misbehaving" all morning. This African American girl knew this and so did most of the other students, but Mrs. Bean still did not say anything to the two girls nor did she respond to the African American girl's comment. In addition, during this same period a Latino boy stood up and went to talk to another Latino boy; and nothing was said. Yet, Dante got up to blow his nose and was given a warning to which he quickly whispered so that others could hear, "Dang, I bet she can blow your nose."

The observations in Ms. Bean's classroom clearly showed differential treatment and were critical for two reasons. First, it heightened our awareness of African American students' consciousness of differential treatment. Secondly, signified that Latina(o) students were ignored and also allowed to disengage from the "academic" program, which might in part explain their academic underachievement at Park Avenue School.

With the pervasiveness of the negative stereotypes of African American men and boys in society coupled with the negative perceptions and differential treatment by teachers, it was not surprising when a Latina looked at one of the African American boys and said, "Shut up, you stink, and you're stupid," that he would say nothing back. It seemed as though her words had been in many ways sanctioned by this environment. This was not just ordinary *kids being kids* stuff. She seemed to have dismissed this little African American boy in her mind as irrelevant, and maybe he had dismissed himself as invisible and irrelevant (see Bush, 2005).

This differential treatment is probably why, during another observation, an African American male student who needed help from his tablemates and was completely ignored. He wanted to know what page the class was on because the teacher was counting to ten and he needed to find the page before she finished. His Latina tablemate looked at the other girl at the table and said to her, "Don't talk to him. He will just get us in trouble." The African American boy then looked sad, never found the right page, and eventually just tuned out. It was obvious these girls had no sense of community, no feeling of camaraderie, and no compassion for their classmate. It appeared that it was not just the teachers who had categorized these boys as *beyond love*, but their Latina(o) classmates as well.

The Impact of Being Beyond Love

Because African American boys were not direct participants in this current study, it was difficult to provide a full account of how teacher and peer perceptions impact their view of themselves. Yet, the data provided some glimpses into the world of African American boys who have been placed outside of the boundaries of love by society, teachers, and peers. In the aforementioned section where the Latina told the African American boy, “Shut up, you stink, and you’re stupid,” he seemed to accept their appellation choosing not to advocate for himself. In other examples, African American boys would leave classrooms on bathroom passes and would not return for hours as if they knew no one would miss them as their teachers and peers said nothing to them upon their return. It is as if these African American boys existed in a strange world of being highly visible as they were habitual targets of discipline strategies while simultaneously being invisible as they were allowed to wander around outside of class and sometimes outside of school grounds as in the next example which was recorded in a field note log.

While walking through the schoolyard, I came upon two of the African American male students from Ms. Walt’s classroom. I asked them where they were supposed to be. One of the students explained that he was going to visit his sister. I explained to them that they should go back to class unless Ms. Walt knew where they were. Michael explained to me that they did not want to go to class because he “hated” their teacher. The other student replied, “Yep.”

Implicit in this example is the belief that one is expendable to the schooling process and therefore one acts accordingly which may manifest in a myriad of maladaptive behaviors including being disruptive in class, but in this case, literally leaving school altogether. This dynamic is reminiscent Steele’s work concerning the *stereotype threat* (Steele, 1997, Steele & Aronson, 1995) which posits that when a person enters a situation in which a stereotype of a group to which the person belongs becomes salient, concerns about being judged and treated according to that stereotype arise and inhibit performance. In our case, we suggest that negative perceptions held by teachers and peers concerning African American boys work like stereotypes as they influence their performance, behaviors, and self perceptions.

CONCLUSION

Johnson and Bush (2004) describe the need for whole-school culturally responsive inquiry in order to transform institutions. They put forth a model of culturally responsive inquiry that suggests that institutions, not just individual teachers, need to be culturally responsive in order to ameliorate underachievement patterns for students of color. They contend that this transformation takes place in stages, including building leadership and data teams, killing myths and building dissatisfaction, assessing where you are and why, creating a vision and plan for your school, and monitoring progress.

To this end, oftentimes teachers and administrators are not fully aware of the data related to disciplinary issues. For example, in this study, the teachers did not know at any time how many of their African American male students had been suspended. They often used approximations when describing discipline actions. The participants also did not keep track of how much instructional time was lost due to disciplinary issues. There was, in fact, a general lack of understanding related to the extent of their discipline situation. Therefore, accurately defining the problem and/or situation becomes the first step in addressing the issues. Hence, the collection of data is the first step in this process. Disaggregated data that should be collected include but are not limited to: detention, suspension, and expulsion data by incident and student identification (including gender and race; data on the number of students sent out of class during instruction, including being placed in the back of the room, in the hallway, or in another teacher's classroom; Referral and placement data related to behavior-related special education classifications disaggregated by teachers; office referrals with reasons for referrals listed; data on other punishments, including the assignment of standards, loss of recess, loss of privileges, or other activities including field trips, library, parties, and so on; and, data regarding the differential punishments for similar offenses.

While we make these necessary recommendations for public schools, we also contend that even in a post Barack Obama era that the majority of African American boys and men still find themselves beyond love. Thus, even as we make recommendations for mainstream schools, we wonder if love can be taught or legislated and continue to raise Du Bois' (1935) question: "*Does the Negro need separate schools?*" in order, among other things, to counter another Jenna six and the narrative of *who they say I am*.

NOTE

1. Pseudonyms are used for the names of the school, district, participants, and staff members.

REFERENCES

Applied Research Center. (2000). *Facing the consequences: An examination of racial discrimination in the U.S. public school*. Retrieved from http://arc.org/erase/FTC2zero.html

Banks, J. (1991). The dimensions of multicultural education. *Multicultural Leader, 4*, 5-6.

Bell, R. (1992). *Faces at the bottom of the well: The permanence of racism.* New York, NY: Basic Books.

Bogdan, R., & Biklen, S. (2003). *Qualitative research for education: An introduction to theories and methods.* New York, NY: Allyn & Bacon.

Bureau of Justice Statistics. (2003). Prison statistics. Retrieved from http://www.ojp.usdoj.gov/bjs/prisons.htm

Bush, L. (2005). Stopping the stereotypes. *Black Issues in Higher Education, 22*(13), 66.

Carby, H. V. (1998). *Race men.* Cambridge, MA: Harvard University Press.

Casella, R. (2001). *"Being down:" Challenging violence in urban schools.* New York, NY: Teachers College Press.

Center for Disease Control. (1994, March). Health risk behaviors among adolescents who do and do not attend school: United States, 1992. *Prevention Morbidity and Mortality Weekly Report, 43*(08), 4.

Chall, J., & Jacobs, V. (2003). The classic study on poor children's fourth grade reading slump. *American Educator, 27*(1), 14-15.

Christle, C., Jolivette, K., & Nelson, M. (2005). Breaking the school to prison pipeline: Identifying school risk and protective factors for youth delinquency. *Exceptionality, 13*(2), 69-88.

Crenshaw, K. W., Gotanda, N., Peller, G., & Thomas, K. (Eds.). (1995). *Critical race theory: The key writings that formed the movement.* New York, NY: New Press.

Darley, J. M., & Gross, P. H. (1983). A hypothesis-confirming bias in labeling effects. *Journal of Personality and Social Psychology, 44*, 249-256.

Davis, J. E. (2003). Early schooling and academic achievement of African American males. *Urban Education, 38*(5), 515-537.

Delgado, R. (1995). *Critical race theory: The cutting edge.* Philadelphia, PA: Temple University Press.

Delgado, R. (1996). *The coming race war? And other apocalyptic tales of America after affirmative action and welfare.* New York, NY: University Press.

Delgado, R., & Stefanic, J. (2001). *Critical race theory: An introduction.* New York, NY: New York University Press.

Diamond, J., Randolph, A., & Spillane, J. (2004). Teachers' expectations and sense of responsibility for student learning: The importance of race, class, and organizational habitus. *Anthropology & Education Quarterly, 35*(l), 75-98.

Du Bois, W. E. B. (1935). Does the Negro need separate schools? *The Journal of Negro Education, 4*, 328-335.

Dunbar, C. (1999). African American males and participation: Promising inclusion, practicing exclusion. *Theory into Practice, 38*(4), 241-252.

Duncan, G. A. (2002). Beyond love: A critical race ethnography of the schooling of adolescent black males. *Equity & Excellence in Education, 35*(4), 131-142.

Ferguson, A. (2000). *Bad boys: Public schools in the making of Black masculinity.* Ann Arbor, MI: The University of Michigan Press.

Fordham, S., & Ogbu, J. (1986). African American students' school success: Coping with the "burden of 'acting White'." *Urban Review, 18*, 176-203.

Foster, H. (1990). Ethnocentrism and racism: The disproportionate representation of minorities and poor in special education programs for the emotionally disturbed. *Perception, 25*(2), 16-19.

Foster, M. (1997). *Black teachers on teaching*. New York, NY: New Press.

Gay, G. (2000). *Culturally responsive teaching: Theory, research and practice*. New York, NY: Teachers College Press.

Gay, G. (2006). Connections between classroom management and culturally responsive teaching. In C. M. Evertson & C. S. Weinstein (Eds.), *Handbook of classroom management: Research, practice, and contemporary issues* (pp. 343-370). Mahwah, NJ: Erlbaum.

Gilbert, S. E., & Gay, G. (1985). Improving the success in school of poor Black children. In B. Shade (Ed.), *Culture, style, and the educative process* (pp. 275-283). Springfield, IL: Charles C. Thomas.

Good, T., & Brophy, J. (1978). *Looking in classrooms*. New York, NY: Harper & Row.

Good, T., & Brophy, J. 1980. *Educational psychology: A realistic approach*. New York, NY: Holt, Rinehart, & Winston.

Greene, J. (2002). *High school graduation rates in the United States*. New York, NY: Manhattan Institute for Policy Research.

Gregory, J. F. (1996). The crime of punishment: Racial and gender disparities in the use of corporal punishment in the U.S. Public Schools. *Journal of Negro Education, 64*, 454-462.

Hilliard, A. (1976). *Free your mind: Return to the source, African origins*. Atlanta, GA: Georgia State University Press.

Hilliard, A. (1991). *Learning styles and cultural diversity*. Pre-conference workshop conducted at the annual meeting of the Association of Teacher Educators, New Orleans, LA.

Hilliard, A. (Ed.). (1991) *Testing African American students: Special re-issue of the Negro Educational Review*. Morristown, NJ: Aaron Press.

Hilliard, A. (1995). *The maroon within us: Selected essays on African American community socializations*. Baltimore, MD: Black Classic Press.

Hirschi, T. (1969). *Causes of delinquency*. Berkeley, CA: University of California Press.

Holzman, M. (2006). *Public education and Black male students: The 2006 state report-card*. Schott Educational Inequity Index, Cambridge, MA: The Schott Foundation for Public Education.

Hosp, J., & Hosp, M. (2001). Behavior differences between African American and Caucasian students: Issues for assessment and intervention. *Education & Treatment of Children, 24*(3), 336-351.

Howard, T. C. (2003). Culturally relevant pedagogy: Ingredients for critical teacher reflection. *Theory Into Practice, 42*(3), 195-204.

Irvine, J. (1990). *Black students and school failure*. Westport, CT: Greenwood Press.

Irvine, J., & Fraser, J. (1998, May 13). "Warm demanders": Do national certification standards leave room for the culturally responsive pedagogy of African American teachers? *Education Week*, 56.

Jackson, J. F. (1999). What are the real risk factors for African American children? *Phi Delta Kappan, 81*(4), 308-312.

Johnson, R. S., & Bush, L. (2004). Leading schools through culturally responsive inquiry. In F. English (Ed.), *Sage handbook of educational leadership* (pp. 269-296). London, England: SAGE.

Kennedy, R. (2001). Racial trends in the administration of criminal justice. In N. J. Smelser, W. J. Wilson, & F. Mitchell (Eds.), *America becoming: Racial trends and their consequences* (Vol. II, pp. 1-20). Washington, DC: National Academy Press.

Kleinfeld, J. (1975). Effective teachers of Eskimo and Indian students. *School Review, 83*, 301-344.

Kunjufu, J. (1985). *Countering the conspiracy to destroy Black boys*. Chicago, IL: African American Images.

Ladson-Billings, G. (1994). *The dreamkeepers: Successful teachers of African American children*. San Francisco, CA: Jossey-Bass.

Ladson-Billings, G. (1995). Toward a theory of culturally relevant pedagogy. *American Educational Research Journal, 32*(3), 465-491.

Lindsey, R., Nuri-Stacys, K., & Terrell, R. (1999). *Cultural proficiency: A manual for school leaders*. Newbury Park, CA: Corwin Press.

Levitt, S. D. (2004). Understanding why crime fell in the 1990s: Four factors that explain the decline and six that do not. *Journal of Economic Perspectives, 18*(1), 163-190.

McFadden, A. C., Marsh, G. E., Price, B. J., & Hwang, Y. (1992). A study of race and gender bias in the punishment of school children. *Education and Treatment of Children, 15*, 140-146.

Merriam, S. B. (2001). *Qualitative research and case study applications in education: Revised and expanded from case study research in education*. San Francisco, CA: Jossey-Bass.

Monroe, C., & Obidah, J. (2004). The influence of cultural synchronization on a teacher's perceptions of disruption: A case study of an African American middle-school classroom. *Journal of Teacher Education, 55*, 256-268.

National Center for Education Statistics. (2003). Status and Trends in the Education of Blacks. Retrieved from http://nces.ed.gov/pubs2003/2003034.pdf

Noddings, N. (1984). *Caring: A feminine approach to the ethics and moral education*. Berkeley, CA: University of California Press.

Noddings, N. (1995). Teaching themes of care. *Phi Delta Kappan, 76*(9), 675-687.

Osher, D., Sims, A. E., & Woodruff, D. (2002). Schools make difference: The overrepresentation of African American youth in special education and the juvenile justice system. In D. Loosen & G. Orfield (Eds.), *Racial inequality in special education*. Cambridge, MA: Harvard Education Press.

Oswald, D., Coutinho, M., & Best, A. (2002). Community and school predictors of overrepresentation of minority children in special education. In D. Losen & G. Orfield *(Eds.), Racial inequality in special education*. The Civil Rights Project at Harvard University. Cambridge, MA: Harvard University Press.

Parker, L., & Lynn, M. (2002). What's race got to do with it? Critical race theory's conflicts with and connections to qualitative research and epistemology. *Qualitative Inquiry, 8*(1), 7-22.

Pigott, R., & Cowen, E. (2000). Teacher race, child race, racial congruence, and teacher ratings of children's school adjustment. *Journal of School Psychology, 38*, 177-196.

Polite, V., & Davis, J. (1999). *African American males in school and society: Practices and policies for effective education*. New York, NY: Teachers College Press.

Poissant, A., & Alexander, A. (2000). *Lay my burden down: Suicide and the mental health crisis among African-Americans*. Boston, MA: Beacon Press.

Raffaele Mendez, L., Knoff, H., & Ferron, J. (2002). School demographic variables and out-of-school suspension rates: A quantitative and qualitative analysis of a large, ethnically diverse school district. *Psychology in the Schools, 39*(3), 259-277.

Reid, R. (2001). Using behavior rating scales for ADHD across ethnic groups: The IOWAConners-attention deficit hyperactivity disorder testing with the IOWA Conners rating scales. *Journal of Emotional and Behavior Disorders, 35*, 1-11.

Rosenthal, R., & Jacobson, L. (1968). *Pygmalian in the classroom: Teacher expectation and pupil's intellectual development*. New York, NY: Reinhart & Winston.

Schiraldi, V., & Ziedenberg, J. (2001). *Schools and suspensions: Self-reported crime and the growing use of suspensions* (Justice Policy Institute Policy Brief). Washington, DC: Open Society Institute.

Serwatka, T. S., Deering, S., & Grant, P. (1995). Disproportionate representation of African Americans in emotionally handicapped classes. *Journal of Black Studies, 25*, 492-506.

Shaw, R. S., & Braden, P. J. (1990). Race and gender bias in the administration of corporal punishment. *School Psychology Review, 19*(3), 378-383.

Siddle Walker, V. (2001). African American teaching in the South: 1940-1960. *American Educational Research Journal, 389*(4), 751-779.

Singer, S. (1996). *Recriminalizing delinquency*. Cambridge, England: Cambridge University Press.

Skiba, R. J., & Knesting, K. (2001). Zero tolerance, zero evidence: An analysis of school disciplinary practice. In R. J. Skiba & G. G. Noam (Eds.), *New directions for youth development* (No. 92: Zero tolerance: Can suspension and expulsion keep schools safe?) (pp. 17-43). San Francisco, CA: Jossey-Bass.

Skiba, R. J., Michael, R. S., Nardo, A. C., & Peterson, R. (2000). *The color of discipline: Sources of racial and gender disproportionality in school punishment*. Bloomington, IN: University of Indiana.

Skiba, R. J., Michael, R. S., Nardo, A. C., & Peterson, R. (2002). The color of discipline: Sources of racial and gender disproportionality in school punishment. *Urban Review, 34*(4), 317-342.

Skiba, R. J., Peterson, R. L., & Williams, T. (1997). Office referrals and suspension: Disciplinary intervention in middle schools. *Education and Treatment of Children, 20*(3), 295-315.

Skiba, R. J., Simmons, A., Staudinger, L., Rausch, M., Dow, G., & Feggins, R. (2003, May). *Consistent removal: Contributions of school discipline to the school-prison pipeline*. Presented at the School to Prison Pipeline Conference, Boston, MA.

Snyder, H., & Sickmund, M. (1999). *Minorities in the juvenile justice system: 1999 national report series, juvenile justice bulletin*. Washington, DC: United States Department of Justice, Office of the Justice Programs, Office of Juvenile Justice and Delinquency Prevention.

Solórzano, D., & Yosso, T. (2001). From racial stereotyping and deficit discourse. *Multicultural Education, 9*(1), 23-31.

Steele, C. M. (1997). A threat in the air: How stereotypes shape the intellectual identities and performance of women and African Americans. *American Psychologist, 52*, 613-629.

Steele, C. M., & Aronson. J. (1995). Stereotype threat and the intellectual test performance of African Americans. *Journal of Personality and Social Psychology, 69*, 797-811.

Strauss, A., & Corbin, J. (1998). *Basics of qualitative research and procedures for developing grounded theory.* Thousand Oaks, CA: SAGE.

Sweet, A. P., & Snow, C. E. (Eds.). (2003). *Rethinking reading comprehension*. New York, NY: Guilford Press.

Tonry, M. (1999). Why are U.S. incarceration rates so high? *Crime and Delinquency, 45*, 419-437.

Townsend, B. (2000). Disproportionate discipline of African American children and youth: Culturally-responsive strategies for reducing school suspensions and expulsions. *Exceptional Children, 66*(3), 381-391.

Tyler, K., Boykin, A. W., Boelter, C., & Dillihunt, M. (2005). Examining mainstream and Afro cultural value socialization in African American households. *Journal of Black Psychology, 31*(3), 291-310.

United States Department of Justice. (1997). *Correctional populations in the United States*. Retrieved from http://www.ojp.usdoj.gov/bjs/pub/pdf/cpus97.pdf

Valenzuela, A. (1999). *Subtractive schooling: U.S.-Mexican youth and the politics of caring*. New York, NY: State University of New York Press.

Weiner, L. (2003). Why classroom management is so vexing to urban teachers? *Theory Into Practice, 42*(4), 319-326.

Weinstein, C., Curran, M., & Tomilson-Clark, S. (2003). Culturally responsive classroom management: Awareness into action *Theory into Practice, 42*(4), 335-350.

Wu, S. C., Pink, W. T., Crain, R. L., & Moles, O. (1982). Student suspension: A critical reappraisal. *The Urban Review, 14,* 245-303.

Zimmerman, R., Khoury, E., Vega, W., Gil, A., & Warheit, G. (1995). Teacher and parent perceptions of behavior problems among a sample of African American, Hispanic, and Non-Hispanic students. *American Journal of Community Psychology, 23*, 181-197.

CHAPTER 5

THE POWER OF ONE

A Case Study of Daniel's Endeavor to Make a Difference

Anthony A. Pittman

> The power of one may be myth or cliché, but when controversy puts any one individual, however small, in the spotlight, we should stop and pay attention.
>
> —Rita Larivee (2008)

INTRODUCTION

DeAndre Swygert, an after-school teacher and basketball coach, is improperly identified as a robbery suspect and is accosted by Berkeley police officers with their guns drawn (Trott, 2008). A former associate vice president of student affairs at a small independent university in the Midwest who holds a degree from Harvard University has launched a new job search process. During multiple interviews, his physical stature leads various interviewers to inquire whether he had ever played football, whether in high school or professionally. Taken aback and somewhat annoyed by

African American Males and Education: Researching the Convergence of Race and Identity, pp. 101–127

such inquiries, the interviewee responds in ways that do not automatically compromise his potential to secure employment. Conversely, his colleague, a doctoral candidate and high-ranking military officer who often faces similar questioning, is amused by such queries and takes pleasure in responding affirmatively to them (Thompson, 2008).

Upon exiting Club Kalua, a nightclub in the Queens borough of New York City, Sean Bell is shot 51 times and is killed by three detectives who are subsequently acquitted of murder charges. Bell was scheduled to be married on the day of his death (Wilson, 2008). Personally, I have witnessed firsthand the visible frenzy of a White woman engulfed by terror as she frantically sought to secure the locks on the doors of her car when it occurred to her that the stoplight would be red at the same time of my crossing the street in front of her vehicle.

What do the aforementioned males have in common? All are African American men who, in one form or another, have been victims of unfortunate circumstance or who have reified for others age old stereotypes about men of African descent as ominous, violent, and predisposed to execute acts that are not only self-destructive but catastrophic to others within their surroundings—views that are countered by prominent scholars (e.g., Austin, Gilmore, & McCormick, 2003; Kunjufu, 2001; & Porter, 1998).

Although a scant body of literature documents and refutes notions that African American men are promiscuous, shiftless, reckless, and irresponsible human beings (hooks, 2004; Kotre, 1999; Reese, 2003), more scholarship about Black males is needed, especially given that many would agree it is no mystery that African American males are among the more commonly misunderstood populations in the United States and wider culture. With this in view, I believed it to be prudent to construct an interview protocol that would examine the experiences of Black males who function in mentoring capacities. Approximately 10 Black men who mentor and/or teach young African American males in various states in the northeast and southeast were invited to participate in this project. Of the invitations extended, one person committed fully and completed the process in its entirety.

CASE STUDY OVERVIEW

The purpose of this qualitative, singular case study is to chronicle the experiences of Daniel, an African American man who mentors adolescent Black males. He endeavors to assist them with positive identity construction as well as to prepare them for reorienting to society subsequent to their release from the juvenile penal system. The Africentric Resistance

Modality Model advocated by Robinson and Howard-Hamilton (1994) is the conceptual framework upon which the study is guided. The paradigm outlines seven principles that may engender a sense of well being for and among people of African descent. However, for the purpose of this work, *Umojo* (unity) and *Nia* (purpose) are referenced expressly. *Umojo* is a unifying premise of family, community, and nation. It affirms positive thoughts and actions and encourages one to contribute to the betterment of the world in which he lives and the people around him. The basis of *Nia* is community building and restoration. Among its foci are to engage spirituality through prayer and meditation. It also avows the exploration of purpose in life as well as collective prosperity through the use of one's talents and the talents of others.

REVIEW OF RELEVANT LITERATURE

For one to fully comprehend the unique challenges that often confront African American males, a review of the literature is paramount. I shall not attempt to provide an exhaustive account of the existing body of research; rather, I compartmentalize this important component of the article in the following ways. First, I synthesize scholarship pertinent to definitions about African American male masculinity and how these views have and continue to evolve. Secondly, I supply an overview of the literature germane to the educational plight of African American males. Some attention is devoted to the perceptions of schooling among many African American males as well as what needs to be done to enhance their educational experiences. Thirdly, I conclude the literature review by providing an overview of some of the special programs and services that have been orchestrated to position African American males more favorably within academic and social contexts.

DEFINING AFRICAN AMERICAN MALE MASCULINITY

The institution of slavery has had residual and devastating effects upon African American men. Among the consequences of this despicable period in the history of America is vacillation and conflict among some African American males about what it means to be masculine. Elkins (1959) introduced literature of the Black man as passive unassuming, and self-loathing. Concomitant with these views were portrayals of African American men as violent and rebellious, resulting in the proliferation of subsequent pejorative stereotypes that also highlighted the alleged absenteeism of the Black male in the Black family structure (Moynihan, 1965).

Since he was perceived to lack the capacity to commit fully to his family, the Black man was also misrepresented as a promiscuous being whose objective was to gratify himself sexually via the pursuit of White women (Broderick, 1965; Reiss, 1964)

Cazenave (1979), Frazier (1939), and Haley (1976) were among initial contenders who began to shift the paradigm related to the aforementioned negative perceptions about what constituted Black male masculinity. Their works suggested that previous beliefs about Black men and the Black family were flawed because the literature failed to acknowledge the social factors extant during slavery. These scholars' comprehensive examinations of the Black family and Black males within broader contexts revealed impediments to Black men's mobility, both educationally and economically. Thus, the aforementioned researchers repudiated the notion that the characteristics of manhood could be determined based solely upon the measure of race. Staples (1982) noted that the normative definition of masculinity, albeit implied, has been achieved by most White males in the United States. However, he referred to Black males' struggles to accomplish this norm as a catch-22, having asserted that the Black man is "damned if you do and damned if you don't" (p. 2).

The entrapment among most Black males that Staples highlights is perhaps best captured by *cool pose*, as advocated by Majors and Billson (1992). *Cool pose* acknowledges the hardships that some African American men experience, causing many of them to adopt the disposition as a method of retaining their sense of manhood in a society that restricts their access to the accoutrements enjoyed by many of their White male counterparts. However, physical, linguistic, and stylistic posturing by many who subscribe to the *cool pose* ideology has, in many ways, reinforced commonly held stereotypes about Black male behavior and has further disenfranchised many Black men from their communities. Traditional definitions of masculinity, irrespective of racial identification, prohibit men from occupying roles perceived to be the territory of the opposite sex. Physical and sexual prowess, fierce competitive approaches, disdain for homosexual relationships between men, and detached interactions with other males are among some of the widely maintained understandings by the general populace, men in particular, about the construct of masculinity (O'Neil, 2002; O'Neil, Helms, Gable, Laurence, & Wrightsman, 1986; Pleck, Sonenstein, & Ku 1993).

THE EDUCATIONAL EXPERIENCES OF AFRICAN AMERICAN MALES

In comparison to the rate of their White male counterparts, the disappearance of African American males from schooling contexts prior to graduation is substantially and significantly disproportionate. Much of Black males' departures from educational settings before school completion may be attributed to substandard academic preparation among some Black males, lower teacher expectations, institutional racism, and a host of social, emotional, and psychological issues that plague Black men. It has been argued that the provision of a strong educational foundation is a prerequisite for helping Black males to combat the myriad challenges that confront them (Akbar, 1996; Kunjufu, 1997, 2001; Porter, 1998). However, many of the instructional processes executed by White, middle-class female teachers are often incongruent with the cognitive profiles of the Black male student clientele (Kunjufu 2002). Similarly, the fact that the curriculum, in many instances, is remote to the lived experiences of the population it intends to serve impacts negatively the ways in which African American males negotiate school.

Much of the literature related to the academic underachievement by African American males fails to scrutinize carefully many of the resulting negative effects that schooling has upon the Black male psyche. Alarming rates of African American males' assignments to special education (Harry & Anderson, 1994), exposing them to biased testing procedures that often relegate them to lower academic tracks (Oakes, 2005), and denying them the opportunities to gain entrée into gifted and talented scholastic programs (Pittman, 2009) are grossly omitted in the research. Analysis of the punitive policies that suspend and expel Black males more frequently than any group of students is also underrepresented in the literature. Davis and Jordan (1994) state, "Suspension is one of the most severe punishments schools administer to students, and previous research has shown that African Americans, males in particular, are disproportionately affected" (p. 579). Perhaps more importantly, the underachievement by Black youth is a by-product of the disparate funding in public education (Fairchild, 1984). All of these factors are widely known to threaten the general welfare of African American males and their posterity; yet, interventions to ameliorate these circumstances are addressed myopically in educational discourse, if they are discussed at all.

Although systematic flaws are unquestionably among the reasons why many African American males are unsuccessful within the academic milieu, some Black males are complicit in their lack of scholastic achievement. For example, referring to some Black males' rejection of academic engagement because the curriculum is disconnected from the realities of their experiences, Davis and Jordan claim that, "Black males are seen as both victims and participants in their own educational demise" (p. 571). When examining African American males' avoidance of schooling, Polite (1994) found that upon given the option to select rigorous courses of study that would prepare them for college and the workforce, some African American males deliberately pursued academic plans that would accommodate minimal graduation requirements. Polite noted that "African American males ... understood the graduation requirements, yet they built their high school program around a mélange of meaningless electives" (p. 591).

Polite (1994) concluded that students' choices were due to their ignorance about how their basic course selections would hold unfavorable consequences for their future employment opportunities. He acknowledged that the lack of intervention from some of the students' parents as well as the lack of proper advisement by teachers or guidance counselors who were well aware of the students' course selections is indicative of the kind of educational malpractice that is common in schools. He states, "Efforts to encourage academic excellence for African American males ... were nonexistent" (p. 593). Unfortunately, remnants of this kind of indifference and contempt for African American male students are pervasive throughout many schools in the country.

Empirical findings also suggest that African American males who are exposed to effective study skills by their teachers at the elementary school level and are encouraged to exercise these methods are more likely to earn high academic marks as they progress through junior high and high schools (Davis & Jordan, 1994). This notion alone speaks to the urgency of school districts' need to employ practitioners who possess the proper disposition to work diligently with their Black male student populations to ensure that they obtain disciplined study habits. However, as previously noted, much of the teaching force in present day public school systems is comprised largely of middle class, White females, many of whom lack the capacity to motivate their students and do not establish harmonious teacher-pupil relationships with the Black males under their tutelage (Delpit, 2006; Kunjufu, 2002).

To the extent that African American males obtain and utilize proper study skills and are permitted to benefit from smaller class sizes that would simultaneously enable them to become more academically engaged in the classroom, African American males are less likely to become truant or drop out of school altogether (Davis & Jordan, 1994). Emphasizing the critically important role that teachers play in the classroom, Davis and Jordan claim that

> lower grading teachers either lack confidence in these [Black male] students, have lower expectancies of them, or both. They assign little homework because they believe their Black male students will not or cannot complete it, and consequently issue low grades because they believe these students neither deserve nor have earned higher grades. (p. 578)

Davis (2006) also addresses the turbulence that some Black males may encounter in schooling and broader social contexts. He interviewed numerous African American males and found that many of them lamented the immature behaviors and actions (e.g. skipping school, physically assaulting other students, and sometimes attending school while under the influence of illegal drugs and alcohol) that resulted in their premature departures from school, what Davis also refers to as the dropout dance. One of his subjects capitulates a regretful sentiment succinctly, "everybody make mistakes. I took the wrong road in life" (p. 298).

Davis makes a convincing case for society in general and academic environments in particular to be willing to offer redemption to and for African American males vis-à-vis second chances. To accomplish this, regular and alternative educational programs are necessary to facilitate Black males' favorable identity construction and to enable them to rebound from hazardous pitfalls as they navigate life's experiences (Horvat & Traore, 2001). In effect, Davis asserts that "we must seek to understand Black males' experiences on their own terms and from their own perspectives ... African American males certainly need multiple chances to succeed ... they need more opportunities to set things right and get things right" (p. 302).

Crippled by the ascension of the feminist movement and an upsurge in scholarship on gender that focuses specifically upon the achievement gap between males and females, generally males have been labeled as "the new disadvantaged" (Foster, Kimmel, & Skelton, 2001). However, specific regard to how Black males have been displaced by this particular paradigm shift has not received commensurate research fervor when compared to White male students (Mincy, 2006). An emerging body of scholarship documents the perceptions by some African American males that the pursuit of scholarship is analogous to femininity. Consequently, some Black males are reluctant to embrace achievement in school because of fears that educational attainment in some way weakens their masculine identity. Dancy and Brown (2008) assert:

> African American men learn to equate the academic world with femininity, perhaps because elementary school teachers consistently reward behavior that is traditionally feminine (conformity, quietness, and cooperation) and punish behavior that is traditionally masculine (independence, adventurousness, and rebellion to authority. (p. 988)

Misunderstanding among some African American males that academic engagement is analogous to the emulation of effeminate behavior warrants closer examination in the research literature. The belief that such attitudes are developed in elementary school presents numerous opportunities for classroom teachers, administrators, parents, and others directly involved in the educational enterprise to combat these kinds of mentalities early on. Under normal circumstances, the minds of most Black males in this formative stage of their educational career can be shaped in ways that will render them impervious to accepting defeatist ideologies. For this to occur, however, a caring and skilled practitioner must be available and accessible in the classroom.

AVAILABLE PROGRAMS AND SERVICES FOR AFRICAN AMERICAN MALES

A recent search on Wilson Web that spans the years of 1990 to the present resulted in seven articles that were closely linked to the topic of mentoring programs for African America males. I excluded four of these available resources because the programs were structured in various areas of the United Kingdom. The fact that such minimal scholarship on the subject is accessible, underscores the magnitude of how urgently this gap should be bridged. One could hypothesize that given much of the negative publicity and character assassinations hyped in the media pertaining to Black males that more literature pertinent to existing mentoring programs and services for Black men would be available. Holland (1996) notes:

> A vast array of intervention strategies have been tried. However, like many programs aimed at correcting societal problems, most academic remediation efforts are introduced after students have already failed. The absence of preventive strategies contrasts sharply with the proliferation of remediation models, and programs whose purpose is to stem the tide of academic failure in young Black males have yet to reach critical mass. (p. 316)

This is not to suggest that there is a shortage of venues that cater to the unique educational, social, and emotional needs of African American men; however, documentation about their efficacy is minimal at best. An example of one program's effect that can be found in the literature is PROJECT 2000.

PROJECT 2000 was founded in the urban center of Washington, DC. The essence of the program was to provide African American males with role models and to prevent Black students from adopting antischooling attitudes. Recognizing that most antischolastic viewpoints tended to emerge in the primary grades as a result of mismatched relationships between Black male students and their White teachers and the limited accessibility to other Black male role models in the home and broader community, especially Black men who were engaged academically, PROJECT 2000 united young Black males with other African American male mentors. The mentors for the program were not selected on the basis of their educational levels; in fact, some of them held blue-collar positions within the community. However, a fundamental prerequisite to becoming a mentor was to be able to identify as a "literate adult male" (p. 317). Mentors also worked under the direct supervision of school personnel.

The program also facilitated professional development seminars for teachers, many of whom were White and female. The intention of these sessions was to inform the educators of sound pedagogy that could be executed without marginalizing the Black male students in their classrooms. PROJECT 2000 had two distinct phases, one at the primary level and another at the secondary level. Regarding the former, participants and volunteers were guided by five tenets: listening, self-control, responsibility, commitment, and work. The cornerstone of the secondary phase of the program is "to provide alternative educational opportunities such as academic support, mentoring, and personal development services that will enable these boys to complete junior and senior high school" (p. 318). Expounding upon the five principles referenced earlier, service, initiative, persistence, and creativity were the foundation for the second phase of the program.

In terms of evaluating the success of PROJECT 2000, an empirically-based, comparative research study revealed higher gains for the elementary school students on achievement tests in the content areas of mathematics, reading, and language arts. According to Holland (1996), "more than 85% of PROJECT 2000 boys were at or above grade level in almost every subject under examination" (p. 320). At the secondary level, preliminary data revealed that "33 out of 38 PROJECT 2000 scholars had earned GPAs of 2.00 or better and were in good standing" (p. 320). According to Holland, PROJECT 2000 has been replicated in numerous other urban centers across the country.

Another program that was launched to propel African American males forward academically, socially and politically, is the MAAT Academy. MAAT is an acronym for Motivated Action toward Achievement and Transformation (Mitchell, Bush, & Bush, 2002). Begun in 2001, MAAT is the namesake of an ancient Egyptian goddess "who symbolized the seven virtues of truth, justice, harmony, reciprocity, balance, order, and prosperity" (p. 143). Initially its mission was to "address the distinct needs of African American male students at the school and counteract their consistent underachievement" (p. 142). The success of the program over the years has led to its addressing issues incident to the environmental and economic health of underserved communities of color.

A multicultural educative approach undergirds MAAT's current mission and is central to its approaches to teaching urban youth how to work collaboratively with people from diverse racial, ethnic, and economic backgrounds to effect change for the better. Likewise, "culturally relevant lesson planning that incorporates the experience and contributions of African people throughout the Diaspora seeks to enhance student learning by incorporating aspects of the students' cultural background" (p. 143). In terms of the program's selection of participants, "the most at risk" (p. 143) African American population is selected including Black males and students from traditionally underrepresented groups.

Unlike PROJECT 2000, MAAT is more stringent in its selection of mentors. Many of the mentors for MAAT serve as full time teachers at the academy. Black male students are able to witness firsthand role models who share their same racial make up, as "Students are required to attend small group counseling sessions with a licensed African American male counselor twice a week for forty five minutes before the start of the school day" (p. 145). Black male students and all program participants are also afforded opportunities to confer with college counselors. The hope of program administrators is that these sessions will generate students' interest in pursuing postsecondary education.

Data about the efficacy of MAAT showed that Black male students experienced significantly fewer disciplinary and office referrals. In addition, qualitative data through interviews revealed that teachers "observed improvements in the classroom behavior, relations with their peers, and increased participation and achievement from participants" (p. 145). More recent benefits of the program for Black males and students in general are inherent in students' opportunities to engage in experiential and inquiry-based learning to resolve numerous health and environmentally-related challenges within their immediate communities. Students sometimes function as ambassadors and often have the listening ears of public and elected officials who attend to the proposals that the students, as agents of change, author. Thus, Black males and other students at MAAT experience education not only within the confines of the hallowed halls of their schools, but they also take advantage of community resources which helps to make their learning more purposeful and enduring.

A common theme in the literature about shielding African American males from many of the perils that may result in their lack of educational attainment and/or complete withdrawal from school suggests that the elementary school age is among the more critical timeframes in which preventive measures need to be implemented. Much of the literature also emphasizes the importance of classroom teachers being aware of and sensitive to the unique traits of any Black male student under their educational charge. However, as noted previously, the racial make up of most elementary school teachers is White and sometimes presents challenges for both the educators and their Black male students. Thus, arguments for gender and racial diversification of schools have been presented (Houston & Calderon, 1991; Nieto, 2007; Skelton, 2009; Tatum, 2008). A recently developed program, albeit at the collegiate level, that has flourished and proposes to diversify the elementary school teaching force both racially and genderwise is Call Me MISTER.

Although the MISTER (Mentors Instructing Students Toward Effective Role Models) program's primary objective is to increase the percentage of South Carolina's Black male elementary school teaching corps, participants, referred to as MISTERs, benefit from academic, financial, and social support. A minimum grade point average is required for maintaining program affiliation. Workshops and seminars that help to prepare its participants for state certification examinations are also offered on a regular basis. The men receive tuition assistance, funds for books, and a stipend that they may use for educational purposes.

According to Hair (2007), the South Carolina Student Loan Corporation instituted loan forgiveness for the MISTERs who complete a 5 year teaching contract in the state. To enhance the social aspect of the males' lives, gatherings are held in various locations between neighboring partner institutions that have Call Me MISTER programs in place. A recent search of the program's website revealed that the organization hosted a national conference and featured prominent keynote speakers like Richard Riley, the former Secretary of Education; Abigail Thernstrom, vice chair of the United States Commission on Civil Rights; and Jawanza Kunjufu, the founder of African American Images. MISTERs also participate in community service projects, especially those that permit them to tutor and mentor Black and other elementary school age boys.

Call Me MISTER has garnered local and national recognition. Since its inception, the model has been replicated across various states in the country. The number of partnering institutions in South Carolina has also increased. This is due in part to the efforts of its program administrators, the MISTERS themselves, and Jeff Davis. Davis is a Clemson University alumnus who appeared alongside several of the MISTER participants during an episode of the Oprah Winfrey Show. Call Me MISTER has also been spotlighted on the South Carolina Education Television Network, ABC News, and other television stations. In terms of accomplishing the purpose for which it was created, Rogers (2007) states, "There are 20 former misters currently teaching in the state.... In addition, there are about 150 misters currently in college in the network, who will almost double the number of Black men elementary school teachers in the state when they graduate" (www.diverseeducation.com).

Speaking of the immediate advantages of the program for the MISTERs and their potential future impact on the students they will serve, Roy Jones, director of Call Me MISTER claims:

> MISTERs learn values, leadership skills, mentoring and how to be role models. They learn to be men. And it is those skills, paired with their academic preparation that will make them distinctive in the classroom. The MISTERs will have a different perspective than most of the other teachers.... Some of them come from a dysfunctional background themselves. All of them represent a new breed of teacher: one uniquely prepared to address the whole child. (www.callmemister.clemson.edu)

Other programs with foci incident to Black males include the 100 Black Men of America, Tomorrow's Black Men, Black Men Rising and a number of Greek-lettered, fraternal organizations. Each of these associations has a mentoring component inherent in their endeavors to improve the academic, social, emotional, and general quality of life for Black males. Generally speaking, little is documented in the research literature about the outcomes of these organizations, particularly in terms of their effectiveness in meeting the distinctive needs of Black men. However, the omission has recently captured the attention of scholars who examine the historical, cultural, and political impact of fraternities and sororities on college campuses throughout the United States (Brown, Parks, & Phillips, 2005; DeSantis, 2007; Ross, 2001).

The goal of this literature review was to briefly spotlight some of the research related to African American male identity construction and the volatility of its calculus. At issue are lingering after effects of slavery which often result in others' negative views of Black men mentally, physically, emotionally, and otherwise. Despite the fact that many men of African descent possess formidable intellect, the research demonstrates that as early as elementary school, many Black males are predisposed to lower teacher expectations, higher incidence of special education, and suspensions and expulsions from school for petty infractions, especially in comparison to their White male counterparts. Similarly, corporeal interest in Black men often results in perceptions of them as hypersexualized and promiscuous beings. Although research suggests that some Black males are complicit in many of the obstacles that confront them, insufficient systematic and programmatic interventions have been executed to support African American men in their quests to more positively direct their paths in a variety of educational and social situations.

METHODOLOGY

A study of this nature is important because it furthers understanding about the critical need for Black males to be mentored and supported. Sharing anecdotal evidence of the participant's successes is also invaluable for a number of reasons. First, it counters popular opinion that African American men are beyond redemption and that they frequently yield to peripatetic winds which direct them nowhere. Secondly, the subject's positive effect upon Black males is showcased as a means of combating fallacious beliefs that men of African descent lack the individual and collective resolve to alter any path that would result in nothing more than their ultimate death and destruction. More importantly, the triumphs that emerge from the participant's relationships with his mentees are conveyed to afford others who would assume African American male mentoring positions with a blueprint of viable strategies that may be enacted to alter many of the less favorable fates to which many Black men often become privy.

The overall research question that framed the study was "Why was Daniel motivated to mentor Black males?" A secondary question included, "What obstacles and/or challenges, if any, did Daniel encounter as he sought to influence younger African American males' understanding of manhood, decency, self-respect, and the implications of their behaviors and actions?" The project employs the case study approach advocated by Yin (2002). He asserts that single cases are permissible when the objective is to accomplish three major components of the qualitative method: to describe, to understand, and to explain (Yin, 1984; 1989). Moreover, this protocol was selected because it facilitated the examination of central themes throughout interview processes. It also proved useful for exploring *Umojo* (unity) and *Nia* (purpose), two key conceptions of the Africentric Resistance Modality Model, as introduced by Robinson and Howard-Hamilton (1994).

Rich data for this study were obtained over 6 weeks in two different ways. Questionnaires were electronically submitted to the participant and follow up, open-ended interviews about the participant's responses were conducted by telephone. Each interview, a total of three, lasted 1 hour and with the participant's consent, was taped. The audio tapes were transcribed verbatim and were electronically resubmitted to the participant. These methods generated several pages of text and afforded me the opportunity to verify and obtain greater clarity about statements that the participant had made.

Pattern analyses were conducted to identify emerging themes in the data (Miles & Huberman, 1994). Repetitions in the language utilized by the participant directed my attention to conceptual relationships in the data (Gadner, Buber, & Richards, 2003). In addition, the two principles *Umojo* and *Nia* of the Africentric Resistance Modality Model assisted with interpreting and understanding the participant's motivation to mentor other African American males. Member checking and peer debriefing with university colleagues confirmed the authenticity and consistency of identified themes and patterns in the data (Patton, 2002).

ABOUT THE PARTICIPANT

Daniel Jean is a 35 year old African American man who began working with youth as a peer educator at a nonprofit theatrical program in Boston, Massachusetts. He was 16 years old at the time and has since amassed over 15 years of experience serving troubled youth and their families in both public schools and outreach environments. After completing high school and throughout college, he maintained his membership at the mentoring program in Boston and was ultimately catapulted to a managerial position. He attended Northeastern University, Massachusetts College of Art, and Roxbury Community College.

Daniel has served as a project manager and is proud of having instituted a citywide HIV/AIDS Prevention Program that was funded by a grant from the Center for Disease Control. He has functioned as a mediator for youngsters during their times of conflict, facilitated gang intervention programs, and counseled drug addicts. He has also lectured throughout the greater Boston community, having conducted workshops in Boston Public Schools, Cambridge Public Schools, the Metro Boys and Girls Club of Boston, the Boston Department of Public Health, and many other programs that cater to young people.

During the initial interview, Daniel described himself in this way:

> My talent and experience has allowed me to work for many youth health programs with diverse populations of all cultures, backgrounds, and age groups. I have a strong knowledge of presenting abstinence, HIV/AIDS prevention, and other health subjects for youth. My background in youth services and development has equipped me with great communication skills as well as the patience and understanding to work with those that I service regardless of age, gender, or ethnicity. I'm a great team player who likes to take advice just as much as I like to give it. Through my years of service to community youth, I have gained experience in many fields. I am strongly equipped with the skills that it takes to work in any office, school, or customer service setting. (personal communication, July 22, 2008)

When asked to explain what motivated him to mentor African American males, he spoke about his troubled past:

> I grew up with a single mom. I've smoked weed. I was drinking alcohol at sixteen. I joined a gang. I've been shot at. I've been jumped and put in a hospital. When I work with Black males, I make it a priority to spend as much time as I can explaining to them where I came from and how I succeeded. I try to explain to them that those experiences were my wake up call, not my ticket to ride. Mentoring Black males is my calling. God gave me the ability to reach young men in a way that others can't. I think sometimes the educated brothers—no disrespect—but it's a little harder for them

> to get through to them because they may not have experienced what some of these guys have experienced firsthand. I have always had a personal connection with the Black men that I've worked with because I see myself in them when I was their age. So I hope I can bring a dual perspective to your topic, one as an educator as well as one of having been a troubled Black youth who successfully made it out of the cycle of despair that African American men in America often face. Why I mentor Black males? It's in my heart. (personal communication, July 22, 2008)

Although he was born in Boston, Massachusetts, Daniel relocated to Snellville, Georgia, approximately twenty minutes east of Atlanta. There, he is employed as an adolescent health educator for an HIV/AIDS service agency. He is a skilled communicator who enjoys being in the company of young people. Each time we spoke, his zeal for doing the best he can to help those in need, especially Black males, manifest in his vocal inflections and the depth of his responses to the interview questions. He was excited to have been invited to participate in the study and commended me for choosing African American men as the focus of the project. He expressed appreciation for my pursuing this research agenda and claimed this would be "a great service to our community." He also suggested that the project is essential because he believes it will help "tackle the issues concerning Black men."

CASE STUDY RESULTS

As previously noted, the intent of this study applies the Africentric Resistance Modality Model to examine the factors that motivated Daniel to mentor other African American males. Also, the study explores how he attempts to help younger Black males reacclimatize to society upon their release from confinement. The findings of Daniel's case correlate with many of the structures inherent in the Africentric Resistance Modality Model, particularly *Umojo* and *Nia*. Of note are indicators that Daniel believes: (1) mature African American men should unite and share the responsibility to mentor other Black males, especially those who are at risk of lagging behind educationally, morally, and socially, (2) that educationally astute and professional Black men should serve as role models and should volunteer some of their time to tutor academically struggling Black males with schoolwork, social skills building, and behavior management, (3) that African American men need to collaborate with community programs, youth service agencies, and detention and health centers to plan and to implement preventive and/or corrective activities and events that help to limit the number of Black males who become juvenile delinquents, (4) that divine intervention instilled within him compassion for humankind, especially Black males such that he believes he has a moral and spiritual obligation to uplift and to redirect the lives of troubled Black youth within his community, and (5) that his purpose in life is to counsel at risk Black youth about what it means to be a man of decency and to warn them about the dangers of unsafe sexual practices, drug abuse, and poor decision making.

This case revealed that Daniel mentors and teaches Black males between the ages of 13-24. The median ages of the Black men he encounters are between 15-17. During the penultimate interview he chronicled his work experiences with Black males in both Boston and the state of Georgia:

> Most of the young men I worked with were from Boston's innercity ... Roxbury, Dorchester, and South End neighborhoods. I saw myself in many of them, but the program I was a part of provided me with a safe haven from the streets and gave me mentors, positive role models, and experiences to learn from. I wanted the youth that I worked with to experience the same thing. I made it my mission to reach out to the young Black men in particular because many of them came from poor neighborhoods, bad schools, and single parent homes. For many of them the path to gangs and drugs had already been laid, and I could see them slipping through the cracks, even while in the safety net of the program. However, I felt that my presence and the presence of the other Black male counselors helped reinforce that safety net.

Researcher: Can you tell me when, how often, and how long you meet with Black males?

Daniel: Since moving, I come in contact with about 100-150 Black males per year. I facilitate an hour presentation to the youth that I work with 6-7 times a week.

Researcher: Where do your meetings with Black males usually take place?

Daniel: My 2008 summer scheduled presentations are presented at the GR Youth Detention Center, RC Adolescent Drug Treatment Program, and the Lawrenceville Boys and Girls Club. Outside of those scheduled presentations I may be requested to present at any number of other youth facilities in Gwinnett County and surrounding areas.

Researcher: Can you describe a typical session?

Daniel: Most of the Black men that I encounter are at the GR Youth Detention Center. Here I might have a classroom of 15-20 incarcerated males. 50-60% are Black males. I begin my sessions by introducing myself as an HIV prevention educator. I lay down a set of ground rules that they need to follow. Then I give them some general statistics about HIV and how it's become a serious problem in young people across the country. I then ask the youth to tell me what they know about HIV and AIDS and follow with a brief "myth and fact" activity to eliminate any false information that they may have about the disease. I follow that with an activity that explains HIV transmission and its progression to AIDS. The remainder of my sessions usually takes place the following day or week, which I use to discuss other STDs, abstinence, condom use, and how to make responsible decisions. Outside of discussing about HIV and STDs, I try to spend some time engaging the young men in general conversations. I talk to them about their future goals and how they plan to reach them, I discuss steps to making better decisions, how to fix a bad decision, how to better resolve conflicts and find alternatives to drugs, gangs, etc. Anything related to being a decent human being ... we talk about it.

Researcher: How are the topics chosen?

Daniel: I usually pick additional topics based on the group's reaction to the general presentation. If I see a lot of gang language, signs or behavior, I use my last session to talk about being decent men and the consequences of making bad decisions. If the young men express a lot of sexual activity, I make an emphasis in talking more about sexual consequences like having a child or getting a non curable STD. Or if I see some of the youth showing interest in changing their lives, or are displaying great talent in art or music, I try and talk about education, goals, and objectives. The groups vary so much and my time can be very short, so often it's very difficult to get my whole message across, but I try to use special activities like videos followed by discussion and role playing.

Researcher: What are some of the videos you have used during your sessions?

Daniel: Most of the videos are approved by the agency. I usually show *Blunted on Reality* and follow up with a good discussion on decision making. I also show *Amanda's Story*. For young men I try to point out that there are a lot of young ladies out there with HIV, so you need to think about that. I give them role-playing situations and ask them in general what are some decisions young people have to make. It works well with the guys who goof off. Sometimes I give

> them condom situations ... like if there's this girl at a party and you know she's having sex with a whole bunch of guys in the room ... would you have sex with her or not. Or if you know you're going to be tested at work to find out if you've smoked weed and you've been offered a blunt ... would you smoke it or not. I talk to them about how to resist pressure or to have sex responsibly if they're going to have sex. I talk to them about being men of integrity. I constantly ask them what they need to do to make things better in terms of making good decisions.

In that Daniel has frequent and consistent contact with Black males, I asked him to describe a recent session that resonated with him and why the meeting had particular significance. He explained that he had been working for a full year with four Black males ages 15-16 who had been detained for robbing a grocery store. He recounted the gathering like so:

> A recent session that I would say sticks out in my mind is four guys I was working with. They were friends who were in jail for the robbery of a grocery store. To me, they were average teens ... silly, defiant, and invincible. However, their crime, armed robbery, was serious enough that they were clearly going to be tried as adults. As time passed and I got to know the boys, two in particular, I realized that their behavior, sometimes boastful and egotistical, was simply a cover up to hide the inevitable, that they were going to be in jail for a long time. I watched their emotions shift from playful and unapologetic to serious and depressed. Two were sentenced early in the year once they turned seventeen, and the other two were sentenced later on in the year. I watched each of them getting closer to being sentenced and sent to their future homes. The drama and pain that was glued to their faces was almost hard to bare. Eventually they were each sentenced to 10 years in prison. The thought pained me, even after watching this cycle play out far too often for the past four or 5 years that I had been presenting at the jail. Working with this particular group of boys was significant to me because it was an example of how so many young Black men carelessly throw their lives away, ignore the consequences of their actions and kill their hopes and dreams. To me, those four young men represented Black boys from all walks of life. Some poor, some smart, some are talented, some come from good families with good values, some are violent and belong in jail, and some are just plain stupid. They represent all the boys that I work with, mostly clueless of how they were being herded into the slaughter house of their demise. So they sit around joke, play, laugh and ignore people trying to help them as the judges, lawyers, juries and law enforcement profit from their failure. Ten years of their young lives thrown away, all for nothing. It's a cycle that's playing itself out all over the country and even outside of the United States,

> the United Kingdom, the Caribbean, and Africa. A lot of our young Black men are wasting away. (personal communication, July 28, 2008)

Among other questions during the third and final interview, I asked Daniel if he had experienced any challenges working directly with Black males. He stated that the most difficult times are when there are few epiphanic moments when the young men he is attempting to help fail to follow his counsel and end up exacerbating already complicated circumstances:

> My biggest challenge working with Black males is not seeing the light bulb go off in their heads ... not seeing enough "ah ha" moments. It frustrates me to see so many of them not getting it, not letting it sink in or letting the hard shell of a few others in the group influence their own common sense. Far too often a lot of our Black boys are too clouded with other influences to change what is their reality into what is our hope. I tell them that any risk that you take that puts your life in danger, or your family's life in danger, is of no real cost to anyone else but yourself and your family. You are the one who is disenfranchised, your families are the ones who must mourn, and they are the ones who must eat the cost of your failures. I tell them not to be careless with their life, to think their actions through carefully and think of all of the important things they jeopardize before they make bad decisions. Sometimes they listen; sometimes they don't ... unfortunately. (personal communication, August 20, 2008)

With regard to Daniel's response about obstacles he has encountered in working with males of African descent, it can be observed that negative peer influence has impacted intermittently his level of progress with some of his mentees. He mentioned that there are sessions in which he encounters what he terms the "alpha male:"

> I have those kids who think they're the alpha male. They're the ones who think they know all the answers. When that happens, I let them have their say. I respect their role and need to be in charge. I usually validate their opinions and try to meet them with a positive response that brings the focus of the lesson back to what doctors say and what statistics show.

Researcher: Is there anything else that you do to overcome these challenges?

Daniel: What I've done to overcome challenges is to consistently reinforce my message. I continue to be very blunt and direct with my message to the boys. I don't sugarcoat their problems, and I try and respect their view even if I disagree. I also seek out the boys who do get it and are trying to change, whether I am the cause or not. I encourage them. I push them, and I congratulate them in every way I can.

Researcher: What would you say motivates you to persevere and to keep mentoring Black males, even when you find yourself facing significant obstacles?

Daniel: (Sighs) I think I do get frustrated a lot ... like ... I can't get this group. My way of dealing with it is to not take it personal and to come back and try another approach. Some of the guys are way more visual, so I have to create a way to make it interactive. I try to prepare my mind for having one or two males who are alpha males, and I have to find a way to include them. I avoid coming into the situation with the attitude that I'm going to save all these kids. If I have a session and it doesn't go well, I'll come back to it another time with a different way of handling it. I don't give up on them, but I always try to find another way of dealing with them. I was also a victim of gang violence, and I think this is also a motivating factor.

Researcher: Do you feel comfortable sharing a little more about that experience ... your being a victim of gang violence I mean?

Daniel: Sure. I was sixteen at the time. I was hanging with a friend of mine who was a gang member. In order to see his girl, we had to go to a certain part of town. God sent me so many messages to go home because we could not find this girl's home for nothing. When we finally found her, we got there and she wouldn't let us in. She actually set him up. All of a sudden, a whole lot of guys showed up and they started attacking us. Most of them followed me (chuckling), thinking I was a part of a gang. They beat me up, and I passed out in an abandoned lot. When I woke up, I was in the hospital. That experience invoked in me the desire to be a killer. These are the experiences our young men are going through. It's stuff like this that makes our young men want to fight and not in a lawful way, but in a way that wanted to make me forget about all my mother taught me about not wanting to get in trouble. It was fight or flight for me at the time. As I got older though, I had a change of mind about fighting other Black men who are being screwed by the system and turned that anger toward fighting a system that's screwing us. Becoming militant made me step back and look at the bigger picture, the conditions of my neighborhood ... our neighborhoods and why many of them are the way they are … the drugs, the guns, the violence. I became smarter. I began to read more. I attribute the change in my attitude to Malcolm X, the activists, the Panthers and realized that I was too smart for taking that negative route. This generation, though, they don't have a message. We had more options like Louis Farakhan and Queen Latifah, and people who had something to say. Now they have Little Wayne—oh God help us. He sold more albums than Michael Jackson, and this is the voice that our young Black men are listening to. God help us. This is why we need more Black mentors out there. This generation needs to hear more positivity coming from people like you and me.

Researcher: Generally speaking, what do you believe is one of the most pressing issues affecting Black men in the United States?

Daniel: The most prominent issue affecting black males in the United States today is a lack of a systematic approach to dealing with the plight of America's Black men. If this were a Jewish problem, that community would be up in arms assuring that the problem was eliminated. If it were a Chinese problem, we would see the Chinese community developing stringent interventions to minimize its effects on their communities. The lack of a rigorous, collective, unchanging approach by black Americans to deal with the problems of black men and the black family as a whole is the greatest issue affecting black men in America. I could tell you a whole lot more, but since you asked for one, I'll stop there, but as far as we have come along, we still have a pretty long way to go.

Researcher: So let's talk about your successes. What are some of them and how do you evaluate the overall success of what you do with these young black males?

Daniel: (Sighs) That's tough. I do have successes. One that comes to mind is when the guards at some of the jails come in and sit in on my sessions. I think this is good because it shows them in a better light, and it creates better bonding opportunities for the guys. But as far as evaluating success, we really don't have an evaluating system. I evaluate my own success by evaluating how many of the young men want to be tested. I offer HIV testing, so that's my best way of evaluating myself at the end of the presentations … are they willing to get tested. At session one, if they're goofing off and nobody's listening and I go back and by session

> four and I have their attention, then I know I've been successful.

Despite the fact that the many of the African American males with whom Daniel works are incarcerated, he validates them and treats them with dignity and respect. He listens carefully to them, and he accepts their points of view, even when his and his mentees' perspectives are dissonant:

> I don't shoot anybody down, because whenever it becomes confrontational, it presents a challenge for me. In class sometimes, the students themselves recognize the machismo of the alpha male and they'll just recognize that the person is trying to be a knucklehead, but a person in my position has to strategize and hold my ground. (personal communication, August 20, 2008)

Perhaps what is most honorable about Daniel's mentorship is his capacity to maintain high expectations for the men with whom he works. He attempts to supply the males with a sense of hope and advice about how they can avoid becoming repeat offenders:

> I give them examples and ask them about their own lives and ask them to write down their future goals and discuss how to reach them. More importantly, I have them express what will happen if they continue down the wrong path. I always tell them to be prepared to change their ways and not wait for someone else to force them to change. The general belief is that every kid in jail is the same, but there are some kids in jail who are from good homes and are victims of circumstance. Many of the youth seriously express wanting to get jobs or start their own business. Some of them talk about going to college, playing sports, or becoming musicians. Others talk about "getting my life right" or getting out of jail, or out of "the system." But since they've been disenfranchised and lack the education and necessary skills, they don't know how to reach their goals. It's my duty to give them advice about their options ... like not giving up, like getting out of jail and staying out, like volunteering, joining a church, and starting a business. (personal communication, August 20, 2008).

IMPLICATIONS

The findings of this case study offer responses to the following inquiries: (1) "Why was Daniel motivated to mentor Black males?" and (2) "What obstacles and/or challenges, if any, did Daniel encounter as he sought to influence younger African American males' understanding of manhood, decency, self-respect, and the implications of their behaviors and actions?" Daniel's experiences, as chronicled throughout this case study, communicates a strong and powerful message about how influential one person can be in making a difference in the lives of African American males. Conversations with colleagues who were familiar with this project and who also confirmed emergent themes and patterns in the study concur that Daniel's devotion to community and his stalwart determination to alter for the better the paths of at risk Black males was very transparent. Likewise, discussions with Daniel over the course of the study revealed that his indomitable energy and purposeful commitment to uplift Black males would continue beyond the culmination of his participation in this research project.

For a variety of audiences, the implications of this study are numerous. Of immediate relevance, however, is the significance of this study to classroom practitioners in particular. As can be observed from Daniel's case, African American males possess the wherewithal to be successful in schooling contexts. To this end, it is of paramount importance that teachers create and foster within their classrooms an environment that is safe for all of their students to take risks. Where Black males are concerned, particularly those who may have been labeled at-risk, the establishment of a conducive haven for learning becomes especially imperative.

Similarly, as reflected in Daniel's pedagogical strategies, notwithstanding the fact that he has not been formally trained as a classroom teacher, he incorporates multimodal teaching practices to capture his audience's attention and diversifies his techniques throughout his presentations to command and to maintain the focus of his groups. The content of his instruction is pertinent to the experiences of those under his tutelage, and the learners under his charge are afforded the freedom to respectfully disagree with their facilitator. He does not disparage dissenting viewpoints, and he positively reinforces individuals for contributing to discussions. In effect, Daniel welcomes and encourages the opportunity for the effective exchange of ideas, understanding that members of his sessions want to learn. He views himself as both mentor and learner; consequently, a reciprocal dynamic is evident in his approaches to educating his audiences about manhood, HIV/AIDS, and diverse topics incident to Black male identity.

Daniel also maintains high expectations for all of his mentees, both academically and behaviorally. He believes in their potential to accomplish realistic goals, despite the fact that many of them are confined. He recognizes that some of the Black males whom he mentors will eventually be released from the penal system and therefore need to learn how not to become repeat offenders. Thus, he differentiates his presentations and provides information that meets the needs of all those who attend his trainings. Ground rules are set at the beginning of the sessions he hosts and order is maintained throughout. He solicits the input of his mentees about the best ways he can enhance the quality of his presentations. This strategy allows him to provide meaningful content to Black males, and it simultaneously commands the respect for all parties involved and engenders acceptable standards of behavior and decorum for the learning context. To the extent that classroom practitioners incorporate similar strategies that Daniel models in this case study, the learning opportunities for Black males may be maximized.

LIMITATIONS

This case study offers a singular point of view about the factors that motivated one man's efforts to mentor Black males and the intersection of the Africentric Resistance Modality Model. This theoretical framework outlines seven principles; however, two key concepts, *Umoja* and *Nia* have been explored. Although this conceptual paradigm helped to frame the examination of the factors that motivated Daniel to mentor Black males, other theoretical models could also be applied. Likewise, other principles within the Africentric Resistance Modality Model could be among the motivational influences. Daniel's single case may also be nonrepresentative of the broader population, one, among other drawbacks of case study research, especially those that are singular in approach. Therefore, additional research that applies other theoretical frameworks to examine the factors that motivate Black men to assume mentoring responsibilities is warranted.

CONCLUSION

The plight of African American men in the United States is like a tide that ebbs and flows and rises and falls in the consciousness of many. At times Black men are appreciated for their contributions, especially when they demonstrate athletic prowess and excel on the basketball court and football field. A similar kind of reception is generally afforded to those in the entertainment industry when they act well and/or supply the funkiest beats and "all that jazz." However, what typically fails to appear on the radar screen are the battles that many Black males experience on a daily basis. Some struggle with masculinity and identity issues while others combat health, employment, and educational barriers each day. The Africentric Resistance Modality Model was employed in this study to explore the factors that motivate Daniel Jean to mentor Black males and to assist them in overcoming some of these hurdles. One can glean much by attending to Daniel's case, especially with respect to understanding that all Black men—bound or free—can benefit from the support of a good mentor.

REFERENCES

Akbar, N. (1996). *Breaking the chains of psychological slavery.* Tallahassee, FL: Mind Productions & Associates.

Austin, B., Gilmore, B., & McCormick, J. (2003). *Wake up and start to live: An analysis of a Gallup Poll and a statistical profile of African American men*, 1990-2000. Lanham, MD: University Press of America.

Broderick, C. (1965). Social heterosexual development among urban Negroes and Whites. *Journal of Marriage and the Family, 26*, 200-203.

Brown, T., Parks, G., & Phillips, C. (2005). *African American fraternities and sororities: The legacy and the vision.* Lexington, KY: University of Kentucky Press.

Cazenave, N. (1979). Middle-income Black fathers: An analysis of the provider role. *The Family Coordinator, 28*, 583-593.

Dancy, E., & Brown, M. (2008). Unintended consequences: African American male educational attainment and collegiate perceptions after *Brown v. Board of Education. American Behavioral Scientist 51*(7), 984-1003).

Davis, J. (2006). Research at the margin: Mapping masculinity and mobility of African American high school dropouts. *International Journal of Qualitative Studies in Education, 19*(3), 289-304.

Davis, J., & Jordan, W. (1994). The effects of school context, structure, and experiences on African American males in middle and high school. *The Journal of Negro Education, 63*(4), 570-583.

Delpit, L. (2006). *Other people's children: Cultural conflict in the classroom.* New York, NY: New Press

DeSantis, A. (2007). *Inside Greek u: Fraternities, sororities, and the pursuit of pleasure, power, and prestige.* Lexington, KY: University of Kentucky Press.

Elkins, S. (1959). *Slavery: A problem in American institutional and intellectual life.* Chicago, IL: University of Chicago Press.

Fairchild, H. (1984). School size, per-pupil expenditures, and academic achievement. *Review of Public Data Use, 12*, 221-229.

Foster, V. Kimmel, M., & Skelton, C. (2001). What about the boys? An overview of the debates. In W. Martino & B. Meyenn (Eds.), *What about the boys? Issues of masculinity in schools.* Buckingham, England: Open University Press.

Frazier, E. (1939). *The Negro family in the United States.* Chicago, IL: University of Chicago Press.

Gadner, J., Buber, R., & Richards, L. (2003). *Organising knowledge: Methods and case studies.* New York, NY: Palgrave Macmillan.

Hair, J. (2007). *South Carolina student loan donates $500,000 to the Call Me MISTER Program.* Retrieved from http://www.scstudentloan.org/

Haley, A. (1976). *Roots.* Garden City, NY: Doubleday.

Harry, B., & Anderson, M. (1994). The disproportionate placement of African American males in special education programs: A critique of the process. *The Journal of Negro Education, 63*(4), 602-620.

Holland, S. (1996). PROJECT 2000: An educational and mentoring support model for inner-city African American boys. *Journal of Negro Education, 63*(3), 315-321.

hooks, b. (2004). *We real cool: Black men and masculinity.* New York, NY: Routledge.

Horvat, E., & Traore, R. (2001). Rebuilding the lives of high school dropouts: Lessons from a successful program. *Journal of Research in Education, 11*(1), 88-95.

Houston, R., & Calderon, M. (1991). Preparing an ethnically diverse teaching force. *Teacher Education and Practice, 6*(2), 43-49.

Kotre, J. (1999). *Make it count.* New York, NY: Free Press.

Kunjufu, J. (1997). *Motivating and preparing Black youth for success.* Chicago, IL: African American Images.

Kunjufu, J. (2001). *State of emergency: We must save African American males.* Chicago, IL: African American Images.

Kunjufu, J. (2002). *Black students/middle class teachers.* Chicago, IL: African American Images.

Majors, R., & Billson, J. M. (1992). *Cool pose: The dilemmas of Black manhood in America.* New York, NY: Touchstone.

Miles, M., & Huberman, A. (1994). *Qualitative data analysis.* Thousand Oaks, CA: SAGE.

Mincy, R. (2006). *Black males left behind.* Washington, DC: Urban Institute Press.

Mitchell, K., Bush, E., & Bush, L. (2002). Standing in the gap: A model for establishing African American male intervention programs with public schools. *Educational Horizons, 80*(3), 140-146.

Moynihan, D. (1965). *The Negro family: The case for national action.* Washington, DC: U.S. Government Printing Office.

Nieto, S. (2007). *Affirming diversity: The sociopolitical context of multicultural education* (5th ed.). Upper Saddle River, NJ: Allyn & Bacon.

Oakes, J. (2005). *Keeping track: How schools structure inequality* (2nd ed.). New Haven, CT: Yale University Press.

O'Neil, J., Helms, B., Gable, R., Laurence, D., & Wrightsman, L. (1986). Gender role conflict scale: College men's fear of femininity. *Sex Roles, 14,* 335-351.

O'Neil, J. M. (2002, August). *Twenty years of gender role conflict research.* Paper presented at the 110th Annual Convention of the American Psychological Association, Chicago, IL.

Patton, M. (2002). *Qualitative research and evaluation methods* (3rd ed.). Thousand Oaks, CA: SAGE.

Pittman, A. (2009). *Whited out: Unique perspectives on black identity and honors achievement.* New York, NY: Peter Lang.

Pleck, J., Sonenstein, F., & Ku, L. (1993). Masculinity ideology and its correlates. In S. Oskamp & M. Constanza (Eds.), *Gender issues on contemporary society* (pp. 85-110). Newbury Park, CA: SAGE.

Polite, V. (1994). The method in the madness: African American males, avoidance schooling, and chaos theory. *The Journal of Negro Education, 63*(4), 588-604.

Porter, M. (1998). *Kill them before they grow: The misdiagnosis of African American boys in American classrooms.* Chicago, IL: African American Images.

Reese, R. (2003). *American paradox: Young black men.* Durham, NC: Carolina Academic Press.

Reiss, I. (1964). Premarital sexual permissiveness among Negroes and Whites. *American Sociological Review, 29,* 688-698.

Robinson, T., & Howard-Hamilton, M. (1994). An Africentric paradigm: Foundations for a healthy self-image and healthy interpersonal relationships. *Journal of Mental Health Counseling, 16* 327-339.

Rogers, I. (2007). *Call me MISTER program expands to 11th college.* Retrieved from www.diverseeducation.com/

Ross, L. (2001). *The divine nine: The history of African American fraternities and sororities in America.* New York, NY: Kensington Books.

Skelton, C. (2009). Failing to get men into primary teaching: A feminist critique. *Journal of Education Policy, 24*(1), 39-54.

Staples, R. (1982). *Black masculinity: The Black male's role in American society.* San Francisco, CA: The Black Scholar Press.

Tatum, B. (2008). *Can we talk about race?: And other conversations in an era of school resegregation.* Boston, MA: Beacon Press.

Thompson, E. (2008). *Mistaken identity.* Retrieved from http://chronicle.com/

Trott, A. (2008). *Misidentification nearly leads to arrest of basketball coach.* Retrieved from http://www.mindfully.org/

Yin, R. (1984). *Case study research: Design and methods* (1st ed.). Beverly Hills, CA: SAGE.

Yin, R. (1989). *Case study research: Design and methods* (Rev. ed.). Beverly Hills, CA: SAGE.

Yin, R. (2002). *Case study research: Design and methods* (3rd ed.). Beverly Hills, CA: SAGE.

Wilson, M. (2008). 3 detectives acquitted in Bell shooting. Retrieved from http://www.nytimes.com/

CHAPTER 6

ACHIEVING MERITOCRACY

The Acculturation Experiences of African American Male Scholars

Darryl B. Holloman

> There are varying levels I think professors work within and upon and across. And so you know the complexity with being young and inexperienced as an African American [faculty member], I don't know which is greater. I think when I first entered the academy I sometimes wondered if I faced issues because I was young, or was it because I was Black, or was it because I was southern and I had a dialect. And so you wonder all these things and you have all these "what ifs." So you make sure that you are prepared and are able to deal with issues and that you are honest [with yourself]. (personal communication, December 29, 2004)

This faculty member clearly displays the complexities that surround his attempts to acculturate as a junior-level scholar to the academy. Although research on African American faculty members at predominately White institutions of higher education are replete with such narratives, few studies have focused on how those scholars meritoriously acculturated to those White environments (Anderson, 1993). Currently, African American

African American Males and Education:
Researching the Convergence of Race and Identity, pp. 129–148

male faculty members in the United States who hold the rank of full professor are only 2.0% of the professoriate, with associate professors accounting for 3.0%, and assistant professors 3.4%. These figures are alarmingly low when compared to White male faculty members who are at 70.1%, 55.7% and 44.1% respectively, and White female faculty members who are at 18.4, 29.3% and 36.1% respectively. Additionally, the percentage of African American male faculty members at 2.6% is only slightly larger at all ranks of the professoriate than African American female faculty members at 2.5% (Department of Education, 2002).

Existing research often reports the acculturation experiences of African American scholars from a deficit model. This deficit model typically focuses on the difficulties that untenured African American junior-level faculty members encounter in their attempts to acculturate to the academic and social environments of predominately White postsecondary settings (Allen, Epps, Guillory, Suh, & Bonous-Hammarth, 2000; Butner, 2000; Davis, 1999; Finkelstein, Seal, & Schuster, 1998; Jackson, 1991; Jones, 2000; Jones, 2001; O'Meara, 2002; Patitu, 2000; Tillman, 2001; Turner, 2003; Weems, 2003). This article contributes to the literature on the acculturation process of Black faculty members at predominately White institutions through an examination of the lives of four tenured senior-level African American scholars who have successfully acculturated to predominately White educational settings. The purpose of the study is to share the personal and professional experiences that these faculty members recounted in their acculturation processes.

THE ACCULTURATION OF FACULTY OF COLOR TO THE ACADEMY

Sadao (2003) suggests that, "Acculturation relates to the introduction of and interaction with a new culture, the emphasis being on the potential for compromising one's previously held beliefs and values to function in the new culture" (p. 399). Sadao (2003) argues that faculty of color actually exist in two distinct cultures: "the ethnic culture where he [or she] was born and raised and the university culture where he [or she] found professional success" (p. 397). Consequently, Sadao (2003) identifies the ethnically biased culture of faculty members and the climate of the university as the main factors that inhibit the successful recruitment, tenure and promotion of faculty of color. In her qualitative study of 19 junior and senior faculty members of color, Sadao (2003) found that for the members of her study, understanding their culture and institutional climate helped them to successfully acculturate to the academy because they developed "the capacity to understand and be part of two cultures" (p. 398).

Sadao (2003) suggests that faculty of color acculturate to predominately White institutions of higher education when they have acquired a bicultural identity. Once faculty members of color establish a bicultural identity, they develop the ability to switch between two cultures, and they learn to balance the demands of their profession (Sadao, 2003). This cultural "code" switching is determined by either the faculty member's situation or their institution. Although an important finding, Sadao (2003) encourages further examination of her bicultural model in other studies. Subsequently, this article used Sadao's framework in conjunction with the literature on Black Faculty to examine the acculturation experiences of the men studied.

CHALLENGES TO THE ACCULTURATION PROCESSES FOR FACULTY OF COLOR

The literature reports that African American faculty members at most stages of their academic careers encounter institutional barriers such as isolation from peers, extensive teaching loads, and inflexible research expectations (Jones, 2001; Turner, 2003). Researchers further report that African American faculty members are often expected to support their institution's commitments to diversity by serving as representative on committees that target minority issues and through extensive mentoring of minority students. In addition, African American faculty members often grapple with issues that surround the societal perceptions of race and its influence on predominately White educational environments. As a result of these inequities the special needs or considerations of these faculty members are often overlooked as they attempt to acculturate to those settings (hooks, 1990; Ladson-Billings, 1997; Patitu, 2000).

In his qualitative study of sixteen faculty members of color, Baez (2000) warns that scholars must condemn higher education practices and norms that reflected differential rewards for faculty members of color—especially for minority scholars who are dedicated to race-based research and service. Essien (2003) states that as minority law professors acculturate to predominately White educational settings they show signs of being overworked, are excluded from informal networks, and function in hostile and unsupportive environments. Essien (2003) surmises that these barriers are caused by the failure of predominately White institutions to ensure that minority faculty members receive mentoring, encouragement for race-based research agendas, and funding to support minority-based research projects. Essien (2003) suggests that institutions of higher education must create a climate of "belonging within the academic community" for faculty members of color as a means of assisting them in their acculturation process (pp. 63-71).

Jackson (1991) suggests that African American faculty members in particular "have a tendency to challenge the contemporary conceptions of scholarship in terms of content, theoretical paradigms, philosophies and methodologies" (p. 145). Jackson (1991) further explains that the scholarly activities of African American faculty members may not always adhere to traditional modes of academic production. Jackson (1991) concludes that these issues affected the acculturation of African American faculty members at predominately White institutions. Allen and colleagues (2000) state:

> The positions of different racial/ ethnic groups within the academic hierarchy are consistent with their differential status, wealth, and power in U.S. society. African American faculty members face barriers due to the historical, cultural, and social factors that frequently have shaped their relations with Whites generally. Pervasive attitudes of racism as well as differential access and power continue to limit educational opportunities for African Americans in the United States. Such inequities produce the achievement discrepancies in contemporary U.S. education that explain the relative scarcity of African Americans as members of the nation's higher education faculty. (p. 113)

Allen et al. (2000) report that as African American faculty members conduct work in predominately White institutions of higher education they in many ways mirror the challenges that African Americans face when working within the larger society.

This body of literature reflects the importance of conducting research that examines the similarities and differences in regards to how minority groups perceive, interpret and respond to their acculturation processes as faculty members. Smith, Altbach, & Lomotey (2002) state:

> A report issued by the UCLA Higher Education Research Institute indicated that most analysis of national data for faculty of color are seldom disaggregated by race, ethnicity, and gender. Data for faculty of color are often aggregated and reported in a homogenous analysis of "minority faculty" that, unfortunately, tends to confound their distinct experiences in the academy, often leading to the erroneous conclusion that all faculty of color share the same sociohistorical experiences, demographic characteristics, professional values, aspirations, and levels of success. (p. 246)

Subsequently, current studies of faculty members of color should seek to reveal the heterogeneity within this group. Exposing the heterogeneity of faculty members of color serve to reflect differences surrounding issues of access, challenges, and barriers faced by minority groups within predominately White educational settings. In addition, studies which explore the perceptions of individuals versus their group dynamics help to display the variance by which people respond and react to being acculturated into a social system (Ladson-Billings, 1997).

RESEARCH DESIGN AND METHOD

This article used life histories to intensely document the experiences of four senior-level African American male faculty members who worked in predominately White institutions of higher education located in the northeast. Life histories are useful to researchers who are interested in examining contemporary events from the living memory of individuals in an effort to place those memories within their larger social and cultural context (McDowell, 2002). By their very nature, life histories are important tools in conveying the lives of individuals to better understanding how those lives are shaped by social and institutional settings (Tierney, 2000).

And whereas life histories are not necessarily generalized, they do provide an opportunity to closely scrutinize cultural notions and issues of identity development which may not be thoroughly captured in more expansive studies. Tierney (2000) finds:

> The life history not only represents the memory of an individual, it also produces identity. The challenge to us as researchers is to ensure that individuals are not the object of our discourses, but rather the agents of complex, partial, and contradictory identities that help transform the worlds they and we inhabit. (p. 540)

Life histories provide a snapshot into the lives of individuals as they perceive and interpret the world from their own perspectives and experiences. Such an intense analysis of a human life is often missed in quantitative studies, or for that matter large qualitative studies, which fail to reveal the complexity of the individual self.

Procedures

Data for this study was collected through a total of twelve in-depth interviews, which were conducted with four senior-level African American male faculty members during the Fall of 2004 and the Spring of 2005. The respondents were selected using purposeful sampling and they were recruited from two national education conferences (Merriam, 1998). The respondents were located in three states: New Jersey, Illinois, and Pennsylvania. They taught and worked at both public and private American research institutions. The respondents held ranks that ranged from associate to full professor. The interview took place in person, and at the institution of each of the faculty members. Each interview was tape recorded by the researcher. The first two interviews were used to capture and record the respondents' perceptions of both their personal and professional experiences. These sets of interviews were 60-90 minutes in length. The last interview was used as a means for the respondents to reflect on their experiences as Black male faculty members in American society. These interviews lasted from 45-60 minutes. At the beginning of each interview, participants were given a brief overview of the purpose of the study, the topics that would be covered, and the probable length of time that the interview required. To allow respondents an opportunity to explore their ideas and areas of personal significance each interview concluded with a short open-ended discussion.

As the data were collected common themes and salient issues were compared, coded, categorized and analyzed according to methods used by Dey (1993) and Seidman (1998). Recognizing that dependability, transferability, credibility, and conformability are important criteria for trustworthiness in qualitative research, the process of verification was used to interpret the data (Morse, Barrett, Mayan, Olson, & Spiers, 2002). Each man was provided with a copy of his original transcript for review and to check for correct content. Member checking was accomplished by each man providing comments on both the written transcriptions as well as the final written account of the study. Peer examination was sought by consistent review from an outside reader as well as colleagues who were familiar with the study. Further, realizing that triangulation of the data is an important component in establishing internal validity; multiple methods were employed as a means of "confirming emerging findings" (Merriam, 1998). Consequently, triangulation was achieved through a combination of interviews, observations, and document analysis. Document analysis and persistent observation were achieved by reviewing each man's curriculum vita, his school's web pages, his work setting and environment, and when possible, his home life.

Data Analysis

Interview data were examined across and within categories where both similarities and differences were sought in the emerging themes. Seidman (1998) suggests interview date be analyzed by either crafting a profile or through thematic content analysis. The researcher used thematic content analysis to search for themes across categorized data (Seidman, 1998, p.

107). The researcher employed a technique called winnowing to begin the coding process (Seidman, 1998). As a result of the winnowing process, fifty-five preliminary categories emerged in the initial larger study. In an effort to provide a further analysis of the data and to "chunk" the information in search of themes, these categories were placed into matrices (Dey, 1993).

Researcher Bias

It is an important element of any qualitative study to acknowledge researcher bias early in the process. Hence, the researcher is an African American man and acknowledged that there were certain times in the study where he and the men agreed on certain points of view. This was particularly true of two respondents, who like himself, were raised in the American South. The researcher did not attempt to eliminate any biases, being keenly aware of the critique that can occur when race-based research is conducted by members of the same race, but he did work to address some of those biases. Although the researcher and respondents self-identify as African American men, each of their individual life experiences have caused them to take very different directions both professionally and personally.

FINDINGS AND DISCUSSION

To capture the repetition of categories in the initial study, 55 categories were collapsed into 15 subcategories: Biography, Family Life, Influences, Educational Experiences, Racial Experiences, Faculty Life, Connections/Disconnections, Research Agenda, Mentorship, Collaboration, Tenure, Teaching/Scholarship/Service, Attraction, and Grants/Funding. Those categories were assigned numbers and placed into a matrix which produced five overarching themes: (1) Respondents' biographical background and influences, (2) Respondents' introductions to the American educational system, (3) Respondents' transitions to faculty life, (4) Respondents' coping mechanisms as faculty members, and (5) Respondents' perceptions of the academy.

Drawing on the work of Sadao (2003) and the literature on faculty of color this article examines the personal and professional experiences that the respondents recounted in their efforts to successfully acculturate to predominately White educational settings. The research revealed that whereas each of the respondents had experiences with being acculturated to predominately White educational settings, each scholar brought his own unique perspective to the acculturation process. This article focused on the acculturation experiences of the respondents primarily as graduate students and professionals in the field but the respondent's early school settings were where they reported being first introduced to the acculturation process.

EARLY ACCULTURATION EXPERIENCES IN EDUCATIONAL SETTINGS

Each of the men in the study entered elementary school at the height of the integration movement in the United States, so they were introduced to the challenges and benefits of acculturation to predominately White educational settings even prior to entering college:

> Another eventful thing about being a Black student in a largely White school was taking shop class. My shop teacher called my mother and informed her of how well I was doing and encouraged her to put me in a vocational school for printing. And my mother, I remembered that evening was livid, that this White guy was suggesting that her son should work in a printing shop and that was all he would be good at doing. (personal communication, January 7, 2005)

> In my high school there was the ability to actually have a play that focused on Black actors—*A Raisin in the Sun*—as a senior play that would never have been thought of in other parts of Delaware. And it even got some flack at my school. But it gave Black students like me an opportunity to be engaged in those types of activities; whereas, some of my friends in other schools were relegated to vocational kinds of activities and automatically stereotyped in a lot of ways. (personal communication, December 2, 2004)

In most instances the men reported that even as youth they were expected to have some level of responsibility in understanding and interpreting their acculturation process within predominately White school settings. The men reported some short comings in their abilities to fully comprehend what was expected of them in those situations; but overall they indicated that they understood that their successes in those environments was largely determined by their ability to acculturate to their school's academic and social environments. Their ability to acculturate to their school's environment was often facilitated by a parent, role model, teacher, or prominent member in their community. The men indicated that those individuals were helpful in their early acculturation experiences because they provided advice and suggestions on how best to navigate their predominately White environments.

Many times the men reported being the only African American male student in their classes and they often spoke of not understanding what made them "special" or "different" from their other Black classmates:

> At a certain point my brother, sister and I all became a part of the advance classes and that led to a difference among our friends, who were not taking those classes with us. There were maybe two or three other Black students besides us who took those classes. No one ever explained to us [what was going on]. No one ever explicitly stated that there was some tracking going on and looking back on it you can see it. But all my friends did not experience that and I wondered about that at times. And sometimes that led to our friends looking at us as if we were not a part of them. (personal communication, December 7, 2004)

During such times the men reported feeling isolated in their early acculturation experiences but they reported that these experiences gave them an opportunity to establish a sense of resilience in the process. Although their early school experiences were instrumental in helping them to acculturate to predominately White environments there were also other experiences that reinforced their need to acculturate to main stream society:

> I recall in high school going to this predominately White area in Brooklyn to buy my mother a fluorescent lamp for her plants. And it was clear to me from the time of getting off the subway—walking to the electrical fixture place—going in the store and not being asked to be helped—and having to fight to get attention for someone to serve me—it was absolutely clear to me that no one in that area wanted me to be there. (personal communication, January 7, 2005)

> I went to a desegregated school with White students when I started the fifth grade and we were excited about the possibility of going to school with White people because they were objectified in such a way. (personal communication, December 19, 2004)

Each of the men reported similar types of occurrences in mainstream society and they reported that experiencing such things increased their desire to acculturate to their school settings. The men agreed, however, that overall their early school experiences had a significant influence on their acculturation processes. The men reported that their efforts to acculturate their school environments continued throughout their undergraduate experience, but it was not until they arrived to graduate school that they reported expanding their views on being acculturated in predominately White educational settings.

ACCULTURATION EXPERIENCES IN GRADUATE SCHOOL

While it is true that by the time the men arrived to graduate school they were somewhat accustomed to being African American men in predominately White school environments, it is in graduate school that these men began to assert themselves more in the acculturation process:

> So when I went to graduate school I didn't want to be known. I played semi-pro soccer for 3 years but I didn't want people at school to know about it because I just wanted to separate those lives. And so the faculty in graduate school tended to be people that I couldn't fully trust anyway because they didn't seem to be open. They didn't seem to be open to diversity even though there was much more openness to diversity than I had ever witnessed. (personal communication, December 2, 2004)

Although these men understood that their successes in predominately White educational settings was linked to their ability to acculturate to those environments, in some cases as witnessed above, the men began to voluntarily withdraw from those settings almost in a sense of defiance. This could be the result of the men moving further away from their earlier protective units (e.g., family, teachers, etc.) or it could be that the men realized that they actually had more influence on their acculturation process than they previously realized. In graduate school the men reported insisting that their schools take a more active role in helping them as students to acculturate to their academic and social surroundings. This assertiveness was strongest in the men who perceived that their graduate schools were unwilling to accept them on their own cultural terms. In some instances this established a contentious rapport between the men and their graduate programs. This negative rapport sometimes led to feelings of mistrust in the men, particularly in regards to how they identified with their professors and the school's administration:

> Being Black I didn't think that any faculty members were interested in any of my issues but I also didn't spend much time bemoaning that because of my social life in graduate school with friends—other folks of color. We created our own intellectual environment. So it was a haven away from the seminary and the psychology program. (personal communication, December 2, 2004)

> I wasn't politically correct because that was not important to me. What was important to me was that [they] were honest with me and then I moved on from there. I challenged faculty in the sense of asking very difficult questions. (personal communication, December 29, 2004)

In graduate school the men also connected more with non-Black minorities or other Blacks from different regions who helped them to view their acculturation process beyond a Black and White racial dichotomy. These new relationships were established because the men reported they were able to personally identify with the acculturation process that their fellow minority groups were experiencing. Such relationships helped the men to realize that they were not in an acculturation "silo" and that various minority groups acculturated differently to predominately White educational environments. Some of the men reported that they even favored a particular academic discipline because of the number of minorities groups who were enrolled and who they believed shared with them in some aspect of an acculturation process. It was during these moments that the men felt their acculturation to graduate school was most successful:

> When I got to graduate school there was a sizable group of Black students from the Deep South in my department. It was extraordinary! I was like this was just so welcoming to me. They already had a Black student organization within the math department that met regularly and they would not only talk about the social problems and issues of Black students within the department or university, but they also did things like sponsored talks from among members of the group. So you would have a math talk to give to the group. So there was this extraordinary combination within the department, within this group, both sort of the social support and the intellectual support. (personal communication, January 7, 2005)

> And you had some interesting racialized theologically views coming from Koreans, some Koreans who gave a lot of money to the theology programs, and who had their own sort of center. It was interesting getting exposed to different cultures where they were fairly racist in their views and studying religion at the same time. (personal communication, December 7, 2005)

Although the men identified with other minority groups, the men reported that there were instances when some of those groups held their own preconceived notions of Black men. Consequently, the men found themselves undergoing a certain type of acculturation process within minorities groups while simultaneously having to acculturate to their predominately White educational environments.

As these men moved through their graduate school experience they learned how to connect to the structures of their departments and institutions as well as structures that sometimes reached even beyond the boundaries of their campuses:

> I traveled to a very rural hamlet outside of New York and it was a highly literate and sophisticated epic center among a largely upstate New York work-

> ing class. It is very different from my rural southern town and I think it was there that I really became a thinking person. So who I was socially, intellectually and developmentally started in graduate school. (personal communication, December 19, 2004)

> As I said the social group that got together was more activist and the writing we did bonded us in a lot of ways. There were Latino, Mexican, Puerto Rican and a few Asian students. (personal communication, December 2, 2004)

Throughout his graduate school experience each man reported expanding his views on how best to acculturate to their predominately White school environments as African American men. For example, the men reported viewing their acculturation process from a more global perspective. And it is in graduate school that the men first attempt to use research as a means of better understanding their role as Black men in society. Whereas the men indicated learning to take a more macro view of their acculturation process, they also reported maintaining a research interest in topics that spoke to the African American community specifically.

The men believed that their experiences in graduate school helped them to solidify their relationships with predominately White educational settings and it is in graduate school that they began to contemplate careers as faculty members. The men indicated that in graduate school they were able to identify personal traits such as patience, discipline, collaboration, tolerance and fortitude. They indicated that these traits assisted in their successful acculturation as Black graduate students in their predominately White graduate programs. The men reported drawing on those personal traits as they transitioned into their professional role as faculty members in the academy.

ACCULTURATION AS FACULTY MEMBERS: INTEGRATING THE PERSONAL AND PROFESSIONAL SELVES

As the men began their acculturation process in their professional role they reported enhancing their abilities on how to best succeed as Black men in predominately White educational settings. Some of their experiences were similar to those in graduate school but as professionals the men reported becoming more astute in their acculturation processes. The men indicated that this was partially based on how faculty work and life are structured. Unlike their previous educational experiences where they could connect to some type of support network, the solitary life they experienced as faculty members, at times made their acculturation process challenging. In some instances this made the men disconnect their personal life from their professional one:

> You know that a lot of people here don't even know that I have a wife who is pregnant and that is fine with me because I don't think that everybody here you can trust to give pieces of yourself but others you can. I also coach, since my son has been four he has played soccer and basketball. And that life [I have kept] very separate from academic life. (personal communication, December 14, 2004)

This respondent in particular reported that in his other professional experiences he worked to integrate his professional and personal lives, but as a faculty member he insisted that those two aspects of himself were not congruent. Subsequently, instead of embracing both cultures simultaneously the respondent insisted that the two remain separate facets. Most of the men reported experiencing moments when they separated aspects of their personal lives from their role of faculty member as they acculturated to the academy as professionals. That separation was sometimes intentional, as is the case with the respondent above, and at other times those separations were spurred more by the profession than by the men's personal choice:

> I think for me it has been more complicated being a gay scholar than a Black scholar, particular among other Black scholars. My White peers have been more willingly accepting of my gayness and it is assumed by White people that I am gay, it is very funny and since they assume that I am gay their point of entry in conversation is with that assumption in mind. For Black people they have to accept it directly and until it is said it is assumed that [I am not gay]. (personal communication, December 20, 2004)

> I try to be the best me that I can be and I think probably the more challenging thing is to try to be Christ like. That is probably the bigger challenge in the academy than being either Black or in a same sex relationship. I haven't found that being in a same sex relationship or being Black difficult. I am not out on an agenda or anything else except following the passion that I think that the holy spirit wants me to follow and so my first duty is to be Christ-like and doing the will that I have for my life. The others are secondary in that sense. (personal communication, December 29, 2004)

These men indicated that their sexuality and spirituality were definitely an integral component of their personal lives, but in their acculturation as faculty members in predominately White environments they learn to treat these aspects of themselves pragmatically. Even though most of the men viewed various aspects of themselves as congruent parts of their role as Black male faculty members, they reported learning to view their personal and professional lives on a continuum. As faculty members the men reported taking this approach because they learned that trying to establish some form of equilibrium between their personal and professional lives sometimes hindered their acculturation efforts. Although achieving a harmonious balance between professional and personal life was challenging, the men reported that the most difficult aspect of their acculturation process as faculty members in predominately White educational settings involved learning how to facilitated aspects of their work as researchers.

INTEGRATING A RESEARCH AGENDA INTO THE ACCULTURATION PROCESS

Most of the men reported that the difficulty in conducting their work as faculty members in their predominately White educational settings surrounded establishing and promoting a race-based research agenda. The primary challenge regarding this aspect of faculty work was how to best incorporate that agenda into their acculturation process. On the one hand the men felt compelled to remain true to their research agendas but on the other hand they felt responsible for accepting the standards set by the academy. Each of the men reported being interested in some aspect of race-based research but they felt that the academy did not always provide a supportive environment for such work:

> I don't think that I fit here well in the terms of ways in which people are learning clinical situations that are very human, relational. I think that the time that we spend on asking questions is too long. So I struggle with that tension with my scholarship being impure and messy. I like being in both worlds but I think you know the world of creating experiments follows some very rigid guidelines. And that is what this world [academe] really wants and needs for us to define ... what is authentic scholarship? (personal communication, December 12, 2004)

> I think in the academy there are those who use quantitative measures in that way and they are smart people who think up knowledge, but I also worry about them as being distant from regular people that are not quantitatively minded and who are still intellectually engaging. But those areas are not always supported in the academy. [I believe] in order to get [to the people] you have to be like them. And those people don't always speak this academic language. So I struggle with that, too! So it is not just quantitative versus qualitative, it is also that we are in a class that is unique, but we are not the only class. How is our work relevant to the rest of the world! (personal communication, December 12, 2004)

Each man spoke of being challenged at various times in their career with conducting research that was acceptable in their predominately White environment but which also spoke to the needs of the African American community at large. The men reveal that this quandary often placed them at a crossroads as African American researchers:

> The freedom of this place is also its limitation. People are not committed to a particular cause like maybe running a program or organization [like when I was a clinical researcher]. As a clinical researcher I could somehow manage and control the kind of services that were provided. The revolutionary stuff doesn't happen in the academy. We spend more time debating on how things should take place and it is so far removed from the rest of society. (personal communication, December 12, 2004)

> You know I have seen a lot of African American faculty members come and go and change institutions. Unfortunately, some of it has to do with money. But the great majority of it comes from the lack of appreciation or acknowledgement that you exist and that you are important. For someone not reaching out and connecting with them. I think that most African Americans go into faculty because they are compelled like I was with making a difference. And when you realize that some of your other colleagues are not serious, that students are not serious, it can become a very frustrating situation, in order to create the kind of change and movement that could be, and so they are frustrated with the whole culture in a sense. (personal communication, December 29, 2004)

To assure that he continued to represent the authenticity of his work as a race-based researcher, each of the men developed strategies which helped him to connect his work to his acculturation process. For example, some of the men reported finding other scholars of color who could provide support for similar types of research projects. Other respondents suggested building collaborative bridges with peers regardless of their race or research interests. Some of the men reported that they worked in highly competitive environments where collaborative work was not seen as favorable, but even those men reported seeking colleagues at such things as national conferences to help create a more supportive environment for their work. These respondents suggested that building those collaborative bridges helped them to stay true to their research agendas but also provided a means to garner the respect of their colleagues.

The difference in the men's perspectives regarding the acculturation of race-based research into their predominately White environments was shaped by their personal style, how they envisioned conducting such work, and the type of institutions where the men conducted their scholarship. The men reported that it is crucial for race-based researchers to work to fulfill their passion, but not at the sake of failing to fulfill their obligations as faculty members first:

> I would say always work at the level of your passion because if you work in areas that you are passionate about it will maintain you and then you can continue to do the work long term. But I want to qualify that by saying work smart with your passion. [It is important to know] if your passion is sort of pragmatic in this environment. You must know your environment, and then you will know how to use your passion. Maintain relationships across ideological lines and even with people who don't value your work. Maintain ties at other kinds of levels, socially as well, so if people cannot really understand and respect your work they understand you as an individual. As someone who is contributing to the field. So they might not necessarily agree with it but they respect your efforts. (personal communication, December 20, 2004)

Each of the men brought varying perspectives regarding the best approach to conducting race-based research. And there was variance in how the men believed that work should be incorporated as minority faculty members move through faculty ranks. Each of the men discussed the importance of conducting thorough research regardless of the topic, but the men differed regarding the best method for conducting such work. Some of this variance was based on the men's respective fields of study or areas of interest. Overall the men indicated that such things as selecting the most appropriate methodology, understanding the type of research that was supported by their institution, or selecting the most appropriate venue to have their scholarship published were helpful in their work being acculturated to their predominately White educational environments. First and foremost, the men attributed their ability to successfully incorporate their race-based research agendas into their acculturation processes because they understood what the academy expected of them as scholars.

CONCLUSION

> I have been very fortunate in the academy in that I have been supported. I've been funded and I have been given an opportunity with fellowship opportunities. So I have had, I think, an unusual academic experience as a young Black intellectual. But I have been cautious of recommendations from some people because they will have very different trajectories than mine. I think that I have been given lots of opportunities, not necessarily that people value my work, or that people see the high quality of my work but I think it is often a reflection of me. Kind of what I bring as a person to my department, to my colleagues. Some of it is just sort of my personal dis-

> position with people. I tend to make people feel comfortable and I am supportive of people and supportive of people's ideas. (personal communication, December 24, 2004).

The men in this article represent a microcosmic view into the social structure of senior-level African American male faculty members who have successfully acculturated to the academic and social settings of predominately White educational environments. And even though their experiences may not necessarily represent the general population of African American male faculty members, these men do provide insight into the life and work of individuals of color in American institutions of higher education. The world of these men was one intersected by race, sexuality, scholarship, expectations, spirituality, perceptions, backgrounds, and experiences but it was also a world where none of these concepts stood as distinct segments of their identity.

The men in some ways supported the work of Sadao (2003) and the literature on Black faculty. The men revealed that there were definitely moments throughout their acculturation process in predominately White educational settings where they felt they were toggling between two cultures; and they indicated that at times this was problematic in their attempts to acculturate to those environments. The men expressed that there were times that they felt misunderstood as Black men in predominately White school settings and that their actions or emotions were misinterpreted. Some of the men reported feeling a sense of isolation which normally surrounded their research agendas or areas of interest. These feelings of isolation often started as early as graduate school and continued throughout their professional career.

But the men did not indicate that they believed that there was a need for them to acquire a bicultural identity as a means of being successful in their acculturation efforts in predominately White college settings. In some cases the men actually seemed to rebuff those settings when they believed that those settings were not supportive of their cultural differences. Throughout their educational experiences the men reported that their identity as Black men remained a central focus of their acculturation experiences and this sense of identity only expanded as they advanced through the educational pipeline. The men reported that by the time they arrived to graduate school that they understood how to acculturate to predominately White educational environments, and even though there were adjustments that needed to be made in the transition to college environments, they did not view themselves as hindrances to the acculturation process. The men revealed that even though they understood their position as Black men in predominately White educational settings their successful acculturation to those settings did not necessarily involve them treating their acculturation process as a binary one. The men revealed that their acculturation process was actually more cyclical in nature and involved the men developing an acculturation approach that was more fluid.

The men indicate that they understood their college environments, and although there were moments when those environments were less than welcoming, they arrived to the academy already equipped with skills to assure that they could successful acculturate to their predominately White college environments. The men noted, however, that oftentimes either the academy or their individual institutions may not have been prepared to receive them as Black male scholars. This was true even when the men understood the culture of the academy. The men described moments when they felt their work as race-based researchers was marginalized and they felt there were times when they believed that the academy did not value them as scholars of color. The men felt that even though they brought different perspectives and backgrounds to the academy, they did not believe that the academy always embraced those differences. They reported that the atmosphere they found in the academy did not always resonate with their previous educational experiences, and even though those atmospheres did not hinder their advancement through faculty ranks, they believed that those environments at times could have been more supportive of their acculturation efforts. Overall the men indicated that they were satisfied with their choices to pursue careers as faculty members in the academy and the men believed that they were meritorious in acculturating to its environments.

IMPLICATIONS

This chapter has relevance for university policies and practices regarding those concerned with the acculturation processes of African American male faculty members. The article suggests that as these men arrive to predominately White college environments they bring their own preconceived notions of how those environments should work best for them. Consequently, it would be important for predominately White college environments to create welcoming environments which acknowledge the varying acculturation expectations among various groups. But it is also important for those environments to understand that these different groups may look to one another for support as they acculturate to predominately White educational environments.

As African American male faculty members arrive to predominately White college campus creating such things as social support groups may assist these faculty members in connecting to the academic and social structures of their educational environments. Such opportunities could not only assist these scholars in their acculturation efforts but it could also assist these individuals in expanding their views of the acculturation process. African American male faculty members may benefit through encouragement to collaborate on research projects as a means of validating their research interests. Such things as collaborative team projects or partnerships with senior level faculty members could help to substantiate the research quality and productivity of these faculty members.

Although African American male scholars share similar experiences it is important that institutions of higher education recognize the differences among these scholars as well. African American male faculty members come to their campuses from different backgrounds and with various expectations. By institutions of higher education acknowledging these differences they validate the heterogeneity found within this group. Validating the heterogeneity among African American male scholars may help facilitate a more holistic experience for these men as they advance through faculty ranks. For example, recognizing the heterogeneity among African American male scholars may encourage these scholars that their works as race-based researchers are also seen as contributing different values to the academy.

REFERENCES

Anderson, J. D. (1993). Race, meritocracy, and the American academy during the immediate post-World War II era. *History of Education Quarterly, 2,* 151-175.

Allen, W. R., Epps, E. G., Guillory, E. A., Suh, S. A., & Bonous-Hammarth, M. (2000). The Black academic: Faculty status among African Americans in U.S. higher education. *Journal of Negro Education, 1-2,* 113.

Baez, B. (2000). Race-related service and faculty of color: Conceptualizing critical agency in academe. *Journal of Higher Education, 39,* 363-391.

Benjamin, B. (2000). Race-related service and faculty of color: Conceptualizing critical agency in academe. *Journal of Higher Education, 39,* 363-391.

Butner, B. K. (2000). Coping with the unexpected: Black faculty at predominately white institutions. *Journal of Black Studies, 3,* 453-461.

Davis, J. E. (1999). What does gender have to do with the experiences of African American college men. In V. C. Pilote & J. E. Davis (Eds.), *African American males in school and society: Practice and policies for effective education* (pp. 134-148). New York, NY: Teacher College Press.

Dey, I. (1993). *Qualitative data analysis: A user-friendly guide for social scientist.* London, England: Routledge.

Essien, V. (2003). Visible and invisible barriers to the incorporation of faculty of color in predominately White law schools. *Journal of Black Studies, 34,* 28.

Finkelstein, M. J., Seal, R. K., & Schuster, J. H. (1998). *The new academic generation: A professor in transformation.* Baltimore, MD: The Johns Hopkins University.

hooks, B. (1990). *Yearning: Race, gender and cultural politics*. Boston, MA: South End.

Jackson, K. W. (1991). Black faculty in academia. In P. G Altbach & K. Lomotey (Eds.), *The racial crisis in American higher education* (p. 135-147). New York, NY: SUNY press.

Jones, L. (2000). *Brothers of the academy: Up and coming Black scholars earning our way in higher education*. Sterling, VA: Stylus.

Jones, L. (2001). *Retaining african Americans in higher education*. Sterling, VA: Stylus.

Ladson-Billings, G. (1997). For colored girls who have considered suicide when the academy's not enough: Reflections of an african american women scholar. In A. Neuman & P. Peterson (Eds.), *Learning for our lives: Women, research, and autobiography for education* (pp. 52-70). New York, NY: Columbia Press.

McDowell, W. H. (2002). *Historical research: A guide*. New York, NY: Pearson Education.

Merriam, S. B. (1998). *Qualitative research and case study applications in education* (2nd ed.). San Francisco, CA: Jossey-Bass.

Morse J., Barrett, M., Mayan, M., Olson, K., & Spiers, J. (2002). Verification strategies for establishing reliability and validity in qualitative research. *International Journal of Qualitative Research, 2,* 1.

O' Meara, K. (2002). Uncovering the values in faculty evaluations of service as scholarship. *The Review of Higher Education, 26,* 57-80.

Patitu, C. L. (2000). African American faculty balancing the triumvirate: Teaching, research & service. *National Association for Student Affairs Professionals Journal, 1,* 46-64.

Sadao, K. C. (2003). Living in two worlds: Success and the bicultural faculty of color. *The Review of Higher Education, 26,* 397-418.

Seidman, I. (1998), *Interviewing as qualitative research: A guide for researchers in education and the social sciences* (2nd ed.). New York, NY: Teachers College press.

Smith, W. A., Altbach, P. G., & Lomotey, K. (Eds.). (2002). *The racial crisis in American higher education*. New York, NY: SUNY press.

Tierney, W. G. (2000). *Undaunted courage: Life history and the postmodern challenge*. In N. Denzin & Y. Lincoln, *The handbook of qualitative research* (2nd ed., pp. 537-553). San Francisco, CA: SAGE.

Tillman, L. (2001). Mentoring African American faculty in predominately White institutions. *Research in Higher Education, 3,* 300.

Turner, C. S. (2003). Incorporation and marginalization in the academy: From border toward center for faculty of color. *Journal of Black Studies, 1,* 112-125.

United States Department of Education. (2002). National Center for Educational Statistics. Washington, DC: Author

Weems, R. E. (2003). The incorporation of Black faculty at predominately White institutions: A historical and contemporary perspective. *Journal of Black Studies, 2,* 101-111.

PART III

THE NEXUS OF IDENTITY

CHAPTER 7

COMING OUT, FITTING IN

Interrogating the Social Experiences of Black Gay Males at White Colleges

Terrell L. Strayhorn

African American males represent an important constituency group in American higher education and in recent years a good deal of attention has been devoted to their alarming high school dropout rates, declining college enrollments, and disproportionately low degree completion rates, all of which have been referred to as the "Black[1] Male Crisis." For example, national statistics indicate that approximately 50% of African American males dropout of high school before earning their diploma (U.S. Department of Education, 2007) and there has been little to no progress in increasing college-going rates among Black men over the past quarter of a century (Mortenson Research Seminar, 2001). Furthermore, more than two-thirds of Black men who start college do no graduate within 6 years, which is the lowest degree completion rate among both sexes and all racial/ethnic groups (Harper, 2006).

Recent headlines, articles, and book titles also allude to the urgency and pervasiveness of this ill-structured problem among Black males. Con-

African American Males and Education:
Researching the Convergence of Race and Identity, pp. 151–170

sider the following: *Where are the Black Men on Campus?* (Roach, 2001); *Brother, Where Art Thou?* (Shabazz, 2006); *Black Male Genocide* (Staples, 1991); *The Trouble with Black Boys* (Noguera, 2003); *Reconsidering the Crisis of the Black Male in America* (Noguera, 1997), *Disappearing Acts: The Vanishing Black Male on Community College Campuses* (Esters & Mosby, 2007), and even *Countering the Conspiracy to Destroy Black Boys* (Kunjufu, 1986). Furthermore, Black men are often described using disparaging terms that may either reinforce negative stereotypes about Black males or imply that the "problem" facing Black men in education is intractable, therefore, insoluble. These terms include: endangered (Jackson & Moore, 2006); invisible (Ellison, 1952; Strayhorn, 2008b); bad boys (Ferguson, 2000); at-risk; threatening; and lazy (Gibbs, 1988; Majors & Billson, 1992).

With few exceptions (Bonner, 2001; Fries-Britt, 1997; Harper, 2003), most empirical research on African American male undergraduates has focused exclusively on the causes and cures of this long-standing problem that seems to defy solutions of a singular nature. Previous researchers have examined the role of family functioning (Mandara, 2006); educational aspirations (e.g., Strayhorn, in press); academic and social integration (Flowers, 2006); campus environments (Davis, 1994); racial identity development (Ford & Harris, 1997), historically Black fraternities (Harper & Harris, 2006); and even student involvement experiences (Harper & Quaye, 2007; Taylor & Howard-Hamilton, 1995). Another line of inquiry explores the experiences of specific Black male subpopulations including athletes (e.g., Messer, 2006), high achievers (e.g., Bonner), graduate students (Strayhorn, 2009); and student leaders (e.g., Harper & Quaye). Surprisingly, virtually all that is known about African American male undergraduates is based on "highly visible" African American males who tend to enjoy the admiration of their peers and oftentimes both faculty and staff members (Ferguson, 2000). Very few studies explore the collegiate experiences of African American gay male undergraduates who represent an "invisible" population (Strayhorn, Blakewood, & DeVita, 2008) and may be marginalized within their own cultural community of origin (Greene, 1994).

Literature on Black Gay Male Undergraduates

Since there is very little written about Black gay male undergraduates, literature on lesbian, gay, bisexual, and transgendered (LGBT) persons in general was drawn upon to inform this study. Research on LGBT adolescents and college students has burgeoned in recent years, largely focusing on the "constructed" identities (Abes & Jones, 2004; Dilley, 2005; Fassinger, 1998) and gay identity development experiences (e.g., Fassinger,

1991; Renn & Bilodeau, 2005) of such students. Still others have focused on the process by which individuals come to understand themselves as LGBT persons and how such understandings are reconciled with previously held perceptions of self (e.g., Cass, 1984; D'Augelli, 1991). For example, Cass identifies stages through which gay individuals struggle to resolve conflicts or tensions between perceptions of self and others (e.g., identity confusion, tolerance). All of this research, however, has been conducted without giving attention to the experiences of African American men who identify as gay.

Only recently have scholars turned critical attention to the lived experiences of African American gay men (AAGM) in general and Black gay male undergraduates in particular. Book chapter and commentaries exist that estimate the number of AAGMs in America, describe the challenges they face as both "Black" and "gay," as well as offer possible solutions to the social pathologies (e.g., racism, homophobia) that seem to stymie their development (Harris, 2003; Washington & Wall, 2006). Another line of inquiry has centered on several major foci related to Black gay males: factors influencing their college choice (Strayhorn, Blakewood, & DeVita, 2008); issues of sexual orientation and racial identity (e.g., Brown, 2008; Icard, 1986), and whether and how they identify sexually (e.g., Brown, 2005). For instance, Brown employed a case study approach to analyze qualitative data from 110 African American men in Atlanta. And although all of his male participants indicated that they have sex with men, relatively few identified as gay (37%); 13% identified as "down low bisexual," 9% as bisexual, 7% as homosexual, and even 17% as straight. He concluded that Black gay men cannot accept a gay identity for three reasons: homophobia, heterosexism, and constructions of Black masculinity.

While certainly useful, the existing literature is limited in several ways. First, those who study African American males focus almost exclusively on highly visible subpopulations that tend to enjoy the admiration of peers and educators, thereby failing to address the experiences of *invisible* or marginalized groups that may face social isolation, lack of support, and hostility on predominantly White college campuses (Allen, 1992; Feagin, Vera, & Imani, 1996; Pound, 1987), such as African American gay male undergraduates. Second, scholars who study Black gay men have devoted most attention to gay men in general or adults who engage one another in everyday life (Brown, 2005; Icard, 1986); no studies, to date, examine the social experiences of African American gay male undergraduates at predominantly White institutions (PWIs). This is the gap addressed by the present study.

PURPOSE

The purpose of this qualitative study was to understand the social experiences of Black gay male undergraduates at predominantly White institutions. Specifically, I sought to understand how Black gay males at PWIs describe their interpersonal relationships with same race and gay peers. A second objective of the study was to discover the frequency of their interpersonal interactions with such peers on campus.

METHOD

This study is part of a larger research project that centers on the experiences of African American gay males at predominantly White and historically Black colleges in the United States. The present study, however, focuses on Black gay male undergraduates at PWIs only. This study employed a constructivist qualitative approach (Merriam, 1998). A constructivist approach was selected on the basis of (a) its epistemic underpinnings about the very nature of knowledge and how participants in a social setting construct multiple realities (Glesne, 2006), (b) its utility in investigating unexplored or *rarely* explored phenomena and its potential for building a foundation upon which future research can stand (Hill et al., 2005), and (c) its congruent positioning with my own ethics and values as a researcher in terms of how invisible and voiceless people can be seen and heard without doing damage or "violence" to their authentic "voice" (Lincoln & Guba, 1986).

Site and Participants

This study was conducted at two 4-year predominantly White research-extensive institutions located in the northeast and southeast regions of the United States. University A (public highly selective university in the southeastern region) enrolls approximately 22,000 undergraduate and over 6,000 graduate students. At the time of this study, approximately 50% were men and only 7% were African American or Black. University B (private highly selective university in the northeastern region) enrolls approximately 6,800 undergraduate and 4,500 graduate students. At the time of this study, approximately 46% of undergraduates were men and just over 7% were "African American or Black," as defined by the university's institutional research office.

Participants were selected purposefully. As Patton (1990) aptly described, "The logic and power of purposeful sampling ... leads to selecting *information-rich cases* for study in depth. Information-rich cases are those from which one can learn a great deal about issues of central importance to the purpose of the research" (p. 46). In other words, participants were sought who would maximize what could be learned about the experiences of African American gay male undergraduates attending PWIs, namely those who had a "lived experience" and the capacity to talk about it. This sampling approach was deemed appropriate for the present study given its goal of understanding the lived experiences and perceptions of a specific, bounded group (Glesne, 2006).

Specifically, members of the research team worked with the President of the gay student alliances on each campus to identify and recruit a pool of prospective participants. Researchers informed the presidents of the sampling criteria. To participate in the study, participants had to (a) be enrolled (either full-time or part-time) at one of the two universities included in the sample, (b) identify as African American or Black and (c) self-identify as "gay," "homosexual," "same gender loving" or a synonymous term (see Brown, 2005). All prospective participants were asked, by the President, to participate in this study and to share their e-mail address with the principal investigator. This resulted in six potential participants.

Willing participants were invited, via e-mail, to participate in a one-on-one, face-to-face, in-depth interview with a member of the research team. All six prospects agreed to be interviewed. As the research evolved, additional participants were identified and invited to participate in the study; this is a form of snowball sampling (Patton, 2002) wherein existing participants were asked to recommend the study to other Black gay men, at their university, with whom they were familiar. These steps yielded three more participants, bringing the total sample to nine. Since we wished for our interviews to be candid, we promised them confidentiality, which proved to be important to several of our participants. For example, a few interviews had to be conducted in clandestine locations away from campus and some participants asked questions about how interviews would be transcribed, who would see the transcripts, and how they would be accessed in the future. Answering their questions, building rapport, and using pseudonyms provided by participants seemed to quell any concerns about anonymity and confidentiality (Glesne, 1989). Although pseudonyms may mask their "real" identities (Grinyer, 2002), participants can be described in "rich, thick" terms (Geertz, 1973). Table 7.1 summarizes details about the sample.

With the limited number of African American men enrolled in American colleges and universities (U.S. Department of Education, 2007) and "gay male" representing a largely invisible identity that is often intentionally hidden or denied in Black male peer groups (Brown, 2005) and thus very difficult to study (Evans & Broido, 1999), I was encouraged by the

Table 7.1. Description of Study Participants (N = 9)

Pseudonym	*Major*	*Minor*	*Clubs & Activities*	*Mom's Job*	*Dad's Job*	*Career Aspiration*
Terrance	Spanish	Dance	Dance company	Office manager	Shift supervisor	Business or education
Leon	Vocal performance	Theatre	All campus theater	State internal revenue specialist	Owner of a construction company	Musical theatre performance
Blake	Finance	Accounting collateral	Cheerleading	House manager for girls program	Manager	Coaching cheerleading
Lamont	Journalism & electronic media and French	N/A	Orientation leader, Model Un, college democrats	Nurse	Manager	Media management
Lawrence	Architecture	Japanese	Employee: Fast food and retail	Self-employed	IT specialist	Business architecture
Desmond	Public relations, psychology	Business administration	NAACP, honor societies, Black cultural programming committee	County health inspector	City clerk's office	Lifestyle public relations practitioner
Sidney	Opera	Dance	Campus opera/theater	---	---	Famous opera singer
Betsy	Regional studies	Latin	LGBTQ association	Missionary	Missionary	City planning and politics
Elliott	International foreign politics	Public administration	LGBTQ association	--	--	Urban planning and fashion

sample size ($N = 9$). Indeed, issues of homophobia, (re) constructions of masculinity within Black male enclaves, and taboo mentalities that encircle "gayness" in the Black community (hooks, 2004) make it difficult, if not impossible, to gain access to this severely understudied group of college men. Building rapport, maintaining trust, and exercising care throughout the research process helped to elicit the information needed to understand the phenomenon under study. Indeed, this "select few" can be used to amplify the voices of many.

Data Collection

Data were collected using semistructured, in-depth one-on-one interviews over a 12-month period. Interviews were conducted in a way to elicit stories from each participant about their experiences since stories reflect human consciousness (Vygotsky, 1987). A typical interview lasted 60 to 200 minutes. In some cases, ambiguities and additional questions were resolved by follow-up correspondence with the interviewee via telephone, electronic mail, or in person. A semistructured interview protocol was used that included questions about each participant's demographic background (e.g., What is your race? Where were you born?); schooling experiences (e.g., What is your major?); and notable people, places, or circumstances that they perceived as influential on their college experience. Additionally, specific questions were included that elicited information about their social experiences with peers on campus. Questions were designed to prompt rich, thick reconstructions of African American gay male undergraduates' collegiate experiences (e.g., "Can you tell me about a time when?...").

As this qualitative study sought to understand one's collegiate experiences and the meanings attached to such experiences, the amount of time required for serious reflection and critical analysis of data is great. Thus, all interviews were digitally recorded and professionally transcribed verbatim for subsequent analysis, in consonance with the high standards of naturalistic research (Miles & Huberman, 1994; Wolcott, 1992).

Data Analysis

Data were analyzed in three stages using the constant comparison method as described by Strauss and his colleagues (Glaser & Strauss, 1967; Strauss & Corbin, 1998). First, transcripts were read and reread to generate initial categories of information or codes that represented "an initial plot of the terrain" (Miles & Huberman, 1994, p. 69); this is known as open coding (Strauss & Corbin, 1998). Coding is the process of "organizing the material into 'chunks' before bringing meaning to those chunks" (Rossman & Rallis, 1998, p. 171).

Next, codes were collapsed by grouping categories that seemed to relate to each other while leaving intact those that stood independent from all others. This smaller list of categories was used to generate "supercodes," or preliminary themes. Lastly, themes were compared and contrasted to understand the degree to which they were similar; closely related themes were collapsed or renamed so that the "whole name" reflected the sum of its parts. This iterative process was repeated until no new codes or themes were found—a point called *saturation* in the literature (Miles & Huberman, 1994). A final list of themes was settled upon to represent the findings of the study. Each participant reviewed the final list of themes and he was able to clarify, revise, ask questions about, and add elements (Miles & Huberman). NVivo, a qualitative data analysis software, was used to store transcripts, save codes, generate reports of common words, and assist in data management.

Trustworthiness and Quality

Several steps were taken to enhance trustworthiness and ensure quality of the data and subsequent findings in this study. Lincoln and Guba (1986) identify four measures by which rigor and accuracy in qualitative research can be evaluated: credibility, transferability, dependability, and confirmability. These four metrics "replace the usual positivist criteria of internal and external validity, reliability, and objectivity" used in quantitative studies (Denzin & Lincoln, 2000, p. 21). Credibility was assured through member checks, follow-up correspondence, and storage of all data sources that could be easily retrieved and (re)tested throughout the entire research process. Additionally, members of the research team discussed presuppositions, preliminary ideas, and interpretations with each other, as well as with three peer debriefers—that is, disinterested but skilled peers who were qualitative research experts and/or were familiar with African American, gay male, or college men's issues.

To ensure transferability, rich, thick descriptions of both sites and participants are provided in the findings section that follows. Findings from this study will likely transfer to Black gay male undergraduates who face similar experiences in other large PWIs. But as many have explained, ultimately, transferability is primarily the responsibility of readers (Denzin, 1989).

Finally, dependability and confirmability were ensured through audit trails conducted by members of the research team (i.e., one African American professor, two White graduate students), peer debriefers, and one campus administrator who became involved in the research. Despite our many attempts to render findings that are credible, transferable, and dependable, like Henstrand (1991), I cannot promise that these findings represent anyone's truth except my own and my attempt to "represent" the lived experiences of participants as told through their stories and their own voices. Indeed, participants' perspectives have been interpreted, and interpretation may distort their intended meaning, although member checking should have reduced, if not eliminated, this effect (Glesne, 2006).

FINDINGS

Three major themes were identified using the analytic process outlined above. First, African American gay male undergraduates at PWIs reported very few, if any, meaningful social interactions with same-race male peers. They also identified several factors that limited the frequency and nature of their social interactions with other Black male collegians. Second, participants shared that most of their social interactions and meaningful friendships were shared with "openly gay" and/or "straight" (i.e., heterosexual) White male peers. Lastly, several participants described meaningful social interactions with African American women on campus, most whom identified as heterosexual. Each of these themes are discussed below, using verbatim quotes from participants to illuminate the context from which themes came, as well as to unpack the meaning and significance of each theme.

Limited Social Interactions With Black Male Peers

African American gay male undergraduates in the sample reported very few, if any, meaningful social interactions with same race male peers on campus. Lamont and Leon shared the following comments, respectively, which reflected that of others:

> I know more White people than people from my own race ... especially Black guys.

> I can't count them all right now but easily almost all of my friends are White ... and if they aren't they certainly aren't Black guys because most Black guys are ignorant about hanging out with gay guys ... thinking you're always trying to date them (laughing).

Participants spoke at length about three factors that seemed to serve as barriers to their interaction with other African American males: issues of masculinity, homophobia, and incongruent personal interests. For instance, all participants talked about how stereotypical masculine behaviors (e.g., violence, displays of physical prowess, bragging about sexual conquests, antagonism toward gay men) made it difficult to hang around Black male peers. Elliott remarked:

> I don't have that many Black male friends because I don't like to do what they do, you know? Sitting around talking about girls, their breasts, and how many I laid over the weekend is not something I can talk about. And I'm not going to change the way I dress just to hang out with other Black guys.

Homophobia, according to participants, virtually prevents them from interacting with Black male peers in meaningful ways, even with Black male peers who might identify *privately* as gay. For example, Quinn became quite emotional when describing how other Black men on campus "act a little undignified toward [him]." He said:

> People might make a comment like people saying I'm gay. But yeah, from Black people, it's been, like mad snide comments. Because gay in the African American community, it seems, to most Black people, it's even like greater fault than … I don't know. Black guys really don't take too well to it. And they're really heinous, sometimes, about it. They always say stuff like "You fu*king faggot."

Quinn went on to describe how his artistic interests also limited his involvement with other African American peers. Consider the following:

> Just because I was, like, a part of a lot of things. And I was on a morning TV show that broadcast every morning with announcements. And I was nominated for superlatives. And I do drama too. I did all these, you know, acting class and all these things that, normally, Black people don't do … so since I didn't hang out with a lot of Black people, it's like, 'Oh, he thinks he's better than us.'

Other participants expressed difficulty in engaging their Black male peers due to incongruent personal interests. For instance, Desmond stated, "It's just difficult to find friends that are like … Black gay men who want to do more than have sex. And that's been the most difficult challenge.…"

Generally speaking, African American gay male undergraduates in the present study reported few, if any, meaningful social interactions with their same race male peers. Issues of masculinity, homophobia, and incongruent personal interests limited the extent to and manner in which these students interacted with their same race male peers on campus.

Social Interactions With Gay and Straight White Male Peers

Although participants reported very few interactions with other African American males on campus, all but one (89%) of the participants in this study reported frequent social interactions and meaningful friendships with "openly gay" and/or "straight" (i.e., heterosexual) White male peers. For instance, when describing the racial composition of his social network and close friends, Bob declared: "One is Italian ... one is biracial ... and the rest are all White."

Not only did African American gay male participants report many more social interactions with White males, but all of them reported "dating" and having "committed love relationships" with White gay males at some point in their life. In fact, almost half ($n=4$) shared that they "only date" White gay men indicating an exclusive preference for White gay men as romantic or sexual partners. Lawrence's comment captures the essence of those shared by others: "It's just so much easier for me to be attracted to White guys than African Americans. It's just that I've been going by this where I just love preppy or whatever. But you don't find too many Black guys like that." Blake puzzled about his preference for White men and wondered if it was related to his limited interaction with other Black males:

> First of all, because I've not been around a lot of other Black people, it's like I'm normally attracted to White guys only. So I don't know how much of that is actually based on me just not being around Black guys ... I'm just attracted to White guys.

Hanging out with White peers, dating White gay men, and having a preference for White men as sexual and/or romantic partners also seemed to be related to how African American gay male undergraduates viewed themselves. For instance, some participants frequently referred to themselves as "the Whitest Black boy," "an Oreo" (implying that he is Black/African American on the outside yet White on the inside), "not really Black," and "White Black boy."

While most participants reported meaningful interpersonal relationships with White male peers, several mentioned problems that emerge between them and their White peers, one of which is racism and discrimination. Specifically, Black gay men in this study reported several instances when racist comments (e.g., "Black people are lazy") or "nigger jokes" were made by their White peers, White gay male friends, or associates of their White peers. Negative beliefs about Black people also led some of their White gay male peers to make prejudicial decisions. For instance, Betsy shared:

> I had a bad experience here when I was sort of dating a White guy. He was like I can't date you anymore and I was just like, why? He said because you're Black. I was just like, okay, this is really bad, like, I'm going to ruin your reputation ... so I mean that's been like a negative side of my dating.

Participants seemed to adopt strategies to cope with the racist jokes and discriminatory behaviors experienced in such social settings. Blake explained how he coped with such problems:

> Well, now I'm usually the one that will make the [Black] joke. [My White friends] know that if something comes up that deals with race, that I'll probably make the joke. I kinda fell into that. I don't think I really mind being that person that will make the Black joke.

Another participant talked, at length, about his experiences facing social "isms" like racism within the White gay community. Name calling was the most common form of racism experienced by participants (e.g., "Nigger" or "Black fag"). Those who did not adopt coping mechanisms, like the one described above, tended to dismiss such experiences as typical, normal, and even expected: "Even though I was called names and even though, like, I get stares once in a while ... I mean I just let it go. It's like whatever. I'm not going to, like, you know ... I just can deal with it ... that's been my experience at [said university]" (Sidney).

Although participants reported frequent and meaningful interactions with White [male] peers, many whom identified as gay, they also reported negative experiences and ways in which they negotiated such encounters.

Girlfriends and "Girl Talk": Interactions With Black Female Peers

The third major finding related to African American gay male undergraduates' social interactions with Black female peers. Virtually all of the Black gay men with whom I spoke identified meaningful interpersonal relationships with Black women on campus. Desmond offered a particularly powerful illustration:

> Most of my friends are heterosexual, Black females ... I met [said girlfriend] through NAACP Youth Council, she was the first vice-president during our

> junior year. It's easy to be friends with Black girls because we can be open without worrying about each other's motives. It's like with my Black female friends we talk constantly about anything but it's all girl talk, you know?

Several participants explained how they tended to gravitate toward Black female peers, rather than their same race male counterparts, when in predominantly Black settings (e.g., scholarship programs, Black Cultural Center). Similarly, Black gay men in this study felt as if they shared more in common with Black women (e.g., interest in men) than other Black men. Subsequently, they tended to establish meaningful interpersonal relationships with Black women, talk with them about their gay relationships, seek as well as offer advice about men's behaviors, and "hang out" with them around campus. Quinn remarked:

> But yeah, during like, my scholarship meetings and we'd have to do community service projects and what not. You know, I would find a Black girl to hang out with. I'd attach myself to a girl and we'd have fun and, you know, buddy up.

Having Black female friends with whom they could communicate about their experiences and upon whom they could rely for advice enhanced the social experiences of African American gay male undergraduates at PWIs.

DISCUSSION

Recall that the purpose of this qualitative study was to understand the social experiences of Black gay male undergraduates at predominantly White institutions. Specifically, I sought to understand how Black gay males at PWIs describe their interpersonal relationships with same race and gay peers. A second objective of the study was to discover the frequency of their interpersonal interactions with such peers on campus. Findings suggest a number of important conclusions related to the study's objectives that make a significant contribution to the existing literature.

First, the AAGMs with whom I spoke reported few, if any, meaningful social interactions with other Black men on campus and they alluded to three factors (i.e., masculinity, homophobia, incongruent interests) that seemed to limit their engagement with same race male peers. These findings are consistent with previous research on the within group heterogeneity that exists among Black male collegians (Harper & Nichols, 2008). Indeed, "Black male students are not all the same" (Harper & Nichols, p. 209); furthermore, differences (e.g., stereotypical vs. alternative masculinities, divergent personal interests) within this group of students may inhibit their interactions and engagement with each other. These findings, however, challenge some previous studies that suggest Black students are most comfortable among Black peers and in Black social enclaves (Feagin, Vera, & Imani, 1996; Tatum, 1997). This study illuminates an important nuance in our understanding—that is, this may not be true for Black students whose backgrounds, experiences, and behaviors differ from normative expectations or those who may face marginalization within their own culture of origin such as Black gay male undergraduates at PWIs.

Second, although AAGM in this study had limited social interactions with other Black men, they reported frequent and meaningful social experiences with White male peers, many whom identified openly as gay. White gay male peers enhanced the social experiences of AAGMs at PWIs and provided a network of social and psychological supports, as found in earlier research (Icard, 1986). In fact, some participants expressed an exclusive preference for White gay men as partners for "dating" and/or romantic relationships. Although this exclusive preference was stated across a significant proportion of the sample, it was less clear just why this is the case. That some Black gay men prefer White men as romantic partners was reported elsewhere; Bell and Weinberg (1978) reported that over 75% of the Black gay men in their study had White gay lovers. This study provides contemporary evidence to show that the same may be true of Black gay male undergraduates enrolled at PWIs.

And although AAGM participants reported spending most of their social time with White, generally gay, male friends, they also reported negative experiences in such social settings with racism and discrimination. This finding is consistent with previous research (e.g., Icard, 1986), but goes beyond previous conclusions to show that the same is true of Black gay male undergraduates at PWIs. On the one hand, establishing meaningful interpersonal relationships with gay peers is developmentally productive as research has shown that well adjusted homosexuals tend to have close, supportive relationships with members of the gay community (e.g., Cass, 1979). That AAGM experienced racism and discrimination in the gay community, however, can be developmentally damaging as they struggle to develop effective responses to racist encounters among the very same people upon whom they rely for much needed support. Similar to Icard (1986), I draw attention to the collateral damage that could result from such negative experiences—"the stigma of inferiority may become internalized and may result in acceptance of a subordinate role" (p. 89). In this way, Black gay men can be placed in a position of psychological imprisonment, triple jeopardy, or as said elsewhere, "betwixt and between" (Strayhorn, 2008a).

Lastly, AAGMs in the present study established meaningful relationships with African American heterosexual female peers for the purposes of talking about their gay relationships, getting women's advice about men as well as offering Black women advice about male behavior(s), and engaging in "girltalk." Based on my findings, it seems clear that positive social interactions and friendships with Black heterosexual women enhanced the social experiences of Black gay men at PWIs. Participants, on average, felt as if they shared more in common with Black women than their same race male counterparts. And it was that which they held in common that became the basis upon which positive relationships were established and meaningful friendships were fueled. Similar to previous research (Battle & Lemelle, 2002), Black heterosexual women tended to have more positive attitudes toward Black gay men than their same race heterosexual male peers according to participants in the present study.

The potential applications of this research to practice are many. The study's findings should be of particular interest to campus constituencies who have a vested interest in improving the experiences of students on campus (e.g., deans of students, resident hall directors) and those who work with African American college students (e.g., multicultural affairs staff, faculty members). Promoting interpersonal engagement among Black gay men and their peers, especially White gay males and Black females, can enhance their college experience. Student organizations (e.g., LGBT student groups) and recent innovations (e.g., living-learning communities) might be effective strategies in promoting educationally purposeful engagement among students.

Counseling and mental health professionals also may benefit from the results of this study. Findings from this analysis highlight the tensions that Black gay men at PWIs may face as they struggle to navigate both racist White gay communities and homophobic Black communities. Counseling staff might use these results to help Black gay male clients anticipate the potential challenges that they may face in such settings. Similarly, counselors can use this information to assist their clients in developing positive, productive responses to negative encounters with racism, discrimination, and homophobia.

Chief diversity and senior student affairs officers at PWIs might benefit from conclusions drawn in this study. In this analysis, I found that Black gay men encounter negative experiences with racism and discrimination among White peers and homophobic antagonism among Black peers on campus. Diversity and student affairs administrators might consider these findings when trying to assess the overall campus climate for various subgroups. Aggregated surveys and generic interviews with campus constituents may mask the experiences and nightmarish realities of particular subgroups (e.g., Black gay males) on campus. Collecting data from specific subgroups, talking with representatives (e.g., heads, leaders) as well as individuals from various social locations, and searching for negative cases may prove useful to understanding the prevailing conditions that characterize a campus's environment for diversity (Hurtado, 1992).

Findings also have implications for future research, which might proceed in any number of directions. For instance, the present study examined the social experiences of African American gay male undergraduates at PWIs using a qualitative approach. Future researchers might build upon this study by exploring the academic experiences of these students at PWIs, the experiences of Black gay men at historically Black colleges and universities, or the social experiences of a larger sample of Black gay men using traditional survey research methods (Suskie, 1996).

In conclusion, Black gay male undergraduates' social experiences at PWIs are, indeed, complex and multifaceted. Although participants in this study reported few, if any, meaningful interactions with same race male peers, most of them reported frequent and purposeful interactions with White gay male peers and Black women. Several factors inhibited their involvement with other Black men on campus, while other factors (e.g., common interests) enabled them to establish friendships with Black women. Despite this study and a number of recent contributions (e.g., Strayhorn, Blakewood, & DeVita, 2008), "there is [still] a dearth of information available on the subject of Black homosexual men" (Icard, 1986, p. 83). More research is needed to understand the experiences of this invisible, arguably voiceless population and their struggles of "coming out" and "fitting in."

NOTE

1. The terms "Black" and "African American" are used interchangeably throughout this manuscript.

REFERENCES

Abes, E. S., & Jones, S. R. (2004). Meaning-making capacity and the dynamics of lesbian college students' multiple dimensions of identity. *Journal of College Student Development, 45*, 612-632.

Allen, W. (1992). The color of success: African American college student outcomes at predominantly White and historically Black public colleges and universities. *Harvard Educational Review, 62*, 26-44.

Battle, J., & Lemelle, A. J., Jr. (2002). Gender differences in African American attitudes toward gay males. *Western Journal of Black Studies, 26*(3), 134-139.

Bell, A. P., & Weinberg, M. S. (1978). *Homosexualities*. New York, NY: Simon & Schuster.

Bonner, F. A., II. (2001). *Gifted African American male college students: A phenomenological study.* Storrs, CT: National Research Center on the Gifted and Talented.

Brown, C. E., III. (2008). *Racism in the gay community and homophobia in the Black community: Negotiating the gay Black male experience* (Unpublished master's thesis). Virginia Tech, Blacksburg, VA.

Brown, E., II. (2005). We wear the mask: African American contemporary gay male identities. *Journal of African American Studies, 9*(2), 29-38.

Cass, V. C. (1979). Homosexuality identity formation: A theoretical model. *Journal of Homosexuality, 4*(3), 219-235.

Cass, V. C. (1984). Homosexuality identity formation: Testing a theoretical model. *Journal of Sex Research, 9*(1-2), 105-126.

D'Augelli, A. R. (1991). Gay men in college: Identity processes and adaptations. *Journal of College Student Development, 32*, 140-146.

Davis, J. E. (1994). College in Black and White: Campus environment and academic achievement of African American males. *Journal of Negro Education, 63*(4), 620.

Denzin, N. K. (1989). *Interpretive interactionism*. Newbury Park, CA: SAGE.

Denzin, N. K., & Lincoln, Y. S. (2000). *Handbook of qualitative research*. Thousand Oaks, CA: SAGE.

Dilley, P. (2005). Which way out? A typology of non-heterosexual male collegiate identities. *Journal of Higher Education, 76*, 56-88.

Ellison, R. (1952). *Invisible man*. New York, NY: Random House.

Esters, L. L., & Mosby, D. C. (2007). Disappearing acts: The vanishing Black male on community college campuses. *Diverse Issues in Higher Education, 24*(14), 45.

Evans, N. J., & Broido, E. M. (1999). Coming out in college residence halls: Negotiation, meaning making, challenges, supports. *Journal of College Student Development, 40*, 658-668.

Fassinger, R. E. (1991). The hidden minority: Issues and challenges in working with lesbian women and gay men. *Counseling Psychologist, 19*, 157-176.

Fassinger, R. E. (1998). Lesbian and bisexual identity and student development theory. In R. L. Sanlo (Ed.), *Working with lesbian, gay, bisexual and transgender college students: A handbook for faculty and administrators* (pp. 13-22). Westport, CT: Greenwood Press.

Feagin, J. R., Vera, H., & Imani, N. (1996). *The agony of education: Black students at White colleges and universities*. New York, NY: Routledge.

Ferguson, A. A. (2000). *Bad boys: Public schools in the making of Black male masculinity.* Ann Arbor, MI: The University of Michigan Press.

Flowers, L. A. (2006). Effects of attending a 2-year institution on African American males' academic and social integration in the first year of college. *Teachers College Record, 108*(2), 267-286.

Ford, D. Y., & Harris, J. J., III. (1997). A study of the racial identity and achievement of black males and females. *Roeper Review, 20*(2), 105-110.

Fries-Britt, S. L. (1997). Identifying and supporting gifted African American men. In M. J. Cuyjet (Ed.), *Helping African American men succeed in college* (pp. 65-78). San Francisco, CA: Jossey-Bass.

Geertz, C. (Ed.). (1973). Thick description: Toward an interpretive theory of culture, *The interpretation of cultures* (pp. 3-30). New York, NY: Basic Books.

Gibbs, J. T. (Ed.). (1988). *Young, Black, and male in America: An endangered species*. Dover, MA: Auburn House.

Glaser, B., & Strauss, A. (1967). *The discovery of grounded theory*. Chicago, IL: Aldine.

Glesne, C. (1989). Rapport and friendship in ethnographic research. *Qualitative Studies in Education, 2*(1), 45-54.

Glesne, C. (2006). *Becoming qualitative researchers: An introduction* (3rd ed.). Boston, MA: Pearson Education.

Greene, B. (1994). Ethnic-minority lesbians and gay men: Mental health and treatment issues. *Journal of Consulting and Clinical Psychology, 62,* 243-251.

Grinyer, A. (2002, Spring). The anonymity of research participants: Assumptions, ethics, and practicalities. *Social Research Update*. Retrieved from http://sru.soc.surrey.ac.uk/SRU36.html

Harper, S. R. (2003). Most likely to succeed: The self-perceived impact of involvement on the experiences of high-achieving African American undergraduate men at predominantly White universities. *Dissertation Abstracts International, A64*(6), 1995.

Harper, S. R. (2006). *Black male students at public universities in the U.S.: Status, trends and implications for policy and practice*. Washington, DC: Joint Center for Political & Economic Studies.

Harper, S. R., & Harris, F. H. (2006). The role of Black fraternities in the African American male undergraduate experience. In M. J. Cuyjet & Associates (Eds.), *African American men in college* (pp. 128-153). San Francisco, CA: Jossey-Bass.

Harper, S. R., & Nichols, A. H. (2008). Are they not all the same? Racial heterogeneity among Black male undergraduates. *Journal of College Student Development, 49*(3), 199-214.

Harper, S. R., & Quaye, S. J. (2007). Student organizations as venues for Black identity expression and development among African American male student leaders. *Journal of College Student Development, 48*(2), 127-144.

Harris, W. G. (2003). African American homosexual males on predominantly White college and university campuses. *Journal of African American Studies, 7*(1), 47-56.

Henstrand, J. L. (1991). *Teacher culture from the inside: A case study of planned change from the perspective of active participant observer* (Unpublished doctoral dissertation). University of Oregon, Eugene, OR.

Hill, C. E., Knox, S., Thompson, B. J., Williams, E. N., Hess, S. A., & Ladany, N. (2005). Consensual qualitative research: An update. *Journal of Counseling Psychology, 52,* 196-205.

hooks, b. (2004). *We real cool: Black men and masculinity*. New York, NY: Routledge.

Hurtado, S. (1992). Campus racial climates: Contexts for conflicts. *Journal of Higher Education, 63,* 539-569.

Icard, L. (1986). Black gay men and conflicting social identities: Sexual orientation versus racial identity. *Journal of Social Work and Human Sexuality, 4*(1-2), 83-93.

Jackson, J. F. L., & Moore, J. L. (2006). African American males in education: Endangered or ignored? *Teachers College Record, 108*(2), 201.

Kunjufu, J. (1986). *Countering the conspiracy to destroy Black boys*. Chicago, IL: African American Images.

Lincoln, Y. S., & Guba, E. G. (1986). But is it rigorous? Trustworthiness and authenticity in naturalistic observation. In D. Williams (Ed.), *Naturalistic evaluation: New directions for program evaluation* (Vol. 30, pp. 73-84). San Francisco, CA: Jossey-Bass.

Majors, R., & Billson, J. (1992). *Cool pose: The dilemmas of Black manhood in America*. New York, NY: Touchstone.

Mandara, J. (2006). The impact of family functioning on African American males' academic achievement: A review and clarification of the empirical literature. *Teachers College Record, 108*(2), 206.

Merriam, S. B. (1998). *Qualitative research and case study applications in education*. San Francisco, CA: Jossey-Bass.

Messer, K. L. (2006). African American male college athletes. In M. J. Cuyjet & Associates (Eds.), *African American men in college* (pp. 154-173). San Francisco, CA: Jossey-Bass.

Miles, M., & Huberman, A. (1994). *An expanded sourcebook: Qualitative data analysis* (2nd ed.). Thousand Oaks, CA: SAGE.

Mortenson Research Seminar on Public Policy Analysis of Opportunity for Postsecondary Education. (2001). College participation by gender, age 18 to 24, 1967 to 2000. *Postsecondary Education Opportunity, 109*, 1-16.

Noguera, P. (1997). Reconsidering the "crisis" of the Black male in America. *Social Justice, 24*(2), 147-164.

Noguera, P. A. (2003). The trouble with Black boys: The role and influence of environmental and cultural factors on the academic performance of African American males. *Urban Education, 38*, 431-459.

Patton, M. Q. (1990). *Qualitative evaluation and research methods* (2nd ed.). Newbury Park, CA: SAGE.

Patton, M. Q. (2002). *Qualitative research & evaluation methods* (3rd ed.). Thousand Oaks, CA: SAGE.

Pound, A. W. (1987). Black student's needs on predominantly White campuses. In D. J. Wright (Ed.), *Responding to the needs of today's minority students* (pp. 23-28). San Francisco, CA: Jossey-Bass.

Renn, K. A., & Bilodeau, B. L. (2005). Leadership identity development among lesbian, gay, bisexual, and transgender student leaders. *The NASPA Journal, 42*(3), 342-367.

Roach, R. (2001). Where are the Black men on campus? *Black Issues in Higher Education, 18*(6), 18-24.

Rossman, G. B., & Rallis, S. F. (1998). *Learning in the field: An introduction to qualitative research*. Thousand Oaks, CA: SAGE.

Shabazz, R. K. (2006). Brother, where art thou? An examination of the underrepresentation of African American male educators. *DAI, 67*(04A), 208.

Staples, R. (1991). Black male genocide: A final solution to the race problem in America. In B. P. Bowser (Ed.), *Black adolescents: Parenting and education in the community context*. Lanham, MD: University Press of America.

Strauss, A., & Corbin, J. (1998). *Basics of qualitative research: Techniques and procedures for developing grounded theory* (2nd ed.). Thousand Oaks, CA: SAGE.

Strayhorn, T. L. (2008a). *Betwixt and between: To be young, gifted, gay, and Black at a White institution*. Paper presented at the National Conference on Race and Ethnicity in American Higher Education (NCORE), Orlando, FL.

Strayhorn, T. L. (2008b). The invisible man: Factors affecting the retention of low-income African American males. *National Association of Student Affairs Professionals Journal, 11*(1), 66-87.

Strayhorn, T. L. (2009). African American male graduate students. In M. H. Howard-Hamilton, C. L. Morelon-Quainoo, S. D. Johnson, R. Winkle-Wagner, & L. Santiague (Eds.), *Standing on the outside, looking in: Underrepresented students' experiences in advanced-degree programs* (pp. 124-146). Sterling, VA: Stylus.

Strayhorn, T. L. (in press). Different hopes, different folks: The educational aspirations of African American males in urban, suburban, and rural high schools. *Urban Education, 44*(6), 710-731.

Strayhorn, T. L., Blakewood, A. M., & DeVita, J. M. (2008). Factors affecting the college choice of African American gay male undergraduates: Implications for retention. *National Association of Student Affairs Professionals Journal, 11*(1), 88-108.

Suskie, L. A. (1996). *Questionnaire survey research: What works* (2nd ed.). Tallahassee, FL: Association for Institutional Research.

Tatum, B. D. (1997). *Why are all the Black kids sitting together in the cafeteria? And other conversations about race*. New York, NY: Basic Books.

Taylor, C. M., & Howard-Hamilton, M. F. (1995). Student involvement and racial identity attitudes among African American males. *Journal of College Student Development, 36*, 330-335.

U.S. Department of Education, National Center for Education Statistics. (2007). *The condition of education 2007* (NCES 2007). Washington, DC: U.S. Government Printing Office.

Vygotsky, L. (1987). *Thought and language* (A. Kozulin, Trans.). Cambridge, MA: MIT Press.

Washington, J., & Wall, V. A. (2006). African American gay men: Another challenge for the academy. In M. J. Cuyjet & Associates (Eds.), *African American men in college* (pp. 174-188). San Francisco, CA: Jossey-Bass.

Wolcott, H. F. (1992). Posturing in qualitative inquiry. In M. D. LeCompte, W. L. Millroy, & J. Preissle (Eds.), *The handbook of qualitative research in education* (pp. 3-52). New York, NY: Academic Press.

CHAPTER 8

THE EVIDENCE OF THINGS SELDOM SEEN

Toward an Understanding of the Educational Choices of African American Male College Football Athletes

Jamel Donnor

> From afar, one may imagine that one perceives the pattern. And one may. But, as one is not challenged by the details, the pattern may be nothing more than something one imagines oneself to be able to remember.
>
> —James Baldwin (1985)
> *The Evidence of Things Not Seen*

INTRODUCTION

The education of African American male athletes has received a significant amount of attention from the popular media and social sciences over the last 2 decades (Braddock, 1979; Davis, 1995; Harrison, 2000; Hoberman, 1997; Lomax, 2000; Trent, 1982). Despite the popular media's

African American Males and Education:
Researching the Convergence of Race and Identity, pp. 171–188

promulgation of sport as the "great racial equalizer," social scientists continue to show that, collectively, these young men are academically tracked and stereotyped more than their White counterparts (Benson, 2000; Edwards, 1984, 1985; Harrison & Malia Lawrence, 2003; Hartmann, 2000; Malia Lawrence, 2005; Singer, 2005).

Despite the increased attention on this topic, implicit within much of the social science investigations is a tendency to view African American males as passive participants in their experience as student athletes. In other words, beyond their perceptions of race and racism (e.g., natural athletic ability and intellectual inferiority) or examining the financial incentives for fielding athletically successful teams, very little is known about how African American male athletes think about postsecondary education (Emerick, 1997; Grant, 2003; Hilbron, 1995; Johnson, 1985; Ornstein, 1996).

This paper discusses how 17 intercollegiate football African American male student athletes think about their postsecondary education and sports. Based on the information provided, the author suggests that involvement in intercollegiate football at Bowl Subdivision level is counterintuitive to the educational interests of the majority African American participants.

Theoretical Framework

When explaining why African American student athletes in high-profile sports are underachieving at a greater rate than White student athletes, social scientists have often utilized two theoretical approaches and quantitative research methods (Donnor, 2005; Hughes, Satterfield, & Giles, 2007). The first theoretical approach, the conflict perspective posits that the academic shortcomings of African American male college football student athletes are attributed to a "win at any cost" culture promulgated within many athletic programs (Eitzen, 2001). Focusing on low graduation rates and the significant sums of money required for operating a major college football program, conflict theorists assert that African American males are exploited for their athletic prowess. When one compares a participant's of major college sports "effective wage" (i.e., the value of an athletic scholarship, room and board, and book allowance) to the revenue a solvent football program receives from merchandising, corporate sponsorship, and boosters, assertions of exploitation possess more than a modicum of credibility (Brown, 1993, p. 671).

The second theoretical approach is the social psychological perspective, which examines the extent individuals with the physical talent to participate high-profile intercollegiate sports identifies with the social role of athlete. According to Watt and Moore (2001), individuals identified as athletes are susceptible to "identity foreclosure" because of the time and psychological commitment required for developing athletic talent (p. 13). In other words, participants of high-profile college sports are more likely to over identify with the athletic role and neglect the "activities and responsibilities necessary for becoming a successful student" (Watt & Moore, 2001, p. 13). Under this theoretical framework, researchers are concerned with understanding "under what social circumstances people behave in predictable ways," rather than how individuals and institutional arrangements influence a situation (Eitzen & Sage, 1997, p. 6). Subsequently, overidentification with the athletic identity for African American males can inadvertently perpetuate the "Black dumb jock" stereotype (Edwards, 1984).

In contrast, Hughes, Satterfield, and Giles (2007) point out that most studies on Black male student athletes contain "very little qualitative insight to help explain why an athlete's academic performance may differ from a nonathlete's academic performance" (p. 113).[1] Similarly, Gaston-Gayles (2004) notes that "poor graduation rates and academic performance associated with various groups of student athletes warrant investigation that goes beyond merely examining the influence of traditional variables" (e.g., high school grade point average and standardized test scores) (p. 75). According to Pascarella and colleagues (1995), researchers interested in understanding intercollegiate athletics' "net effect" on student athletes, must take into account the "constellation of secondary school experiences, aptitudes, and socioeconomic perspectives" they arrive to campus with, otherwise, "it is likely that comparisons of athletes and nonathletes will simply reflect individual differences at the time of entrance to college rather than the net effects of athletic participation during college" (p. 370).

While the aforementioned theories and method have illuminated the contradictions and complexities of student involvement in intercollegiate athletics, very little information exists on how African American male student athletes make sense of the relationship between low academic achievement and college sports in general, and the role race plays in the process in particular (Comeaux & Harrison, 2007; Singer, 2005). Sociologiat Harry Edwards (1984) contends that race plays a significant role in the education of African American male student athletes three ways. First and foremost, African American male student athletes "must contend with the connotations and social reverberations of the traditional 'dumb jock' caricature" (p. 8). Second, Black male student athletes are "burdened with the insidiously racist implications of the myth of 'innate Black athletic superiority" (p. 8) Third, African American male student athletes must also deal with the "more blatantly racist stereotype of the 'dumb Negro' condemned by racial heritage to intellectual inferiority" (p. 8).

Critical Race Theory

To attend to the aforementioned shortcomings of the aforementioned theoretical frameworks, I used critical race theory (CRT), specifically Derrick Bell's interest-convergence principle to examine how African American college football players at the Football Subdivision level interpret the relationship between athletics, academic achievement, and race. Premised on the legal history of non-Whites, CRT posits that racism and racial stratification are endemic in American society (Bell, 1995). Treating race as a sociocultural construct, critical race theory rejects the mainstream notion that race is simply a matter of physical difference in order to posit how the life chances and lived experiences for people of color are fundamentally distinct from Whites (Bell, 1995). Race from a CRT point of view is a salient social and cultural artifact that serves ideological, social, political, and economic interests of Whites (Zuberi, 2001).

An outgrowth of the critical legal studies (CLS) approach toward law and legal reasoning, critical race theory offers a more expansive explanation of racial inequality by utilizing the following epistemic, analytical, and methodological approaches: (a) history and context, (b) rejecting colorblindness and neutrality, and (c) incorporating experiential knowledge to illustrate how reality is situational and socially constructed (Crenshaw, Gotanda, Peller & Thomas, 1995; Ladson-Billings, 1998). In contrast to overt individual acts of racial discrimination, critical race theorists posit that societal governing institutions, such as law, maintain the racial status quo by privileging and normalizing cultural messages, and existing social and political arrangements that directly and indirectly benefit Whites. From the critical race theoretical point of view, people of color, collectively speaking, have been and remain marginalized on purpose (Bell, 1999, p. 6). Moreover, the goal of CRT is to create a more socially just society by exposing the complexities of racial oppression (Matsuda, Lawrence, Delgado, & Crenshaw, 1993).

In education, scholars have used critical race theory to explain how the learning opportunities for the majority of students of color are distinct from Whites. Specifically investigating the quality of instruction and academic content, school funding inequities, and learning outcome disparities, critical race theorists in education contend that the foregoing issues and barriers, which disproportionately affect schools with large non-White student populations, cannot fully be understood solely through class or gender analyses (Ladson-Billings, 1998; Ladson-Billings & Tate, 1995;

Parker & Lynn, 2002). Given the complexities and insidious ways race and racism operate in education, CRT provides education researchers with the capacity to deal with paradigmatic and epistemological issues by "uncover[ing] and unmask[ing] the persistent and oppressive nature of the normativity of Whiteness, the cooption and distortion of oppositional discourses," and the paradoxical ways education policies designed to address the achievement gap reify the racial status quo (DeCuir & Dixson, 2004, p. 30; Ladson-Billings, 2000). Like legal critical race scholars, critical race theorists in education are committed to social justice by highlighting students of color's equitable access to quality learning opportunities.

RESEARCH METHOD

The data presented in this article comes from a larger study exploring the educational experiences of 17 African American student athletes at three Midwest universities with football programs at the Football Bowl Subdivision level. The young men in this study were asked a series of semistructured ethnographic interview questions focused on gaining their understanding on the relationship between race and athletics on their secondary and collegiate education, respectively. By suggesting that the college education of African American FBS student athletes is a convergence of interests, I am particularly concerned with identifying and giving meaning to a set of attitudes, interactions, and outcomes within a particular setting. Therefore, the findings presented and discussed in this article address the extent football related responsibilities (i.e., pressure from coaches, and actions by academic support staff in the athletic department) limit African American student athletes' ability to enroll in courses of interest and academic majors.

RESEARCH SITES

The fieldwork was conducted at the following universities that satisfied the NCAA's institutional criteria to participate at the Football Subdivision level: Big State University (BSU), Scarlet University (SU), and Tech University (TU). Similar in academic reputation, research tradition, and level of athletic competition, these three institutions represented the ideal site to conduct a study on the impact of participation intercollegiate football on the education of African American male student athletes. For example, at the time of data collection, both BSU and the SU were ranked in the top 10 Public National Universities according to *U.S. News and World*

Report, while TU, a private institution, ranked among the top 15 institutions of higher education for undergraduate students. Site access was obtained through formal and informal methods (Yin, 2003). Big State and Tech universities were accessed formally. Specifically, I mailed letters to associate athletic directors and directors of student athlete academic services at 14 universities with football programs at the FBS level, Big State and Tech were the only institutions to respond favorably to my request. Conversely, access to the Scarlet was obtained through a faculty colleague who served as a mentor to African American males on the team.

SELECTION OF PARTICIPANTS

As a result of obtaining formal access to TU and BSU, participants were selected with the assistance of the Director of Academic Services for Student Athletes at both institutions. For example, the Director at Tech solicited and identified participants. Due to the nature of the research question guiding this project, first-year and sophomore participants were desirable. The rationale for this was twofold. First, as a recent enrollee to an institution of higher education, first-year student athletes are best situated to render a rich description on the difference in expectations between high school and higher education. Second, sophomore student athletes were selected for ability to explain how their advanced participation FBS football has and has not shaped academic-related decisions, in addition to, provide information on strategies they developed as a result of their experience to better navigate their undergraduate education forward.

Student athletes from SU were identified through snowball selection, which resulted in a sample population of participants academically classified as seniors. The faculty colleague identified Robert (pseudonym) as an individual willing to recruit teammates interested in participating in the research study. The data provided by the seniors was particularly illuminating due to their advanced involvement with intercollegiate football. In other words, because these young men were close to earning an undergraduate degree and had used most or all of their athletic eligibility, the UM student athletes were able to offer a comprehensive assessment of the attitudes, institutionalized practices, and actions on the part of education stakeholders and themselves postsecondary education.

The total participant sample for the study consisted of: 10 first-year student athletes (3 from UW; 6 from NU), 5 sophomores (4 from UW; 1 from NW), and 3 seniors from UM. The academic majors for participants from BSU varied from undeclared to mechanical engineering, while the grade point average for the group was 2.63.[2] Majors for TU participants fell into three categories: (1) undeclared, (2) communications studies, and (3) film and media studies. The GPA for Tech student athletes was 2.23.[3] Two of the student athletes from SU declared general studies as their major, while the third studied kinesiology. The grade point average for the Michigan student athletes was 2.77.[4]

DATA COLLECTION PROCEDURE

All 17 ethnographic interviews were conducted face-to-face and varied in length from 45 minutes to 3 hours. The interviews were audio taped and transcribed for data analysis purposes. While a formal interview protocol was used to interview participants, the questions were open-ended to allow the participants to share additional information. In addition to the research literature and theoretical framework, the interview questions were shaped by three pilot studies. The first pilot study was conducted with the director of academic services for student athletes at Big State. A former participant of FBS student athlete, the director, an African American, had the experiential knowledge of the actions, attitudes and interactions with others necessary to create either a positive or negative educational experience for student athletes. An interview question derived from this pilot study was: *If discipline is required of your sport and necessary for success, what are some reasons why it may not carry over into education for Black student athletes?* The director used the term discipline to describe the effort required on the part of student athletes to advance in sport and academically.

The second pilot interview was with a first-year Black football student athlete with a 3.02 GPA. This pilot study was useful for framing questions specific to first-year participants. For example, an interview question developed specifically for first-year student athletes was: *How have you found your high school education helpful in college?* The final pilot study was with a student athlete academically classified as a junior. An education major, the pilot interviewee was key in helping to craft questions for participants who were advanced in their academic standing and athletic participation. A question derived from this pilot interview was: *How are you prepared for life after football? What classes have you taken or experiences have you had supports this?* All three pilot studies were instrumental to the design, development, and refinement of the formal data-generating instrument used in the larger study.

The interview questions were grouped into the following four categories: (1) *descriptive*, (2) *structural*, (3) *contrasting*, and (4) *interpretive* (Spradley, 1979; Merriam, 1998). The descriptive questions sought to elicit a "large sample of utterances in the informant's native language" (Spradley,

1979, p. 85). An example of a descriptive question posed was: *How would you describe your educational experience before being identified as possessing the athletic ability to play for a major college program in high school?* Structural questions were adapted specifically to the particular participant (Spradley, 1979). A structural question asked in this study was: *I am interested in knowing what you know about the graduation rates of FBS African American student athletes; and what do you think are the factors responsible for it?* Contrasting questions sought to discover variations among participants, and between peers of different racial, socioeconomic, and athletic status. An example of a contrasting question was: *Do you think there is a difference in the education of White student athletes?* Interpretive questions allowed for reliability because it enabled me to check for an understanding of the informant's responses (Merriam, 1998). For example, I asked: *Do you think you are stereotyped by your professors? How much does being an athlete contribute to this? What about your race?*

DATA ANALYSIS

Data analysis was an ongoing process. Three analytic strategies were used throughout the course of this study. The first data analysis method was pattern matching (Yin, 2003). Once the interviews were transcribed, each transcript was photocopied and read twice. The first reading was necessary to develop a general sense of the data (Yin, 2003). According to Yin (2003) pattern matching compares an empirically based pattern with a predicted one" (p. 116). If the patterns can coincide, the result can help "strengthen internal validity" (Yin, 2003, p. 116). The initial coding of data occurred during this reading.

The second reading of transcripts occurred while simultaneously listening to the participants' responses to the interview questions. In addition to checking for omissions and typographical errors, this microanalytical approach was used to attend to "certain data and ignore other data" (Yin, 2003, p. 112). In other words, by hypothesizing that education of African American FBS student athletes is a convergence of interests, I am attempting to explain a particular phenomenon with a presumed set of causal links (Yin, 2003). Similar to the first transcript reading, the data was coded during the second reading. Subsequently, both sets of coded data were compared in order to identify reoccurring patterns among the participants' correspondence. Afterwards, a master list representing the most salient categories and codes was established. Determining which coded pieces of data best answered the research question was based upon its ability to represent the critical race theory dimensions of this study (Graue & Walsh, 1998; Lynn, 2006).

The second data analysis method used in the study was triangulation. Three types of triangulation took place to address internal validity (Merriam, 1998; Stake, 2000; Yin, 2003). The first triangulation method used was member checking. Here, the data was presented to the interviewees through informal follow-up sessions to confirm their responses and findings. Along with focusing on the participants' academic status (i.e., grade point average and class schedule), specific queries were posed exploring their academic major and what they wanted "to do with it?" Responses to the follow-up questions were compared with those provided during the formal interview and their academic transcripts.

The second method of triangulation was peer examination (Merriam, 1998). The aim of this approach was to corroborate the emergence and convergence of data points. In this instance, I met weekly with a senior scholar who served on the faculty advisory board for the Big Ten athletic conference. The external investigator was particularly helpful with exposing and clarifying the researcher's assumptions about the findings and theoretical orientation of the study by comparing the emerging themes with her experience on the advisory board and scholarship on critical race theory.

The third triangulation method used and a corollary was theoretical propositions. In utilizing a CRT perspective to frame this study, specifically its history and context tenet, I was able to formulate a richer meaning of the rules, institutionalized behaviors and practices that marginalize African American male student athletes. Additionally, the use of critical race theory helped to situate the findings as systematic.

The third method of data analysis was analytical memo writing and analyzing field notes, which also occurred throughout the data collection process. The analyzing of field notes and writing of analytical memos involved using Derrick Bell's interest-convergence principle (ICP) to identify, understand, and connect the disparate data points of this study. An analytical construct of critical race theory, the interest-convergence principle explains how race and racism are perpetuated and sustained by society's dominant group vis-à-vis an elaborate process of marginalization utilizing governing institutions. This process of racial marginalization accommodates the rights of the subordinate groups only when it converges with the political economic interests of the social status. A realist assessment of the collective status of racial groups, the interest-convergence principle explains how public policies intended to promote social equality circuitously perpetuates inequality by not dismantling the fundamental structures and processes responsible for establishing racial inequities.

Theorized by Bell, a constitutional law scholar, to explain the U.S. Supreme Court's decision to abolish state-sponsored racial discrimination in *Brown v. Board of Education* of 1954 (*Brown I*). Bell utilized the legal history of African Americans to explain the Court's decision to break away from precedent. Put directly, *Brown I* "can[not] be understood without some consideration of the decision's impact on interests other than those of long-suffering Black children and their parents" (p. 640). Consider that prior to *Brown I*, for more than a century African Americans had argued that racially segregated schools were inferior (Anderson, 1988 Watkins, 2001). Indeed, lower Federal district and State regularly responded to African Americans' claims by simply ordering facility equalization. It was Bell's (1980) contention, that the image of America legally subordinating its non-White citizens would undermine its global fight against Russia during the Cold War. Hence, *Brown I* served as a symbolic linchpin to advance America's political economic interests of becoming an international superpower, more than reconciling a fundamental democratic discrepancy. Under the interest-convergence construct, *Brown I* is social progress requiring the coincidence of a pressing national issue rather than an altruistic commitment to racial justice.

For this study, the interest-convergence principle was used to analyze how the participants made academic-related decisions in relationship to sport-related obligations. For example, if a participant stated that he matriculated to his respective university with the intent on selecting a particular academic major and was able to enroll in and complete the requisite courses for the intended major a convergence of interests occurred. Conversely, if a student athlete stated that he was unable to enroll in or complete the coursework for his preferred academic major due to his involvement with football a divergence of interests took place (Guinier, 2004).

FINDINGS

Framing a College Education: How African American Male Student Athletes Select a University

A major theme in the student athletes' accounts was the desire to earn a college degree. The young men understood the significance of having a college degree in order to compete successfully in the labor market once their athletic careers—intercollegiate, professional or both—were complete. Their remarks reveal how athletics afforded them the opportunity to earn an undergraduate degree from a reputable institution of higher education. The following comments are a sample of the college athletes' reasons for attending their respective universities:

Chris: I was looking for a school that was good academically and provided good competition athletically. I was recruited by Duke, the University of Illinois, and Stanford, but Tech seemed like a pretty nice fit. I feel like this is a high caliber school like Stanford.

James: I was recruited by different schools, mostly from the Big 10, and the Big 12. I guess I was looking for a school that had a football reputation per se, but TU was the best one from an educational opportunity standpoint.

Paul: I had a couple of offers from different colleges, Tech was the first D-I school to come and offer me a scholarship. At first Tech was the only school to look at me, but once I committed to them, other big time schools started checking me out. I stayed loyal to Tech because their motto is you get a good education here. I wanted to get a good education. The NFL is not guaranteed to everybody, so why not get an education.

In discussing their selection criteria, these college athletes present a range of thoughtful or rational choices in which they attempted to "achieve optimal results within an incentive structure" prior to arriving on campus (Pedriana, 2005, p. 345). Moreover, rather than rely solely upon geographic preference, type of athletic scholarship offered (i.e., full or partial), or the football program's athletic conference as the primary factor in the decision making process, the young men referred to their universities' academic reputation as the reason for matriculation. While the athletes did not identify explicit areas of study, their responses suggest that they will have the opportunity to access a number of quality classes, academic programs or both as a result of their enrollment decision.

As stated earlier, the young men acknowledge that their physical talent facilitated access to a top-tier institution of higher education. However, it is important to note that they also recognize the additional responsibilities (and pressures) athletics require. While the latter is understood by those familiar with this topic, it is critical to present information on the athletic experiences of these young men to better understand their academic decision-making processes.

Coming Up Short: Navigating Athletics to Foster Educational Attainment

Rather than describe the quality of the education they received, the young men discussed in detail the conflicts and setbacks their participation in college football presented. All of the athletes recalled early in the (college) education process the extent to which football limited their access to courses aligned with personal/professional aspirations. In one instance, the desire to attend law school outweighed the idea of playing an additional year of intercollegiate football. Overwhelmingly, the recollections focused on the student athletes' response to overcoming the frustration and disappointment of selecting an academic major divergent from their initial interests. Julian provided a typical response:

> I initially wanted to be a computer science major, but I didn't think I could do it and play football, because football alone is just so time consuming. With computer science you have all those labs and they really couldn't work around my practice schedule and things like that ... the computer science department has set times and it's up to the student to work around that, and with football I cannot compromise one for the other. Subsequently, I chose English, but I was just taking English classes. Then I got into African American Studies ... I am at the point where general studies is the major I have chosen. As a general studies major you can take what you want, and have areas of concentration which is what I have done.

As explained by Julian, general studies is considered a "football major," meaning that football players, African Americans especially, select this academic program and others, including communications and kinesiology, in order to remain academic eligible. To the contrary, the young men enrolled in so-called less reputable academic majors explained that in spite of the inability to align their initial academic aspirations with subsequent academic choices, they were able to configure a meaningful education:

Julian: In general studies I have the option to take whatever classes I really want. I have taken all the required English classes. All the CAAS [Courses in African American Studies] classes, which are the African American Studies courses, and I've taken math, and language. You got football players who major in general studies and take the easiest classes they can find and get through, and that's fine for them. I am trying to get something out of it. I took a language course, you don't have to a foreign language.

Leon: I first majored in kinesiology, but it was not interesting to me. When I first came to Scarlet, I wanted to study computer science or something similar. Unfortunately, I knew it would not fit into my schedule because of football. That is something I regret, and will regret for a long time that I did not get a chance to study what I wanted. I subsequently chose general studies because I did not want to focus solely on one thing. I wanted a broad understanding of different topics and subjects, and general studies give me a chance to not focus on one thing. I don't have to set my major on a specific thing to get my degree.

Alternatively, Robert decided to forego an additional year on athletic scholarship to graduate early and attend law school. According to Robert:

> when the coach asked if I was coming back for a fourth year it was like 'oh I have got to make a choice.' I originally told him I was coming back, but it didn't feel right. There was a whole big rigmarole about that, but I changed my mind and made my choice that I was not coming back. I remember I went outside and cried in my car. It wasn't like a shock, but it was like 'man, no one told me I was a senior, no one told me I had to start making choices' ... it was jolting. I said to myself 'you have to wake up, are you going to go to law school or are you going to come back for a fifth year.' If I came back for a fifth year that would have meant that I had taken the LSAT for nothing. I was preparing for the possibility that I might not come back, but I did not make the decision until the time actually came and it was a shock. If I came back for a fifth year it would have been totally different. But I was at a point in my life where I had to make a choice, football was my dream and I had to cut it short.

While a divergence of interests exist between initial academic expectations and subsequent choices, all of the student athletes spoke forthrightly about the need to earn a quality education, in relative terms. Their views reveal that attaining a "good degree" is more than simply attending any university. In addition to enrolling at an institution with an academic reputation, a good degree consists of intellectually stimulating coursework and having the opportunity to access desired curricula resources.

DISCUSSION

While efforts to ensure data trustworthiness were taken, there are methodological and analytical shortcomings. The first and most significant limitation was the inability to conduct follow-up interview sessions with the participants from TU and the University of Scarlet, respectively. Attempts were made via e-mail to follow up with participants from NU and UM respectively, however I was unsuccessful. Thus, I acknowledge that this particular method of triangulation is limited, because of a lack of member checking by all of the participants (Graue & Walsh, 1998; Ladson-Billings, 1994; Merriam, 1998).

A second limitation of this study is its use of interest convergence. As Taylor (2000) points out, interests defined as White or belonging to the dominant group run the risk of homogeneity. Hence, I recognize the shortsightedness to view the experiences of similarly situated Whites as nonproblematic (Castagno & Lee, 2007). While intercollegiate football at the FBS level is overwhelmingly governed at every level by White men, both the pressure to win and the amount of resources available to White football student athletes are similar to their Black counterparts. A third limitation and a corollary, is interest-convergence inability to examine the impact of choice within a capitalist society and its role in shaping the material reality that guide an individual's action and inaction (Darder & Torres, 2004).

The follow-up sessions were informal due to the respondent's academic and athletic schedules, and the exhaustion of financial resources. As a result, all of the follow-up sessions took place at BSU. Multiple attempts were made via e-mail to follow up with participants from Tech and Scarlet, respectively, but were unsuccessful.

Despite the foregoing limitation, by documenting their academic decision-making processes, this article introduces a nuanced understanding of the educational experiences of African American males participating in college football at the Bowl Subdivision level. In doing so, a space has been created for rethinking the relationship between sports and academic achievement. While the popular media and supporters of college sports posit that participation leads to better grades, higher academic aspirations, and a positive self-conception on the part of student athletes, the empirical information presented in this article suggests otherwise. In fact, one could logically conclude that based on the personal accounts presented in this paper, that involvement in major college sports is counterintuitive to its participants' educational interests.

Interest convergence theory's focus on motivation allowed for a (re)evaluation and reassessment of the factors informing the education of Black male college athletes. This reconceptualization included viewing African American college athletes as active agents in the schooling process. In other words, Black male student athletes possess the capacity both to interpret their experience as a highly structured phenomenon and to develop a set of options for educational advancement. Indeed, conventional theories used to examine this topic have illuminated the impact of intercollegiate sports on student athletes; however, very little has been done to affirm their agency as a resource for making meaning of the interrelationship between education, sport, and academic achievement.

In demonstrating how Black male college athletes navigate their unique experience, new epistemologies are created. Thus, what might be construed as apathy or antiintellectualism on the part of African American male student athletes (e.g., reasons for their low graduation rates), instead may reflect an accumulation of obstacles to a particular condition. Therefore, it is important that future analyses consider how academic-related choices are specifically influenced by institutionalized practices (and ideologies), which subsequently create divergent experiences for African American male college athletes. In doing so, social scientists are more likely to debunk the "dumb Black jock stereotype," and the popular perception that Black males are overwhelmingly preoccupied with athletic achievement rather than academic advancement (Edwards, 1984, p. 8). In the final analysis, if the education interests of African American male student athletes are to advance, it is paramount that the complexity of pre-college experiences such as the role of parent(s), high school teachers, and school capacity also be considered to improve theory and strategies on their behalf.

NOTES

1. Studies that compare athletes to nonathletes according to Coakley (2007) "produce inconsistent and sometimes misleading evidence" because sport-related experiences are "defined and incorporated into people's lives in various ways depending on the social and cultural contexts in which they live" (p. 101).
2. The grade point averages and academic majors were provided from the participants' official transcripts.
3. Like the participants from the University of Wisconsin, this information was obtained from the participants' official transcript.
4. Unlike UW and NU, the grades ad academic majors for these interviewees were self-reported.

REFERENCES

Anderson, J. D. (1988). *The education of blacks in the south, 1860-1935.* Chapel Hill, NC: The University of North Carolina Press.

Bell, D. (1980). *Race, racism and American law* (3rd ed.). Boston, MA: Little, Brown & Co.

Bell, D. (1995). Racial Realism. In K. W. Crenshaw, N. Gotanda, G. Peller, & K. Thomas. (Eds.), *Critical race theory: The key writings that formed the movement* (pp. 302-312). New York, NY: The New Press.

Bell, D. (1999). Symposium: The power of narrative. *The Legal Studies Forum, 23*(315), 1-31. Retrieved from LexisNexis database.

Benson, K. F. (2000). Constructing academic inadequacy: African American athlete's Stories. *The Journal of Higher Education, 71*(2), 233-246.

Braddock, J. H. (1979). *Academics and athletics in American high schools: Some further considerations of the adolescent subculture hypothesis.* Baltimore, MD, The Johns Hopkins University.

Brown, R. W. (1993). An estimate of the rent generated by a premium college football player. *Economic Inquiry, 31,* 671-684.

Brown v. Board of Education of Topeka, 347 U.S. 483. (1954).

Castagno, A. E., & Lee, S. J. (2007). Native mascots and ethnic fraud in higher education: Using tribal critical race theory and the interest convergence principle as an analytic tool. *Equity & Excellence in Education, 40*(1), 3-13.

Comeaux, E., & Harrison, C. K. (2007). Faculty and male student-athletes: Racial differences in the environmental predictors of academic achievement. *Race, Ethnicity, and Education, 10,* 199-214.

Crenshaw, K. W., Gotanda, N., Peller, G., & Thomas, K. (Eds.). (1995). *Critical race theory: The key writings that formed the movement* (pp. xiii-xxxii). New York, NY: The New Press.

Darder, A., & Torres, R. D. (2004). *After race: Racism after multiculturalism.* New York: New York University Press.

Davis, T. (1995). The myth of the superspade: The persistence of racism in college athletics. *Fordham Urban Law Journal 22*(1), 616-698.

Decuir J. T., & Dixson, A. D. (2004). "So when it comes out, they aren't that surprised that it is there:" Using critical race theory as a tool of analysis of race and racism in education. *Educational Researcher, 33*(5), 26-31.

Donnor, J. K. (2005). Towards an interest-convergence in the education of African American football student athletes in major college sports. *Race, Ethnicity and Education, 8*(1), 45-67.

Edwards, H. (1973). *Sociology of sport.* Homewood, IL: The Dorsey Press.

Edwards, H. (1984). The Black "dumb jock:" An American sports tragedy. *The College Board Review, 131,* 8-13.

Edwards, H. (1985). Educating Black athletes. In D. Chu, J. U. Segrave, & B. J. Becker (Eds.), *Sport and higher education* (pp. 373-384). Champaign, IL: Human Kinetics.

Eitzen, D. S. (2001). Big-time college sports: Contradictions, crises, and consequences. In D. S. Eitzen (Ed.), *Sport in contemporary society: An Anthology* (6th ed., pp. 201-212). New York, NY: Worth.

Eitzen, D. S., & Sage, G. H. (1997). *Sociology of North American sport* (6th ed.). Boston, MA: WCB McGraw-Hill.

Emerick, M. L. (1997). The university/student-athlete relationship: Duties giving rise to a potential educational hindrance claim. *UCLA Law Review, 865*(44), 865-912.

Grant, O. B. (2003). African American college football players and the dilemma of exploitation, racism and education: A socioeconomic analysis of sports law. *Whittier Law Review, 645*(24), 645-662.

Graue, M. E., & Walsh, D. J. (1998). *Studying children in context: Theories, methods, and ethics.* Thousand Oaks, CA: SAGE.

*Green, R. L., McMillan, J. R., & Gunnings, T. S. (1972). "Blacks in the big ten." *Integrated Education, 3*(1), 32-39.

Guinier, L. (2004). From racial liberalism to racial literacy: Brown v. Board of Education and the interest-divergence dilemma. *The Journal of American History, 91*(1), 92-118.

Harrison, C. K. (2000). Black athletes at the millennium. *Society, 37*(3), 35-39.

Harrison, C. K., & Malia Lawrence, S. (2003). African American student athletes' perception of career transition in sport: A qualitative and visual elicitation. *Race Ethnicity and Education, 6*(4), 373-394.

Hartmann, D. (2000). Rethinking the relationships between sport and race in American culture: Golden ghettos and contested terrain. *Sociology of Sport Journal, 17*(3), 229-253.

Hilbron, H. B. (1995). Student–athletes and judicial inconsistency: Establishing a duty to educate as a means of fostering meaningful reform of intercollegiate athletics. *Northwestern University Law Review, 89*(741), 741-784.

Hoberman, J. (1997). *Darwin's athletes: How sport has damaged Black America and preserved the myth of race*. Boston, MA: Houghton Mifflin.

Hughes, R. L., Satterfield, J., & Giles, M. S. (2007). Athleticizing Black male student-athletes: The social construction of race, sports, myths, and realities. *NASAP Journal, 10*(1), 112-127.

Johnson, D. Q. (1985). Educating misguided student athletes. *An application of contract theory, 85*(1), 96-129.

Ladson-Billings, G. (1994). *The dreamkeepers: Successful teachers of African American children.* San Francisco, CA: Jossey-Bass.

Ladson-Billings, G. (1998). Just what is critical race theory and what's it doing in a nice field like education? *Qualitative Studies in Education, 11*(1), 7-24.

Ladson-Billings, G. (2000). Racialized discourses and ethnic epistemologies. In N. K. Denzin & Y. S. Lincoln (Ed.), *Handbook of qualitative research* (2nd ed., pp. 257-277). Thousand Oaks, CA: SAGE.

Ladson-Billings, G., & Tate, W. F., IV. (1995). "Toward a critical race theory of education." *Teachers College Record 97*(1): 47-68.

Lomax, M. E. (2000). Athletics vs. education: Dilemmas of black youth. *Society 37*(3), 21-23.

Lynn, M. (2006). Dancing between two worlds: A portrait of the life of a Black male teacher in South Central LA. *International Journal of Qualitative Studies in Education, 19,* 221-242.

Malia Lawrence, S. (2005). African American athletes' experiences of race in sport. *International Review for the Sociology of Sport, 40*(1), 99-110.

Matsuda, M., Lawrence III, C. R., Delgado, R., & Crenshaw, K. W. (Eds.) (1993). Introduction. *Words that wound: Critical race theory, assaultive speech, and the first amendment* (pp. 1-17). Boulder, CO: Westview Press.

Merriam, S. B. (1998). *Qualitative research and applications in education.* San Francisco, CA: Jossey-Bass.

Ornstein, J. K. (1996). Broken promises and broken dreams: Should we hold college athletic programs accountable for breaching representations made in recruiting student-athletes? *Seton Hall Journal of Sport Law, 6*(1), 641-668.

Parker, L., & Lynn, M. (2002). What's race got to do with it? Critical race theory's conflict with and connections to qualitative research methodology and epistemology. *Qualitative Inquiry, 8*(1), 7-22.

Pascarella, E. T., Bohr, L., Nora, A., & Terenzini, P. T. (1995). Intercollegiate athletic participation and freshmen-year cognitive outcomes. *The Journal of Higher Education, 66*(4), 369-387.

Pedriana, N. (2005). Rational choice, structural context, and increasing returns: A strategy for analytic narrative in historical sociology. *Sociological Methods and Research, 33*(3), 349-382.

Singer, J. N. (2005). Understanding racism through the eyes of African American male student-athletes. *Race, Ethnicity, and Education, 8*(4), 365-386.

Spradley, J. P. (1979). *The ethnographic interview.* New York, NY: Holt, Rinehart & Winston.

Stake, R. E. (2000). Case studies. In N. K. Denzin & Y. S. Lincoln (Eds.), *Handbook of qualitative research* (pp. 435-454). Thousand Oaks, CA: SAGE.

Taylor, E. (2000). Critical race theory and interest convergence in the backlash against affirmative action: Washington State and Initiative 200. *Teachers College Record, 102*(3), 539-560.

Trent, W. T. (1982). Contributions of athletic participation in high school to adult outcomes for college and non-college trained young men. *Journal of Social and Behavioral Sciences, 28*(4), 104-112.

Watkins, H. W. (2001). *The White architects of Black education: Ideology and power in America, 1865-1954.* New York, NY: Teachers College Press.

Watt, S. K., & Moore III, J. L. (2001). Who are student athletes? *New Directions for Student Services, 93*, 7-18.

Yin, R. K. (2003). *Case study research: Design and methods* (3rd ed.). Thousand Oaks, CA: SAGE.

Zuberi, T. (2001). *Thicker than blood: How racial statistics lie.* Minneapolis, MN: University of Minnesota Press.

CHAPTER 9

FACTORS THAT ATTRACT AFRICAN AMERICAN MALES TO COMPUTING SCIENCES

A Study of Aspiring and Computing Scientists

Jerlando F. L. Jackson, LaVar J. Charleston, Phillis L. George, and Juan E. Gilbert

The United States is currently seeing a shortage of skilled workers in science, technology, engineering, and mathematics (STEM) fields that has not been experienced since the mid-1950s (ACT, 2006). Moreover, while college enrollment has increased within the past decade, the share of students acquiring degrees in STEM fields has decreased (Gilbert & Jackson, 2007). Students' lack of adequate preparation to succeed in college level coursework is among the top reasons interest in STEM is declining (ACT, 2006). However, with the propagation of technology within the national and global economy, adequate preparation in STEM-related fields are increasingly becoming a required acquisition for access into today's infor-

African American Males and Education:
Researching the Convergence of Race and Identity, pp. 189–201

mation-based and knowledge-driven society (ACT, 2006; Gilbert & Jackson, 2007; Maton, Hrabowski, & Schmitt, 2000; Moore, 2006).

Within the STEM disciplines, computer science has moved to the forefront of this information age as computer usage cuts across diverse aspects of modern culture (Carver, 1994). Moreover, economic and societal ills have prevented many ethnic minorities from productively contributing to the growing field of computer science, most notably African American males. However, the United States can no longer rely solely upon White and Asian males as the only source of viable scientific and technical talent if they are to remain internationally competitive and keep up with labor market demands (Gibert & Jackson, 2007). While the United States government passed legislation to assist in the educational equity of African Americans to their White counterparts several decades ago, this disparity remains existent (Maton, Hrabowski, & Schmitt, 2000; National Task Force on Minority High Achievement, 1999).

Within the body of literature relative to STEM participation and African American males, there is a scarcity of research on African American males and computer science in particular. Hence, the underlying rationale for this qualitative study was to synthesize the prominent factors that contribute to African American male participation in the STEM field of computer science. Moreover, this study provided a forum for aspiring and current African American male professionals in the field to depict the factors that attracted and retained them in this specific area. Accordingly, the guiding research question for this study was: what are the key factors that contributed to the attraction of African American males to the field of computer sciences?

RELEVANT RESEARCH

In 1971, Toffler predicted a dichotomy within the United States labeling it an "information-rich" vs. an "information-poor" dynamic. The educational, societal, and economical discrepancies within our society have propelled this dichotomy into fruition today, with minorities and African American males in particular, on the "information-poor" side of the spectrum (Carver, 1994). Conversely, many scholars believe that computer technology can be used as a tool to circumnavigate an inadequate educational system, enabling would-be at-risk students to not only succeed within the STEM education pipeline, but to also become contributing members of this information-based society (Carver, 1994; Casey, 1992; Merrell, 1991). This body of literature also iterates that if African American students are to be successful in STEM-related disciplines, it is imperative to spark students' interest at an early age and cultivate that interest throughout the educational pipeline.

Although most African Americans have access to computers within the U.S. public school systems, the computer interaction experienced by African American students within urban public schools are starkly different from their White counterparts within suburban school districts (McAdoo, 1994). The computers interactions within urban public schools generally aim to provide instruction for isolated skill development and remedial work—tasks that do not ignite students' interest into the pursuance of STEM related disciplines. A 2007 study, which focused on a vital region that greatly contributes to the state of Wisconsin's economy, asserted that in order to increase STEM participation among the underserved, states must actively and aggressively cultivate interest in the STEM disciplines from an early age by gaining and maintaining student's interest (Gilbert, Jackson, George, Charleston, & Daniels, 2007).

The researchers (e.g., Gilbert et al., 2007) further iterated that increasing STEM participation can be achieved by cultivating students' interest through precollege, enrichment, internship and cooperative programs, and creating a welcoming environment that would retain and cater to individuals' health, financial, and cultural needs (Gilbert et.al, 2007). Furthermore, research conducted by the Educational Planning and Assessment System (EPAS) for ACT states that, "The students most likely to major in STEM fields in college and persist to earn degrees are those who develop interest in STEM careers through early career planning and take challenging classes that prepare them for college-level science and math coursework" (ACT, 2006, p. 1).

Results from a 2005 national survey demonstrated that boys and girls are equally likely to use computers at an early age (Calvert, Rideout, Woolard, Barr, & Strouse, 2005). However, as a consequence of a socioeconomic divide in early access to computers, these experiences were more prevalent among White children, higher income families, and families from higher education attainment levels (Calvert et al., 2005). Likewise, the research literature posits that the inability to afford various technologies is responsible for the lower sense of value among technology as well as technological applications (Ching, Basham, & Parisi, 2003); thereby making it increasingly difficult for African Americans, who are largely represented among those who are lower socioeconomic status, to pursue careers involving these technologies. Accordingly, a 2003 study suggested that the issue of technology ownership may play a significant role in how individuals value and align themselves with various technologies (Ching et al., 2003). These aforementioned studies collectively suggest that it is necessary for researchers to not only continue to monitor the role of technologies in children's lives, but to also assess the impact of their experiences with technology on their development.

The literature (e.g., Leslie, McClure, & Oaxaca, 1998; Meece et al., 1982; Sherman, 1980) expresses the importance of recognizing the connection between self-concept or confidence and ability in STEM education. Additionally, students are more apt to enroll in optional or additional math and science courses if they perceive themselves to maintain a higher level of ability in these subjects. In most cases, it is the contribution or input of teachers, parents, mentors, counselors, or peers that are believed to have an influence on a student's persistence in STEM, though this evidence is more inexplicit rather than hard (Haven, 1971; Jacklin, 1979; Leslie et al., 1998; Nash, 1979). However, by the time students reach the undergraduate and graduate levels, ethnic minorities are highly underrepresented in STEM-related majors (Gilbert & Jackson, 2007; Graham, 1997; Hill, 2001; Hines, 1997; Hrabowski & Maton, 1995; Moore, 2006). African American males are frequently poorly advised and often discouraged from pursuing advanced courses within STEM education which contribute to the disproportioned participation within STEM disciplines (Davis, 2003; Hrabowski, Maton, & Greif, 1998; Moore, 2006).

METHOD

A qualitative inquiry is appropriate for the study of a phenomenon for which researchers have very little previous empirical knowledge (Shank, 2002). Creswell (2002) stated more eloquently that "qualitative research examines a research problem in which the inquirer explores and seeks to understand a central phenomenon" (p. 52). Within this context, an exploration means that little is known in the literature about the phenomenon and the researcher in turn will use data from participants to develop foundational knowledge. In order to achieve this goal, it is often recommended to employ a comprehensive interview protocol using open-ended questions (Brenner, Brown, & Canter, 1985; Flowers & Moore, 2003; Rubin & Rubin, 1995).

Research Design

This study used a descriptive research design that was primarily qualitative in nature. While in the field, researchers posed a series of closed and open-ended questions that were original in design to examine factors which might attract African American males to the field of computer sciences. Questions were posed during one-on-one interviews—which were approximately 45 minutes in duration. Informed consent was given orally, and participants were made aware of their right to suspend the interview at any given time. Interviews were conducted by members of the research team and were videotaped. Each tape was then transcribed and manually coded for content analysis.

Research Site

Subjects for this study were recruited from the 2006 African American Researchers in Computing Sciences Conference.[1] The conference, held annually at Auburn University, is the first of its kind, as it caters specifically to the needs of African American researchers (i.e., undergraduates, graduates, faculty, and corporate/industry affiliates) within the computing sciences. Although grand in scope, the conference's primary focus is to bring together diverse constituents from within the computing sciences and to offer training (e.g., in specialized computing areas), networking and mentoring opportunities, so as to increase the number of African Americans in pursuit of faculty and research appointments in the designated field(s).

Participants

This study included a total of 12 African American males. Study participants either majored or were majoring in one of the following undergraduate, computing and/or computing related disciplines: computer engineering, computer sciences, mathematics, and math education. Approximately 64.3% of all study participants were classified as graduate students; whereas, 21.3% were classified as undergraduates. The remaining 14.3% were employed as computing sciences faculty/researchers within academe and had received terminal degrees within the computing sciences.

Data Analysis

Using Conrad's (1982) constant comparison method, emergent themes were analyzed after all data were collected through participant interviews. Themes of particular interest to the researchers were those associated with elucidating the research question for this study. These themes were labeled and described independently by two researchers. These themes and their descriptions were then cross verified by the researchers together, relabeled, and defined. Each researcher then reexamined the original transcripts for separate verification of the presence of the emergent themes. Original transcripts from these data were extracted as supportive evidence for the existence of each theme. The researchers together combined findings from the separate analyses to produce a final description of each theme, along with their properties and dimensions.

FINDINGS

Findings for this study suggest there are three major factors that attract African American males to the field of computer sciences and related disciplines. In no particular order, the factors are as follows: (a) cultural specific mentorship; (b) propensity for solving problems in real time/immediate gratification; and (c) universal application of computing/potential for social integration into daily life and living.

Cultural Specific Mentorship

Each of the study participants indicated their interest in computer sciences began in either middle or high school as a result of mentorship they received from African and/or African American male computer scientists. For some, the mentorship was initiated via participating in culturally specific, summer and after school enrichment programs in the math and sciences, during which time they were partnered with African and/or African American male role models in computing. As one graduate student shared:

> When I was really young … let's say middle school … there was a program called MSEN … Math, Science, and Education Network where they took children and gave them enrichment programs in the math and sciences. So, I took a lot of those classes, and they also had a lot of computing in those classes to show you how to use the computers and stuff. So, that's when I really got interested in math and computer science. There was this guy in the MSEN Program. He was a computer scientist. He was an African dude. He was really into computers. So, I hung with him a lot. I think he was dealing with Basic, but that was back then in the late 80s. He mainly dealt with Basic. That was my first introduction to computing sciences.

This particular graduate student, whose name is not listed for anonymity purposes, participated in the same enrichment program in the math and sciences from middle school through college. While in college, he majored in mathematics and minored in computer sciences and attributes his decision to do so to the mentorship he received early in his academic career as a middle school student, and he is not alone. When asked about his initial experiences within the computing sciences, an undergraduate shared:

> I was in a computer science program at the college I attend now, and the summer program was called Computer Science and Pre-Engineering (CSPE). I learned about Dream Weaver web design and visual basic, and I was really good at it.

In this particular instance, the undergraduate African American male elected to change his major from the physical sciences to computer science, as participation in the summer enrichment program and mentorship received while in the program helped boost his confidence and compelled him to pursue a degree in computer science.

> At first I was going to major in Biology because I had been watching CSI: Miami, but when I got the [computing] training and started getting the grades back, I was like ... "I'm good at this, and it's fun."

In addition to participating in culturally specific, summer and after school enrichment programs in the math and sciences, study participants also indicated they received formal as well as informal mentorship from African and African American male, computer scientists through completing programming classes in high school as well as computing/research internships early in their collegiate careers (i.e., freshmen and sophomore years). One graduate student shared:

> My first experience with computers was in high school, and that was playing around with a Macintosh machine that did Pasquel and that moved the turtle around the screen. I thought that was cool. The only class I enjoyed because I got to play with the computer. That was my first actual interaction with a PC, and then we finally got one at home. My high school teacher was a computer science teacher, and he was a Black guy. He was the first one that showed me about programming and so forth.

This graduate student was not alone in his sentiment. Each of the study participants shared anecdotal stories of how enrolling in programming classes and computing/research internship programs with African and African American male mentors in high school and college, respectively, positively influenced their decisions to pursue careers and degrees within the computing sciences.

Solving Problems in Real Time/Immediate Gratification

All of the study participants indicated that their interests in computing and the computer science were sustained primarily because of their love of solving problems and seeing the results. One graduate student shared:

> I like solving problems. You have to come up with an algorithm first, and then you have to match up the code. Once you finish, you can see your output. So, I like the fact that it [computing] solves problems, and you can see results to your problems.

In addition, an undergraduate offered the following:

> I was introduced to computer science when I began taking programming classes in high school. I liked the fact that I could take this problem and solve it and could then say, "Ooh, look at what I can do." I kind of liked that. That was a real introduction to computer science.

Although these two students focused on solving problems and seeing the results, others focused more specifically on computing artifacts that could be generated in real time and, therefore, could yield immediate gratification. Such is evidenced by the following:

> In some fields, you have delayed gratification where you do something, and then you get recognized much later. But in computer science, you write a program, and as soon as you compile it, it works immediately. So, anything that you do, you get immediate gratification for it. I always liked it [computing] because I felt like I could generate something. In sixth grade, we developed this girl rating program where you put in numbers for certain criteria ... you know, eye color and stuff like that ... and we'd rate the girls in our sixth grade classroom. So, that type of stuff where you can generate things in real time and actually see the results of your work is what sustains me.

Universal Application/Potential for Social Integration

This particular factor is inextricably linked to the aforementioned (i.e., solving problems in real time/immediate gratification) as it references the application and social integration of solutions to computer problems that have been solved in real time. Each of the study participants indicated they were attracted to computing and the computer science because of the universal application, limitless possibilities, and/or the potential for social integration into daily life and living (i.e., of solutions to problems solved in real time). One student shared the following:

> I like how it [computing] is kind of integrated into almost every aspect of society. Like ... if you know just a little bit about computers, you can take that and almost apply it anywhere else.

Another student shared:

> Ultimately, I'm really interested in helping people. I would like to be able to extend the quality of life. So, that's kind of related to why I like the computing sciences. I would like to extend the quality of life for somebody like a senior or elder. That way, they can extend their quality of life without having to live with assisted living. Or someone who is seeing impaired or in a wheelchair can do a bit more without the assistance of others. I like working and doing research in those areas.

A third student offered the following statement:

> Computing is everywhere. It helps with finding movies and what's on TV. It helps find recipes to cook. You know, it's just an integral part of everything we do, day out and day in. What interests me the most about computing are the possibilities. You know, there's really no limit to what you can do. You can create so many artifacts to save. You can do so much in the computing sciences. That's what I like. It's being an architect of a virtual world. You can develop your own world ... your own environment. You can develop robots to do your bidding basically. So, it's every way in which you can let your imagination run wild.

A fourth and final student offered the following sentiment:

> There are so many different things that you can do, and computer science is becoming so interwoven with all the other fields. You know, everybody needs computing these days. I mean you can't go to a single department in a university where they're not using computing in one way or another. So, I think that's what's most exciting about it [computing] ... the fact that everywhere there are so many applications, and there are so many needs for advances in computing. And that's what keeps me interested.

CONCLUSION

In this information age of advanced technology, it is important to increase the participation rates of computer scientists in order for the United States to remain globally competitive (Gilbert & Jackson, 2007). Though Whites and Asians account for the majority of the labor force in computer science, the United States is seeing a shortage of skilled workers in science, technology, engineering, and mathematics (STEM) fields that has not been experienced since the mid-1950s (ACT, 2006). It is now, more than ever, imperative to recruit a labor force that is representative of the demographics within our society to the field to not only diversify, but to also narrow the gap regarding labor shortages within the field of computing. The small portion of African American males participating within the field of computer science, as compared to their share in the population, makes them an ideal population to target. This study provides a window into the factors that attract African American males to the field of computer science, thereby implicating factors that if fostered, have the propensity to increase the participation rates among African Americans males.

There were three general themes that emerged within the findings as key factors that attract African American males to the field of computer sciences. Those factors are culturally specific mentorship, propensity for solving problems in real time/immediate gratification, and universal application of computing/potential for social integration into daily life and living. These findings demonstrate the significant role mentorship plays in an African American male's decision to pursue the field of computer science. Likewise, it is within these mentoring relationships that these individuals gained the confidence and computer-related content knowledge that fostered their desires to persist. Therefore, it is reasonable to conclude that enrichment programs or activities that provide such mentorship can play a significant role in increasing the number of African American males who pursue the field of computer sciences as an undergraduate major or profession.

While mentors clearly played an intricate role in the academic and career decisions among the study participants, the mentors honed in on a desire already present within these African American males. That is, the desire to receive immediate gratification for solving problems. Moreover, instructors, policy makers, and parents have the unique opportunity to foster this desire early in a child's life by recognizing it, as well as providing the opportunity for the child to explore this desire by making use of computers and its various applications. However, this would merit that instructors, policy makers, and parents pay closer attention to the student's needs in an effort to provide the adequate support with regard to constructive applications of these desires as early in life as possible.

A driving component of participants' desire to pursue the field of computer science rests in the fact that they saw computers as an intricate part of society—the integration of computers into every day life. This factor demonstrates that members of the targeted population must understand the increasing importance of computers and technology to every facet of life, as this understanding sparked an increased interest among the participants. Simply put, based on the results of this study, the more African American males understand the essential role computers and computer-related technology plays in the day-to-day functions of life, the more interested in the subject they will become. In conjunction with adequate mentorship or direction, their interests are increasingly likely to develop into a career in the computing sciences.

In closing, though African American males are continually being placed at-risk due to societal ills, with the adequate support systems, the participation rates of African American males within the field of computer sciences could increase by fostering activities based on the key factors identified in this study. These factors include, but are not limited to effective culturally specific mentorship, the realization of the integration of computers throughout society and the necessity of technological proficiency for future success, and the ability to connect theories and applications with tangible and immediate results. However, to accomplish the goal of increased participation, administrators, teachers, and parents alike must put more effort and dedication into facilitating the academic progress of African American male within the field of computer science.

NOTE

1. The 2006 Researchers in Computing Sciences Conference was part of a demonstration project, sponsored by the National Science Foundation (NSF), to increase African American participation in the computing sciences. The conference was held in the summer of 2006 at Auburn University and included African American, computing researchers at all levels (i.e., undergraduates, graduates, faculty, and corporate/industry affiliates).

REFERENCES

ACT. (2006). Developing the stem education pipeline. Retrieved from http://www.act.org/research/policymakers/pdf/ACT_STEM_PolicyRpt.pdf

Brenner, M., Brown, J., & Canter, D. (Eds.). (1985). *The research interview: Uses and approaches* (pp. 1-8). Orlando, FL: Academic.

Calvert, S. L., Rideout, V. J., Woolard, J. L., Barr, R. F., & Strouse, G. A. (2005). Age, ethnicity, and socioeconomic patterns in early computer use: A national survey. *American Behavioral Scientist, 48*(5), 590-607.

Carver, B. A. (1994). Defining the context of early computer learning for African American males in urban elementary schools. *The Journal of Negro Education, 63*(4), 532-545.

Casey, J. A. (1992). *Counseling using technology with at-risk youth* (Report No.EDO-CG-92-14). Ann Arbor, MI: ERIC Clearinghouse on Counseling and Personnel Services. (ERIC Document Reproduction Service No. ED 347 480)

Ching, C. C., Basham, J. D., & Parisi, J. (2003, April). *Artifacts and identity: Factors affecting technology use among young adults.* Paper Presented at the American Educational Research Association annual meeting, Chicago, IL.

Creswell, J. W. (2002). *Educational research: Planning, conducting, and evaluating quantitative and qualitative research.* Upper Saddle River, NJ: Merrill Prentice Hall.

Conrad, C. F. (1982). Grounded theory: An alternative approach in higher education. *The Review of Higher Education, 5*(4), 259-269.

Davis, J. E. (2003). Early schooling and academic achievement of African American males. *Urban Education, 38,* 515-537.

Flowers, L. A., & Moore J. L., III. (2003). Conducting qualitative research on-line in student affairs. *Student Affairs Online, 4.* Retrieved from http://www.studentaffairs.com/ejournal/Winter_2003/research.html

Gilbert, J. E., & Jackson, J. F. L. (Eds.). (2007). Introduction and State of the STEM World. *M7 STEM White Paper: Final Report* (pp. 7-13). Milwaukee, WI: Marquette University.

Gilbert, J. E., Jackson, J. F. L., George, P. L., Charleston, L. J., & Daniels, B. D. (2007). SWOT analysis of stem education: A study of the M7 region. In J. E. Gilbert & J. F. L. Jackson (Eds.), *M7 Whitepaper: Final report* (pp. 38-66). Milwaukee, WI: Marquette University.

Gordon, E. T., Gordon, E. W., & Nembhard, J. G. (1994). Social science literature concerning African American men. *The Journal of Negro Education, 63*(4), 508-531.

Graham, L. P. (1997). *Profiles of persistence: A qualitative study of undergraduate women in engineering* (Unpublished doctoral dissertation). Virginia Polytechnic Institute and State University, Blacksburg, VA.

Haven, E. W. (1971). Factors associated with the selection of advanced academic mathematics courses by girls in high school. *Dissertation Abstracts International, 32,* 1747a. (University Microfilms No.71-26027)

Hill, S. T. (2001). *Science and engineering degrees, by race/ethnicity of recipients: 1990-98.* Arlington, VA: National Science Foundation, Division of Science Resources Statistics.

Hines, S. M. (1997). *Factors influencing persistence among African American upperclassmen in natural science and science-related majors* (Report No.HE-030-071). Annual Meeting of the American Educational Research Association, Chicago, IL. (ERIC Documentation Reproduction Service No. ED 406 898)

Hrabowski, F. A., III, & Maton, K. I. (1995). Enhancing the success of African American students in the sciences: Freshman year outcomes. *School Science and Mathematics, 95,* 19-27.

Hrabowski, F. A., Maton, K. I., & Greif, G. L. (1998). *Beating the odds: Raising academically successful African American males.* New York, NY: Oxford University Press.

Jacklin, C. (1979). Epilogue. In M. Wittig & A. Petersen (Eds.), *Sex-related differences in cognitive functioning: Developmental Issues* (pp. 357-371). New York, NY: Academic Press.

Leslie, L. L., McClure, G. T., & Oaxaca, R. L. (1998). Women and minorities in science and engineering: A life sequence analysis. *The Journal of Higher Education, 69*(3), 239-276.

Maton, K. I., Hrabowski, F. A., & Schmitt, C. L. (2000). African American college students excelling in the sciences: College and postcollege outcomes in the Meyerhoff scholars program. *Journal of Research in Science Teaching, 37*(7), 629-654.

McAdoo, M. (1994). Equity: Has technology bridged the gap? *Electronic Learning, 13*(7), 24-30, 34.

Meece, J. L., Eccles, J. S., Kaczala, C. M., Goff, S. B., & Futterman, R. (1982). Sex differences in math achievement: Towards a model of academic choice. *Psychological Bulletin, 91,* 324-348.

Merrell, J. G. (1991, May). *Let's prepare-not repair-our at-risk students.* Paper presented at the annual meeting of the International Reading Association, Las Vegas, NV.

Moore, J. L. (2006). A qualitative investigation of African American males' career trajectory in engineering: Implications for teachers, school counselors, and parents. *Teachers College Record, 108*(2), 246-266.

Nash, S. C. (1979). Sex role as a mediator of intellectual functioning. In M. A. Wittig & A. C. Petersen (Eds.), *Sex-related differences in cognitive functioning: Developmental issues* (pp. 263-302). New York, NY: Academic Press.

National Task Force on Minority High Achievement. (1999). Reaching the top: A report of the national task force on minority high achievement. New York, NY: College Board. Retrieved from http://www.collegeboard.com/research/abstract/3876.html

Rubin, H. J., & Rubin, I. S. (1995). *Qualitative interviewing: The art of hearing data.* Newbury, CA: SAGE.

Shank, G. D. (2002). *Qualitative research: A personal skills approach.* Upper Saddle River, NJ: Merrill Prentice Hall.

ABOUT THE EDITORS

T. Elon Dancy II is assistant professor of Higher Education at The University of Oklahoma in Norman. He joined the OU faculty following faculty appointments at the University of Arkansas at Little Rock and the University of Arkansas at Pine Bluff. Prior to becoming a professor, Dr. Dancy held various administrative posts in both university advancement and health care settings. His research agenda investigates the experiences and sociocognitive outcomes of college students, particularly related to nexus of race, gender, and culture. More specifically, Dr. Dancy's research informs the scholarly literature and institutional practices incident to African American males in K-20 educational settings. With more than 40 publications to his credit, He is the author/editor of *Managing Diversity: (Re)Visioning Equity on College Campuses, The Brother Code: Manhood and Masculinity among African American Males in College*, and *Educating African American Males: The Challenges of Context and the Possibilities for Practice*. Dr. Dancy's research on African American male identity constructions, access issues for college students from underrepresented groups, and the environmental contexts for fostering college student success has appeared in the *American Behavioral Scientist* journal, the *Journal of School Leadership*, the *Journal of Negro Education*, and the *Gender and Education* journal. He has given more than 50 peer-reviewed papers at scholarly and professional conferences. Additionally, Dr. Dancy is senior editor of the *College Student Affairs Journal*. Dr. Dancy's honors and awards include the 2005 Association for the Study of Higher Education-Council on Ethnic Participation Emerging Scholar Award and the 2008 American Educational Research Association Citation for Dissertation Excellence in Postsecondary Education. He was twice named an Emerging Education Policy Scholar from both the Thomas B. Fordham and American Enterprise Institutes. Dr. Dancy received his BS with honors in psychology from the University of Arkansas at Pine Bluff and his Master of Health Administration from the University of Arkansas at Little Rock. He received a PhD with distinction in higher education from Louisiana State University in Baton Rouge with a cognate in sociology.

M. Christopher Brown II is the 18th president of Alcorn State University in Lorman, Mississippi. President Brown is the former executive vice president and provost at the historic Fisk University in Nashville, Tennessee. Prior to this appointment, he served as dean of the College of Education at the University of Nevada, Las Vegas, vice president for Programs and Administration at the American Association of Colleges for Teacher Education, director of Social Justice and Professional Development for the American Educational Research Association (AERA), as well as executive director and chief research scientist of the Frederick D. Patterson Research Institute of the United Negro College Fund. Dr. Brown has held faculty appointments at The Pennsylvania State University, the University of Illinois at Urbana-Champaign, and the University of Missouri-Kansas City. President Brown earned a national reputation for his research and scholarly writing on education policy, governance/administration, and institutional contexts. He is especially well known for his studies of historically black colleges, educational equity, and professorial responsibilities. Dr. Brown has lectured and/or presented research in various countries on six continents—Africa, Asia, Australia, Europe, North America, and South America. Dr. Brown lists among his many honors and awards, the 2001 Association for the Study of Higher Education's Promising Scholar/Early Career Award, the 2002 AERA Committee on Scholars of Color Early Career Contribution Award, the 2007 Philip C. Chinn Book Award from the National Association for Multicultural Education, and the 2008 Association of Teacher Educators Distinguished Educator Award. His research has been supported by the Lumina Foundation, Spencer Foundation, AT&T Foundation, the Pew Charitable Trusts, the Sallie Mae Fund, as well as other foundations and corporations. Additionally, President Brown is the author/editor of 15 books and monographs—*The Quest to Define Collegiate Desegregation* (1999), *Organization and Governance in Higher Education* (2000), *Black Sons to Mothers* (2000), *Equity and Access in Higher Education* (2002), *Studying Diverse Institutions* (2003), *Black Colleges* (2004), *Unique Campus Settings* (2004), *Achieving Equitable Educational Outcomes with All Students* (2005), *The Politics of Curricular Change* (2005), *The Children Hurricane Katrina Left Behind* (2007), *School Matters* (2007), *Still Not Equal* (2007), *Ebony Towers in Higher Education* (2008), *The Broken Cisterns of African American Education* (2009), and *The Case for Affirmative Action on Campus* (2009). He is the author or coauthor of more than 100 journal articles, book chapters, and publications related to education and society. Dr. Brown received the Bachelor of Science in elementary education from

South Carolina State University, the Master of Science in educational policy and evaluation from the University of Kentucky, and the Doctor of Philosophy in higher education from The Pennsylvania State University with a cognate in public administration and political science.

ABOUT THE CONTRIBUTORS

V. Lawson Bush is the Director of the CSULA/UCI Joint EdD Program in Urban Educational Leadership. His research interests include African American educational history, African-centered education, school desegregation, and Black male schooling and developmental issues. His aforementioned research foci situate him as the leading expert on the relationship between Black mothers and their sons and the development of Independent Black Institutions. He teaches such courses as culturally responsive institutions and qualitative research.

LaVar J. Charleston is a senior research associate and lab manager at Wisconsin's Equity and Inclusion Laboratory (Wei Lab) at the University of Wisconsin-Madison (UW). He also serves as an adjunct professor in the department of Educational Leadership and Policy Analysis at UW. Dr. Charleston's research focuses on the trajectory of underrepresented populations into highly technological positions and broadening participation for underrepresented groups in Science, Technology, Engineering, and Mathematics (STEM). Dr. Charleston's work addressing the understanding of interventions and/or broadening participation in STEM has been supported by thought-leading agencies such as the Lumina Foundation, the National Science Foundation (NSF) and the American Association for the Advancement of Science (AAAS). Dr. Charleston currently serves on the review board for the *Journal of African American Males in Education* (JAAME), and has served as the associate editor for the *Annuals of The Next Generation* Journal and as the assistant director for development and marketing at the Center for African American Research and Policy (CAARP).

Denise L. Collier, EdD, has almost 20 years of experience as a public school educator. Currently, she is an administrator for the Pasadena Unified School District. She also provides professional development for teachers throughout the United States. Her research interests include African American language, African American males and schooling, culturally responsive pedagogy, and classroom management.

Jamel K. Donnor is an assistant professor in curriculum and instruction in the School of Education at the College of William and Mary. His research interests include examining race in education and society as it relates to theory, policy studies, and the experiences of African American males throughout the K-16 education pipeline. Dr. Donnor is the author of "Towards an interest? Convergence in the education of African? American football student athletes in major college sports" published in the *Race, Ethnicity, and Education* journal.

Phillis L. George is an assistant professor of social science and director of the Center for Service-Learning at the College of Coastal Georgia (University System of Georgia). As a scholar-practitioner, she is firmly committed to excellence in teaching, research, and service and possesses numerous years of experience in academic and student affairs, including service as a former assistant director of the Chancellor's Scholarship Program (a national, merit-based program for academically talented minority students at the University of Wisconsin-Madison). Her research interests include: service-learning and the impact on student engagement, program evaluation and assessment, and faculty development. She completed her doctorate in Educational Leadership & Policy Analysis (University of Wisconsin-Madison), Master's in Sociology (Oxford University, UK), and Bachelor's in Sociology and Communicative Disorders (University of Wisconsin-Madison).

Juan E. Gilbert is an IDEAS Professor and chair of the Human-Centered Computing Division in the School of Computing at Clemson University where he leads the HCC Lab. He is also a professor in the Automotive Engineering Department at Clemson University. Dr. Gilbert is a Fellow of the American Association for the Advancement Science (AAAS), an ACM Distinguished Scientist, National Associate of the National Research Council of the National Academies, an ACM Distinguished Speaker and a Senior Member of the IEEE Computer Society. He obtained his BS in Systems Analysis from Miami University, his MS and PhD degrees from the University of Cincinnati.

Darryl B. Holloman serves as vice president for Student Affairs and Multicultural programs at Georgia State University. Dr. Holloman has worked in student and academic affairs for over 20 years. His research agenda examines the retention and persistence of at-risk populations on college campuses. Dr. Holloman has several articles and book chapters to his credit (e.g. the *Journal of Christian Education, Threshold in Education Journal, NASPA Journal* and the *Metropolitan Universities Journal*). His most recent work involves a biography of the noted scholar C. Eric Lincoln with Mercer University Press.

Jerlando F. L. Jackson is a professor of higher and postsecondary education in educational leadership and policy analysis at the University of Wisconsin-Madison. He also serves as the coordinator for the Higher, Postsecondary, and Continuing Education Program and as a faculty affiliate for Wisconsin Center for the Advancement of Postsecondary Education. In addition, he serves as director of Wisconsin's Equity and Inclusion Laboratory (Wei Lab). Dr. Jackson's central research interest has been to explore workforce diversity and workplace discrimination in higher education. More recently, he has focused on interventions designed to broaden participation for underrepresented groups in the scientific workforce. He is credited with over 100 publications, 175 presentations, and has published the following books: *Introduction to American Higher Education* (2010), *Ethnic and Racial Administrative Diversity: Understanding Work Life Realities and Experiences in Higher Education* (2009); *Strengthening the African American Educational Pipeline: Informing Research, Policy, and Practice* (2007); and *Toward Administrative Reawakening: Creating and Maintaining Safe College Campuses* (2007).

Anthony A. Pittman earned his PhD in Curriculum and Instruction from the University of Connecticut, Storrs. He is a former educator for the South Carolina Public Schools and now serves as an assistant professor in the College of Education at Kean University in Union, New Jersey. Dr. Pittman is the author of *Whited Out: Unique Perspectives on Black Identity and Honors Achievement.* His research areas include classroom pedagogy, honors education, and the role of schools in student development.

Terrell Strayhorn is associate professor of Higher Education at The Ohio State University, where he also serves as a faculty research associate in the Kirwan Institute for the Study of Race & Ethnicity, and Senior Research Associate in the Todd A. Bell National Resource Center for African American Males. Dr. Strayhorn's research agenda consists of two major streams of scholarly inquiry: (a) the social psychological impact of college on students and (b) the study of inequality in education based on race, gender, and social class. His research has appeared in *The Journal of Higher Education, Journal of College Student Development, NASPA Journal, Journal of College Student Retention, Urban Education,* and the *National Association of Student Affairs Professionals (NASAP) Journal.* Dr. Strayhorn is recipient of a prestigious Faculty Early Career Development (CAREER) grant funded by the National Science Foundation (NSF) for his project titled, "Investigating the Critical Junctures: Strategies that Broaden Minority Participation in STEM Fields."

Zachery Williams is associate professor of African American History at the University of Akron, Ohio. He is the author of *In Search of the Talented Tenth: Howard University Public Intellectuals and the Dilemmas of Race, 1926-1970* and the editor of *Africana Cultures and Policy Studies: Scholarship and the Transformation of Public Policy* (Contemporary Black History Series). Dr. Williams has also published articles in the *Journal of Pan African Studies, Journal of Religious* Thought, the *Journal of American Studies of Turkey,* and the *Journal of African American Men.*

Printed in Great Britain
by Amazon

63847873R00127